The Hamlyn Family Pet Care Encyclopedia

A practical guide to choosing
and caring for your pets

David Alderton

HAMLYN

The Hamlyn Family Pet Care Encyclopedia

C O N T E N T S

1 Small mammals

2 Dogs

3 Cats

4 Birds

5

Reptiles and
Amphibians

6

Fish

7

Invertebrates

First published in 1997 by Hamlyn,
an imprint of Reed Books
Ltd, Michelin House, 81 Fulham Road,
London SW3 6RB
and Auckland, Melbourne, Singapore
and Toronto

Publishing Director   Laura Bamford

Executive Editor   Simon Tuite
Project Editor   Katie Cowan
Editor   Jane Royston

Art Director   Keith Martin
Executive Art Editor   Mark Stevens
Designer   Steve Byrne
Illustration   Line and Line
Picture Researcher   Wendy Gay
Photographers   Laura Wickenden,
                       Paul Forrester
                       and Colin Bowling

Production   Mark Walker

British Library Cataloguing-in-Publication Data
A catalogue record for this book is available
from the British Library

ISBN 0 600 59240 5

Typeset in Gill Sans

Produced by Mandarin offset

PREFACE

PEOPLE have been keeping pets for at least 10,000 years, and there is undoubtedly something deep-rooted in us which responds to our animals. One of the first words of many young children brought up in a household in the company of pets is often 'dog' or 'cat', and as a child grows older he or she may come to view the family pet as a protector, providing assurance in what at times can be quite a frightening world. A pet can be talked to and confided in, and this allows a child to rationalize his or her decisions without adult pressures.

Human situations are also frequently mirrored through pet ownership – albeit in a less emotionally charged environment – and this in turn can help children to deal with circumstances that they will inevitably face in life. Sex, illness and death are all likely to be features of owning pets, and from a parental viewpoint these can provide a helpful starting point for discussions with children about such topics.

Interest in pet care may assume more of a social dimension by the teenage years, and taking part in club meetings and exhibiting pets at shows can help young people to gain confidence and develop their communication skills. For owners of this age, keeping pets may also serve to encourage curiosity in what might otherwise seem rather dull classroom topics, such as genetics and nutrition.

WHAT PETS DO FOR US

Research into why we keep pets is a relatively recent phenomenon, but what is now beyond doubt is that pet-keeping members of the public tend to be generally healthier than average, can recover more rapidly from illness and are also likely to have a better life expectancy. Children who have grown up with pets are usually more self-reliant and less self-centred than those living without any daily contact with a pet, and their general level of activity is also likely to be higher.

While pet owning is generally most common among families with children, keeping a pet can be just as significant to the health and happiness of other groups in society. A good example of this was shown in a study carried out with elderly people living alone. Each member of one group was given a young budgerigar as a pet, whereas those in the other group were given pot plants. It quickly became obvious that the people who were looking after budgerigars had found a fresh interest and purpose in their lives. They became very fond of their new pets, and even insisted on going out to buy food for them.

The study also revealed another significant fact: that owning the birds caused the elderly people to be less introspective, and gave them renewed confidence to deal with the world beyond their homes. Conversations about their budgies, and their progress in terms of tameness and talking, soon replaced mundane grumbles about the weather and minor ailments.

Outside the home, the role of domestic pets is also increasingly valued by health-care professionals. In the UK, for example, the Pro-Dogs Active Therapy (PAT) scheme now involves over 8000 volunteers and specially screened dogs. These are taken to visit long-stay patients in hospitals and in other care centres, who all benefit enormously from this interaction. At the University of Nebraska Medical Center in the USA, it has also become clear that giving people who are suffering from Alzehimer's syndrome contact with pets helps to encourage socialization on the wards between patients.

Children with learning difficulties such as autism may also benefit from a pet in their educational environment. They often enjoy direct contact with pets at home, too, while being unable to communicate fully even with the members of their own family.

CHOOSING A PET

People hope for different things from their pets: for some it may be the loyalty and companionship of a dog or cat; while for others the talking ability of a bird, the stunning coloration of a tropical fish or the bizarre breeding behaviour of a scorpion can be equally significant in their choice.

However, other practical factors must also play a part in shaping your decision about which pet (or pets) to choose. Its cost and upkeep, the time that you will have to devote to its needs, and whether you can find someone to care for it if you go away are just some of the considerations.

The level of pet ownership in all parts of the world is continuing to rise. At present, over 50 per cent of households in the UK own at least one pet, and multi-pet households are also common, especially in those families with children. The purpose of this Encyclopedia is to provide a single reference source for anyone thinking of acquiring or already keeping a pet, or seeking to expand his or her interest; the animals featured are representatives of the groups which are generally available from pet stores or specialist suppliers, and which are relatively easy to keep either indoors or outside the home.

There may be circumstances in which a particular type of pet is not advisable for medical reasons. For instance, allergies to cat fur are not uncommon (although preventive vaccines are being developed to try to resolve these); this type of allergy can also worsen cases of asthma. This may mean that you cannot have a cat in your household, but there are many other animals which will make excellent pets – reptiles, amphibians, fish and invertebrates are all ideal in this situation.

As our choice of pets continues to grow it will become easier to select not only a group of animals, but also a particular creature from within a category that will be best suited to your needs and requirements. This book will help you to compare all the potential pets in detail before making your final choice, and will then guide you in caring for your new companion.

Key to icons and symbols

Icons are used throughout the book at the top right of the pages; these are an easy reference guide to the subject covered on a particular page.

Choosing and buying

Housing and equipment

Feeding

General care

Breeding

Health care

Training

7

These symbols are used in the text on animal breeds, and denote average statistics for the species concerned.

Pregnancy

Average number of offspring

Weaning

Weight

Height

Incubation

Fledging

Independence

Length

Sexing

Small mammals

With the exception of the guinea-pig, small mammals are relative newcomers to the domestic scene. Rats and mice, for instance, were not widely kept as pets until late in the 19th century, while gerbils and hamsters only became well known in the 1960s. However, with over 1700 species of rodents in existence around the world there will almost certainly continue to be additions to the group, and a number of animals that are currently kept mainly by specialist breeders could soon become much more popular as pets.

INCREASING POPULARITY

It is not only rodents that are attracting increasing attention: in the USA, for example, the term 'pocket pets' is now used to describe the growing range of small mammals which appeal to pet owners, with African pygmy hedgehogs (see page 41) being one of the most visible signs of the trend.

Although the members of the small-mammal group often used to be regarded mainly as children's pets, they can also have a strong attraction for adults. This is reflected by the rapidly growing number of house rabbits which, like cats, can be trained to use litter trays and may be allowed to run freely around the home. Rabbits kept like this can become very tame, yet they do not have to be exercised outdoors like dogs; nor is there any risk of them being run over on the roads – a common fate of cats. House rabbits are ideal for today's urban lifestyle, particularly for people living in flats or apartments without a garden.

Some rodents – notably mice and rats – can be off-putting because of their odour, but others – such as guinea-pigs and chinchillas – do not have this drawback. Many of these small mammals are now being bred in an ever-increasing range of colour varieties; they are also often exhibited, offering another aspect of interest to their care. As a potential owner, visiting shows is a very good way to become familiar with the different breeds and to contact breeders (look in specialist magazines or contact club societies for details of forthcoming shows). Rabbits are particularly popular for showing purposes, with some of the larger events drawing thousands of entries.

MAINTENANCE COSTS

The cost of keeping small mammals, in terms of expenditure on food and housing, is relatively low (if you plan to buy a rabbit or a guinea-pig, it may be an even cheaper option to build a hutch and run yourself, rather than buying these ready made –

see pages 14–15). Although exhibition stock or rare colours may be more expensive, the price of small mammals – with the exception of chinchillas – is also low, which is a reflection of these animals' general readiness to breed.

The disadvantage of small mammals is that, in many cases, their lifespan is fairly short. For instance, hamsters may only live for two years, although the larger rodents and rabbits are likely to have a life expectancy of between five and eight years. However, this is not to say that small mammals are prone to illness, because they are generally very healthy. Veterinary costs – aside perhaps from routine claw clipping – are usually fairly negligible, although vaccination to protect a rabbit against myxomatosis and viral haemorrhagic disease (VHD) is often advisable (this will depend on the area in which you live, so ask your vet for advice).

KEEPING SMALL MAMMALS SAFELY

One aspect of caring for small mammals that you should take into account – both for handling purposes and to prevent them from escaping – is their ability to gnaw (the description 'rodent' actually comes from the Latin word *rodere*, meaning 'to gnaw'). The incisor teeth at the front of rodents' mouths (and those of rabbits, although these animals form a separate group known as lagomorphs) grow constantly throughout their lives, and the edges of the upper and lower incisors are sharpened to points by the gnawing action of the jaw muscles. So critical are the incisor teeth to a rodent's lifestyle that, if they do not meet properly in the jaws – a condition known as malocclusion – it is likely to starve.

Behind the incisors is a gap, which is called the diastema. Rodents have no canine teeth, because – unlike cats and dogs – they do not need them to tear food apart. The diastema allows gnawing activity at the front of the mouth to be separated from grinding movements further back in the jaws so that, for example, inedible shells can be kept apart from nut kernels, which are ultimately swallowed while the shells are discarded.

Myomorphs (mouse-like rodents) – a group of small mammals which includes hamsters and gerbils as well as rats and mice – lack premolar grinding teeth. These creatures rely instead entirely on their molar teeth, which have broad surfaces to crush their food into pieces that can then be swallowed very easily. In contrast, guinea-pigs and chinchillas (both members of the caviomorph group) do possess premolar teeth, which are smaller in size and are also located further forward in the mouth than the molars themselves.

9

Choosing and buying small mammals

Your choice of one or more small mammals as pets will be less influenced by your surroundings than if you were buying a dog or a cat. All the animals in this section can be kept in the home, and will not occupy a great deal of space. If you have access to a garden, you can house a rabbit and/or guinea-pig in an outdoor hutch and allow it out to run about on the lawn, but this will not be essential to its well-being. In fact, in a cold climate you may need to bring your pet indoors during the winter. Contrary to popular belief, rabbits are not entirely hardy – their ancestors originated in the Mediterranean region, and a rabbit may succumb to respiratory illness if left outdoors in cold, wet, foggy weather.

There are a number of issues that you will need to consider carefully when choosing a small mammal as a pet, and these are discussed here.

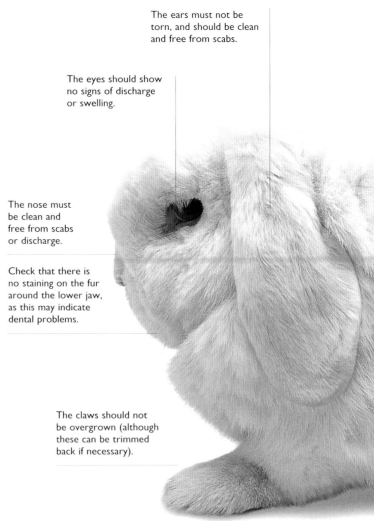

The ears must not be torn, and should be clean and free from scabs.

The eyes should show no signs of discharge or swelling.

The nose must be clean and free from scabs or discharge.

Check that there is no staining on the fur around the lower jaw, as this may indicate dental problems.

The claws should not be overgrown (although these can be trimmed back if necessary).

A plastic carrier with ventilation holes in the lid, lined with some bedding material, is ideal for transporting a small mammal safely.

EASE OF HANDLING

This is an important consideration. If you are buying a pet for a child, a guinea-pig or a rabbit will probably be a better choice than a hamster, as both of these animals will be highly unlikely to bite when being handled. The only time a child may be nipped is if offering food with fingers too close to a rabbit's or a guinea-pig's mouth, so this is a first rule to teach.

SIZE

This should be taken into account with rabbits, as the larger breeds can become as heavy as some dogs (see pages 38–9), making them difficult to carry. If you have a young child, it is therefore sensible to choose a smaller breed. Even then, you must teach the child to handle the animal safely: rabbits especially are susceptible to injury if they fall from a height.

GROOMING REQUIREMENTS

The amount of grooming needed will be a significant factor in small mammals that have long-haired varieties. A teddy hamster, for example, may look extremely appealing, but it will need regular daily grooming to maintain its appearance; this will also apply to an Angora rabbit or to a Peruvian guinea-pig. Remember that, while a child may start out with good intentions, he or she will almost certainly need some adult help at times. Smooth-coated breeds with short hair are much easier to look after, and will become just as friendly as their more cuddly-looking cousins with regular handling.

ONE OR MORE ANIMALS?

You may need to buy more than one animal. Mongolian gerbils, for example, are highly social creatures and should be kept in pairs (not necessarily of the opposite sex, or you may be swamped with unwanted offspring). In distinct contrast, Syrian hamsters are strictly solitary creatures – even matings

What to look for in a healthy small mammal

Look for a good overall body condition.

The area around the vent must be clean – any staining here could indicate diarrhoea.

The fur should be clean with no bald patches; part the fur in places and check that there are no scabs on the skin.

need to be carefully supervised. If you are looking for two pets, therefore, opting for these hamsters will inevitably cost you more because you will need to house them separately.

Mice and rats are both social animals, although it is less important than with gerbils to house them in pairs. Guinea-pigs will also live quite happily together in suitably spacious surroundings. Pairs of females tend to be more compatible than boars, which may scrap on occasions, although there is really little to choose between their temperaments.

When keeping more than one small mammal, it is best to introduce them to their quarters at the same time if possible, as this will minimize the risk of fighting. If you are interested in breeding your animals, make sure that they are unrelated.

AGE

Starting out with a young animal (or animals) is important. This is partly because, as already mentioned, most of the small mammals have a relatively short lifespan and it is not possible to tell the exact age of an adult animal (although certain signs – such as hair loss along the back of a hamster – may be indicative of advancing age). Perhaps more significant, however, is the fact that a youngster of any of these animals can be tamed satisfactorily with regular handling, whereas an adult that has not experienced close contact with people will be far less friendly.

WHERE TO BUY SMALL MAMMALS

A good selection of young animals should be available for much of the year. Pet stores frequently stock a range of small mammals, but if you would like a particular breed or colour you may have to seek out a specialist breeder. As a starting point, ask in your local library for addresses of any national societies for the animal concerned, or look for advertisements carried in specialist magazines.

Before buying any small mammal, you should check it over thoroughly to make sure that it is fit and healthy (see above).

Indoor housing and equipment

The destructive front teeth of small mammals (see page 9) mean that their housing needs to be suitably robust. Although today's modern plastic-based cages are more hygienic than those made of metal, and will not rust, they are certainly more vulnerable on exposed edges to a rodent's sharp teeth. Hamsters – often the worst offenders – are unlikely to gnaw their way out overnight, but they will rapidly expand any hole until it is large enough for them to squeeze through and escape.

A wide range of other equipment is also sold for small mammals, from special drinking bottles and food containers to toys and exercise wheels.

CHOOSING A CAGE

Make sure that the top of the cage fits snugly into its base, so that the plastic rim is properly protected by the mesh. In this type of cage the two sections are often held together by rigid plastic clips. If you were accidentally to leave these loose it could be disastrous – particularly if you or someone else then picked up the cage from the sides rather than from underneath – so always check that they are secure. It can be difficult to find replacements for the plastic clips if they snap, so make sure that these are strong and will be able to withstand plenty of use.

A well-fitting cage door is another point to look for: if the door does not close securely, a larger rodent such as a rat may be able to force its way out and escape. It can be safer to choose a cage with a door in the roof, although if this is small it may be awkward to lift out your pet. Reinforcing the door catch with a second clip, or even with a small padlock, will provide extra security. You should also check the door regularly, as it may fit less snugly if the hinges start to suffer from wear and tear over time.

The different small mammals have different needs, and you must provide the correct type of accommodation and conditions to keep your pet or pets healthy and happy. Some of their specific requirements are given here.

(Below) Hamsters like snug retreats in which they can sleep undisturbed. Placing a nest such as this one in the cage will also provide opportunities for climbing.

LIVING WITH A RABBIT

Unlike the pet rodents – with the possible exception of guinea-pigs – you can allow a rabbit to roam freely in the home, and even train it to use a litter tray if you buy it as a youngster. However, it will still be useful to have a suitable hutch available, where you can confine your pet when necessary. Special indoor hutches for rabbits (and guinea-pigs) are available from pet stores. Always ensure that your pet can come to no harm, or do any damage to your home, before you let it out (see page 19).

Hamsters

Tubular systems are popular for housing hamsters, and can be expanded by adding extra sections. Sleeping and feeding chambers are incorporated into the design, and the animal is easy to see as it moves through the network of tunnels. Hamsters can destroy the components with their sharp teeth, so look for a design with rounded corners, which is harder to gnaw. As your pet grows, check that its expanding waistline does not cause it to become wedged in the narrower tubes.

Special snug bedding should be incorporated into one section, where the hamster can sleep. Avoid using household substitutes such as cotton wool for bedding, as these could cause a fatal blockage of the hamster's gut if swallowed.

Gerbils

These animals need a fairly deep enclosure in which they can burrow. Specially designed plastic tanks are now available for gerbils, and have secure, ventilated hoods as well as colour-co-ordinated drinkers and other equipment. Alternatively,

(Left) A spacious double-tier cage being used for a pet rat; note the water bottle and food on the lower level. The base of the cage can be easily detached, using the metal clips, for cleaning.

AN EXERCISE WHEEL

In the wild a Syrian hamster will often forage for food miles away from its burrow, and a pet hamster will usually appreciate a play wheel on which to exercise. Other rodents are often less enthusiastic about this type of toy, which could actually prove dangerous for an animal with a long tail as it could become caught in the wheel. If a gerbil's tail is injured in this way it is especially likely to bleed, as the skin covering the tail tip is very thin and easily damaged.

If you do decide to provide a wheel for your pet, an enclosed design (as shown above) will be much safer than the traditional open-mesh style.

you could convert an unused aquarium, provided that you fit it with a suitably ventilated hood. This will give your pets much more space than most conventional cages, although the aquarium may be more awkward to clean out. To make cleaning easier, line the base with a plywood tray so that you can simply lift out soiled bedding and replace it. There will be far less likelihood of gerbils escaping from an aquarium than from a cage, and lifting them out via the top of the tank will be much easier than through a cage door.

Chinchillas and chipmunks

These active animals need large cages, which will be available from specialist suppliers or can often be ordered through a pet store. The cages are usually made entirely of mesh, held together with clips, and give their occupants plenty of space.

Rats, guinea-pigs and rabbits

The housing for these pets must include a suitable retreat where they can rest and escape from public view whenever

they wish. Some cages or hutches come already equipped with a designated sleeping area, or you will be able to buy a special retreat separately for a rat's cage. All you will then need to do is to add some safe bedding (paper or hay) to create a snug interior.

To provide an absorbent lining on the floor of a rat's cage, you should buy woodshavings sold specifically as animal bedding. Do not use sawdust, as specks of the dust could irritate the rat's rather prominent eyes.

A hamster emerging from a tube. Many rodents enjoy exploring this type of tunnel.

Outdoor housing and equipment

An outdoor hutch for a rabbit or a guinea-pig needs to be sufficiently well-made to provide dry, snug quarters all year round, particularly in wet or cold weather. A hutch should be divided into two parts: one with a front made of wire mesh, and the other with a solid wooden door to provide a sheltered retreat in bad weather. A dividing door between the day and sleeping quarters is also very useful and will allow you to clean each section in turn, with the rabbit or guinea-pig secure in the other part of the hutch. To provide your pet with the opportunity to exercise in safety, you will also need to buy or make a suitable outdoor run.

A typical ready-made guinea-pig hutch (a hutch for a rabbit will need to be much taller). The felt roof will provide protection against rain, and there is also a cosy sleeping area which should be lined with hay. For outdoor use a more secure door fastening will need to be added to the latch on this hutch, to be sure of excluding potential predators such as cats and foxes.

A HUTCH

Pet stores sell a range of rabbit hutches. Choose one that is high enough to allow your rabbit to sit up without difficulty: many designs are too low for this, although they are adequate for guinea-pigs. If you have a young rabbit, remember that the hutch will still need to be large enough when it reaches its adult size. As a guide, a rabbit hutch should be about 91cm (3 ft) long, and mounted about 60 cm (2 ft) off the ground on stout legs. This is especially important if you live in an area where there are wild rabbits about, as these could otherwise make contact with your rabbit through the mesh and spread disease, including myxomatosis (see page 25).

Waterproofing and security

The roof of the hutch should slope towards the back to help rain to run off rapidly, and a weatherproof covering – such as roofing felt – should be attached over this entire area. Oil the door hinges and hasps when you first buy the hutch and then at regular intervals to reduce the risk of them rusting up and starting to stick. Ensure that all door fastenings are secure – a simple latch can easily be undone by a fox, which will disappear with your pet if given the opportunity. Remember that foxes are now well established even in urban areas, so fit a small hasp and padlock to the frame and door of the hutch for extra security. A combination lock is ideal for this, as it will save you having to keep a key in a safe place; it is also less likely than a bolt to freeze solid during a spell of cold weather.

This type of outdoor combined run and shelter is ideal for use in the warmer parts of the year, and can be moved easily around the garden. Drinking water must always be available.

Hygiene

Placing lining trays within the floor areas of the hutch will not only make cleaning easier but, by keeping urine away from the wood, will also prolong its life. You could make up metal trays for this purpose, with their edges bent over so that they cannot cut your pet's paws; or use a sliding wooden tray with a plywood base and metal sheeting underneath.

A RUN

When the weather is warm you can let a rabbit or a guinea-pig out to roam freely around the lawn, but even in a secure walled garden it will not be safe to allow it out unsupervised. Urban foxes can be active during the day, and some cats will not hesitate to tackle even a relatively large rabbit – quite apart from a guinea-pig.

A ready-made run

You can buy a ready-made run from a pet store, although, as with hutches, many runs sold for rabbits are too low. Rabbits naturally sit on their haunches and also sometimes stand up on their hindlegs, so they will be happier when housed in a sufficiently tall run.

Another flaw of some ready-made runs is that they ignore the fact that rabbits are burrowing animals, and that a run without a base section is likely to be very unsafe. Even if the rabbit does not dig itself out and escape, a fox may be able to force its way in. A base is especially important if the run is to sit on uneven ground in which there may already be gaps, perhaps hidden by grass.

Building a run

You should be able to make a run yourself fairly easily, and this may be a good option as you can construct it to your own dimensions. If you have the space available, a run measuring 1.8 m × 91 cm × 91 cm (6 × 3 × 3 ft) is a useful size. In any case, try to design the run so that you can build it around 91 cm (3 ft) units, as wire mesh (used to cover the panels) normally comes in this width. This will save on unnecessary cutting and wastage, and will also leave fewer sharp edges to be covered with wooden battening. You will be able to buy suitable mesh from a DIY store, garden centre or similar outlet. For durability, this should be no thinner than 19-gauge (the lower the figure, the thicker the mesh). The strand size should be 2.5 × 1.25 cm (1 × ½ in), to keep the inquisitive paws or noses of other animals out of the run.

For the frame, 2.5 cm (1 in) square timber should be adequate. It is a good idea to make the unit using a series of individual frames that you can screw together; this will also make it easier to dismantle the run for storage in a garden shed during the winter, when rabbits and guinea-pigs are normally confined to their hutches. Treat the timber with a preservative before assembling it into frames: make certain that this is non-toxic and allow it to dry thoroughly before putting your rabbit or guinea-pig into the run, in case it decides to nibble the woodwork. Attach the wire mesh to the run using netting staples spaced every 5 cm (2 in) around the frame, on what will be the outer face once all the components are assembled. Trim cut edges as closely as possible to horizontal strands, to avoid leaving sharp ends.

You will need to make the floor section slightly differently from the rest of the run, as it should fit inside the base of the unit and be screwed securely to the sides. Cover this using mesh with more wider-spaced strands so that the grass can grow through easily for your pet to eat.

The roof section of the run should be removable so that you can lift out the rabbit or guinea-pig easily. Attach bolts to the uprights around the run to hold on the roof securely. For protection from rain, you could cover one end and the adjacent sides of the run (as well as the roof section) with plastic sheeting, although the temperature under this on a hot summer's day may rise considerably. Weather-boarding nailed to this part of the run is another option, and may keep the area cooler. In cold weather, a sturdy box placed on its side and partially lined with hay will provide additional shelter for your pet.

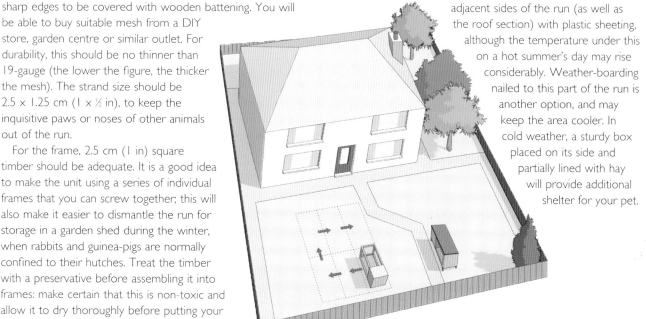

Suitable housing for an outdoor rabbit or guinea-pig: a spacious run, with a covered end to provide shelter (shown on the left), and a ready-made hutch with separate sleeping quarters (right); these should both ideally be in a back garden where your pet or pets will be safer from vandals. Move the run around regularly to provide a fresh supply of grass and to prevent the lawn from dying back beneath the structure.

Feeding

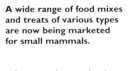

A wide range of food mixes and treats of various types are now being marketed for small mammals.

The nutritional requirements of most small mammals kept as pets are now very well understood, and prepared rations are readily available for them. Feeding a diet of this kind has a number of advantages, the most important of which is that a good-quality food should contain virtually all the nutrients that your pet needs to stay healthy and happy. Manufacturers can now easily produce foodstuffs containing not only all the required proteins, carbohydrates and fats, but also essential vitamins and minerals in well-balanced proportions. Medicines to protect animals against a number of illnesses such as coccidiosis (see page 24) can also be incorporated into foods such as pellets.

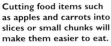

Seed stick treat

BUYING AND STORING FOOD

Prepared foodstuffs may seem quite expensive, but they do actually represent good value and are easy to use and store. If you follow the manufacturer's instructions carefully, you should also have no worries about your pet developing any health problems linked to its diet. Store prepared foods in a cool, dry place, as a damp atmosphere could turn them stale or even cause them to disintegrate. A metal dustbin is ideal for storage if you are using an outbuilding such as a shed, and will prevent wild rodents such as mice from gaining access to the food; these can spread diseases to their domesticated relatives, and must be excluded from any contact with them.

Although bulk buying may be cheaper, avoid purchasing an excessive quantity of food so that you do not exceed the recommended 'use by'

date on the packaging, or your pets will not receive the full benefit of the food's vitamin content. This is especially important with guinea-pigs, which are vulnerable to a deficiency of vitamin C in their diet. Like us, they are unable to manufacture this vitamin in their bodies and, if it is not available in their food, they will develop the cracked skin characteristic of scurvy. If you are keeping a rabbit and a guinea-pig together, you should therefore never feed only rabbit food, as this will not be supplemented with vitamin C at the required level for the guinea-pig.

WHEN TO FEED

Small mammals tend to eat small quantities frequently, rather than consuming all their food at one sitting: a domestic rabbit will eat as many as 40 meals in a day. You must therefore ensure that your pet does not run out of food during the day, as this will interfere with its natural feeding habits. Provide the food in a small but heavyweight earthenware bowl that the animal will not be able to tip over easily.

GREENSTUFF AND FIBRE

There is an increasing tendency among rabbit breeders not to feed greenstuff of any kind to their animals for fear that this could cause a

Cutting food items such as apples and carrots into slices or small chunks will make them easier to eat.

Broccoli is a valuable source of vitamin C.

digestive upset, and under no circumstances should you ever suddenly provide a rabbit with a large amount of greenstuff (or any other unfamiliar food). You will also need to 'acclimatize' your pet by adjusting its diet before allowing it into an outdoor run (see also pages 20–1).

However, fibre is an important part of the diet for a number of small animals, so you should offer good-quality hay to eat on a regular basis (it is an essential source of fibre for rabbits – see page 21). You can also use hay for bedding, to provide a snug nest in your pet's sleeping quarters. Fresh hay should be clean and relatively free from dust, and should not smell musty. Never be tempted to economize on the quality of hay, as this could trigger respiratory illness and have serious effects on your pet's health.

FEEDING A HAMSTER

If you have a hamster you may need to restrict the amount of food that you offer at one time, because of the unusual hoarding habits of these rodents. Your hamster will fill up its cheek pouches with food and then head back to its burrow, where it will build up a store of food. In the wild, this behaviour helps to ensure that the hamster is exposed to danger for the briefest possible time while collecting food, which it can then eat in the safety of the burrow. It can also take advantage of nature's bounty by storing food when it is plentiful. However, this habit can be very wasteful in a cage, and fresh foods may turn mouldy if left uneaten in the nest, threatening the hamster's health.

SEEDS AND OTHER FOODS

A selection of seeds – such as wheat and sunflower – should feature in the diets of pet rodents, including mice, hamsters and gerbils. However, variety is important: you should not rely too heavily on sunflower seeds, for instance, as they are oil-based and contain a relatively high level of fat. This could lead to obesity (particularly in gerbils) and related problems, shortening a rodent's life as a result.

Suitable seed mixes are available from pet stores, but, unlike pellets, these do not offer a complete, balanced diet and need to be supplemented by other items such as a little cheese and pieces of fresh vegetables and fruit. You should provide these foodstuffs regularly, particularly if you are hoping to breed your pet, as studies have shown that breeding results are depressed if these items are withheld from rodents' diets. Special vitamin-and-mineral preparations are also available in powder form for small rodents, and will help to prevent any nutritional deficiencies. Simply sprinkle the required quantity of the supplement over the cut surface of a piece of fruit; the powder will stick to this, and should then be eaten readily.

Mice and rats in particular really enjoy small pieces of hard cheese. 'Treats' like this can be useful in helping to tame a pet, but take care when offering such foods by hand, as the sharp incisor teeth at the front of the mouth can inflict a painful nip (this may not be deliberate, but most rodents have fairly poor eyesight), so keep your fingers well out of the way when you offer a titbit. Remember that you should only give treats to your pet in moderation.

DRINKING WATER

Always provide your pet with a supply of fresh, clean drinking water. This should be in a suitable bottle attached securely to the side of its cage or hutch with a metal clip, or firmly suspended from the roof (provided of course that this is within easy reach).

Change the water every day, and clean the drinker thoroughly using a bottle brush at least twice a week.

(Above) Hook-on stainless-steel food container.

(Below) A drinking bottle such as this one will be supplied with a metal clip to attach it securely to the side of the cage.

17

General care indoors

If you keep a small mammal indoors, you will need to clean out its quarters at least once or twice a week. The frequency of this will depend to some extent on the animal: for instance, gerbils are tidy creatures in their habits and so require less cleaning out than hamsters. A cheap plastic carrier with a ventilated hood, bought from a pet store, will make a good temporary home for a rodent while you clean its cage. A wire-mesh carrier (normally sold for a cat) is ideal for a guinea-pig or a rabbit; alternatively, in an outdoor hutch which has a run attached, you can shut the animal out in the run while you clean its sleeping area.

CLEANING A CAGE OR HUTCH

With an indoor plastic cage, remove the soiled litter and wash the tray with hot water (this should not be boiling, or it may discolour the plastic), using a nylon brush to scrub right into the corners. Rinse the tray and leave it to dry thoroughly, then add fresh litter before clipping the two halves of the cage together again securely.

To clean a guinea-pig or rabbit hutch, sweep it out and disinfect the interior using a veterinary disinfectant. Rinse the hutch and leave it to dry, then put in fresh litter or hay.

HANDLING

When you are removing a rodent from its quarters, you must handle it correctly. If the cage has a door in the roof (rather than at the side), lifting the animal out may be more awkward, particularly at first until it is used to being handled. Most rodents will bite if they become alarmed, so reassure your pet before picking it up: scent is much more significant than eyesight in providing a rodent with information about its environment, so always give it time to smell your hand first. Wearing gloves initially may be a good idea if you are a little nervous, but the rodent will then not be able to pick up your scent, so put out a finger first for it to sniff. As you become more confident and the rodent less shy, you can dispense with the gloves. Always lift a larger rodent with cupped hands. Encourage your pet to walk about on your hand as well, and in time you will be able to handle it without problems. Remember that attempting to grab a rodent is usually a sure way of being bitten!

When lifting a guinea-pig or chinchilla, both of which are relatively heavy, you must provide it with adequate support. This may entail holding the animal's body directly, although, in contrast to some rodents – such as Syrian hamsters – it is very unlikely to bite.

Never lift a rabbit by its ears, but support its body from beneath. A hand placed over the ears will help to quieten a nervous rabbit. Beware of the claws as they can inflict a painful scratch.

Indoors, never take your pet out of its quarters until you have checked that the room is secure, with no gaps in the flooring and ideally no pieces of large, heavy furniture for it to hide behind. Keep any other pets well out of the way.

HOUSING WEAR AND TEAR

Check your pet's quarters regularly for any signs of gnawing, which could ultimately lead to an escape; hamsters are often the worst culprits (see also page 12). If you see signs of gnawing damage, there is really no solution other than to buy a new cage. Rabbits are not exempt from attacking their quarters either, typically by gnawing on the back or sides of their hutches. Although they are unlikely to escape, you will need to repair the damage as soon as possible.

This type of behaviour may not be entirely your pet's fault, as it is often linked to a lack of other opportunities for gnawing. To try to regulate this destructive habit in a rodent or a rabbit, provide crusts of bread dried in the oven, or special gnawing blocks sold by a pet store.

FOILING ESCAPES

In spite of all precautions, pets – especially small rodents – occasionally escape, and this can cause major disruption in the household. If your pet escapes, the first thing to do (if you have not already done so) is to close the door so that the animal will at least be confined to the room and so easier to recapture.

Search very cautiously, because if your pet is hiding behind a heavy piece of furniture and you move this suddenly you could crush it. Bear in mind that you are more likely to hear the animal rather than to see it at first, so listen out carefully for any sounds of scratching. The best time to

(Below) Always handle small mammals gently, bearing in mind that some – such as rats – may bite if forcibly held. Never hold the animal tightly: simply restrain it in your hands, as shown.

(Bottom) When lifting and carrying a rabbit you must provide adequate support beneath its hindquarters, as these pets are especially prone to back injuries.

Potential hazards for an indoor rabbit

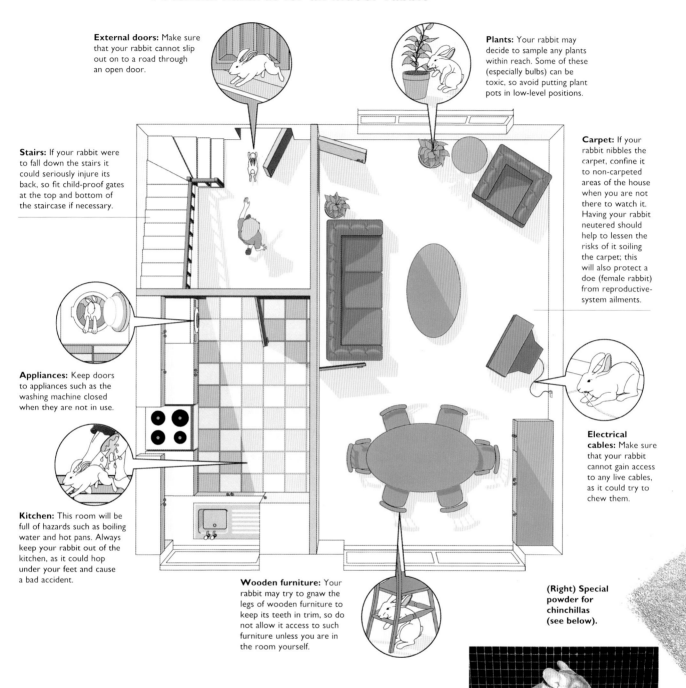

External doors: Make sure that your rabbit cannot slip out on to a road through an open door.

Plants: Your rabbit may decide to sample any plants within reach. Some of these (especially bulbs) can be toxic, so avoid putting plant pots in low-level positions.

Stairs: If your rabbit were to fall down the stairs it could seriously injure its back, so fit child-proof gates at the top and bottom of the staircase if necessary.

Carpet: If your rabbit nibbles the carpet, confine it to non-carpeted areas of the house when you are not there to watch it. Having your rabbit neutered should help to lessen the risks of it soiling the carpet; this will also protect a doe (female rabbit) from reproductive-system ailments.

Appliances: Keep doors to appliances such as the washing machine closed when they are not in use.

Electrical cables: Make sure that your rabbit cannot gain access to any live cables, as it could try to chew them.

Kitchen: This room will be full of hazards such as boiling water and hot pans. Always keep your rabbit out of the kitchen, as it could hop under your feet and cause a bad accident.

Wooden furniture: Your rabbit may try to gnaw the legs of wooden furniture to keep its teeth in trim, so do not allow it access to such furniture unless you are in the room yourself.

(Right) Special powder for chinchillas (see below).

search for a rodent is at dusk, as this is the time when these animals tend to become more active. Once you discover your pet's whereabouts, a fishing net may come in handy for recapturing it, as it may move extremely quickly. Try to 'steer' the animal into the net so that you can scoop it up before returning it to its cage.

If there is no sign of your pet, and only when you have searched the room thoroughly, spread your search further afield. It is essential that you recapture an escaped pet rodent not only for its own sake, but also to prevent any damage within

your home. If it were to escape under the floorboards it could even gnaw at electrical cabling, with disastrous results.

You may be able to trap the escapee by setting up a pile of books in 'steps', connecting to a bucket lined with paper towelling on the floor. Place plastic film over the books, and smear this with cheese leading to the bucket, putting some just out of reach on the rim. With luck, your pet will follow the trail, slide down the plastic and topple in!

Chinchillas have more specific needs than many other small mammals, but they are not difficult to care for in the home. This chinchilla is having a dust bath (see page 35), which will help to keep its soft fur in top condition.

General care outdoors

(Right) Always transfer your pet in a secure carrier from its hutch to an outdoor run. This is an important safety precaution: for instance, if a child were carrying a guinea-pig and the family dog jumped up at him or her, the guinea-pig could fall to the ground with serious – possibly even fatal – consequences. You should obviously also try to keep any other pets in your home away from small mammals to avoid the risk of accidents.

Once the grass is growing in the spring and the weather is warmer you may want to put a rabbit or guinea-pig in its outdoor run, but you must take great care when doing so. The digestive system of rabbits in particular is not well adapted to cope with a dramatic change of diet, and a sudden surfeit of fresh grass in place of its regular food will probably cause diarrhoea at the very least, and possibly even death. If you have fed a rabbit or guinea-pig mainly on dry food and little greenstuff over the winter, start adding more grass to its diet a few weeks before leaving it in an outdoor run for any length of time, to give its digestive system time to adapt.

THE RABBIT'S DIGESTIVE SYSTEM

The rabbit's sensitive digestion stems from the fact that it depends largely on beneficial bacteria in its digestive tract to break down food. Although all rabbits are vegetarian, they lack

(Below) Before allowing a rabbit out into its run, be sure to acclimatize it carefully by gradually increasing the amount of greenfood in its diet. Otherwise it could suffer badly from diarrhoea, which can be very serious in these small mammals.

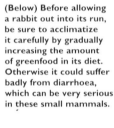

the necessary enzymes to digest the cellulose that makes up plant cell walls, so they would not normally obtain any significant nutritional benefit from such food.

However, in the digestive tract, near the point at which the small and large intestines join, is a long sac called the caecum. This is populated by bacteria and protozoa which digest cellulose and also produce important vitamins, and some of these nutrients are taken up from here into the rabbit's body. Unfortunately the absorption of foodstuffs through the large intestine is very poor, and so a greater proportion of the nutrients would be lost – leaving the rabbit at the risk of starvation – were it not for the fact that it has evolved an unusual means of obtaining maximum benefit

from its food. It literally 'eats' it again, in a process sometimes described as refection.

Rabbits living a natural life in the wild are not exposed to sudden dietary changes. If one food becomes less readily available they will switch gradually to another, and the bacteria in the digestive tract can adjust. If there is a sudden change, harmful bacteria or protozoa may invade the digestive tract, with fatal results.

The importance of diet

The peculiarities of the rabbit's digestive system also mean that treating bacterial illness is more difficult than in animals such as dogs. This is because not all antibiotics are 'selective' as to whether they act on harmful or beneficial bacteria. As a result, if a rabbit is given certain antibiotics, the beneficial bacteria within the caecum may be badly damaged along with the harmful bacteria. Having killed off the beneficial bugs, the drug creates a favourable environment for other, harmful bacteria: notably a type called *Clostridia*. Before long these will have established themselves and released toxins into the rabbit's body, with deadly results.

Recent studies on farmed rabbits have revealed that cases of enterotoxaemia, as this distressing condition is known, are far less likely to arise in those fed a high-fibre diet. This emphasizes the need to provide good-quality hay for pet rabbits at all times, rather than relying simply on pellet food.

OTHER HEALTH HAZARDS

Other possible dangers to your rabbit's health will also be lurking in the garden. If you live in an area where wild rabbits are numerous, try to prevent contact between them and your pet because of the risk of diseases such as myxomatosis (see page 25). You must also have your rabbit vaccinated against myxomatosis before allowing it out in the run, as the disease is easily spread.

Never be tempted to leave your pet in its run overnight, as rabbits – and also guinea-pigs – will be an easy target for foxes. Move the run every few days so that your pet can gain access to fresh grass, but be sure to avoid any area of lawn that has recently been treated with chemicals.

WEATHER CONDITIONS

As the weather changes through the seasons, you must look after your pet accordingly.

Hot weather

When the days become sunnier you will need to choose a shaded location for your pet's run – perhaps under a tree. Both rabbits and guinea-pigs must have adequate opportunity to escape from sunshine, or they could suffer and even die from heatstroke. Always ensure that fresh drinking water is available, in a bottle attached to the side of the run.

Cold and wet weather

In winter, you must protect a rabbit or guinea-pig kept outdoors from the worst of the elements. If your pet has a run with its hutch attached it will have a natural retreat available in bad weather, and you can confine it here safely at night. Site the hutch in a sheltered spot, out of the direction of winds which could drive rain or snow inside.

FOOD, BEDDING AND WATER

Supply a good layer of quality hay for a warm bed; this will also help to supplement the animal's regular diet. At this time of year you should be providing a good level of concentrated energy in the form of a rabbit or guinea-pig mix or pellets, with less green food. Never feed any frosted leaves straight from the garden, as this could upset your pet's digestive system, but thaw them out first.

Check the water supply frequently and, if the temperature is likely to fall below freezing, do not fill the bottle up to the top or it may crack as the water expands and turns into ice. Even if the water in the bottle itself is unfrozen a small volume in the spout may form a plug of ice, so always check the flow from the tip of the bottle.

MOVING YOUR PET INDOORS

You may prefer to move a rabbit's or guinea-pig's hutch into a conservatory or garden shed during the coldest part of the year; this is particularly advisable during damp, foggy weather, which can result in respiratory ailments.

If you do decide to move your pet's hutch indoors, do not put it outside again for long periods until you are sure that the weather is likely to remain mild, or your pet may find the sudden change to colder conditions uncomfortable.

BASIC HOUSING REPAIRS

It is easy to overlook the base area of a hutch, but if it stands on wooden legs you should check them periodically to ensure that they have not started to rot, especially where they touch the ground. If there is any weakness here, the hutch could be blown over or collapse in a storm or high wind.

During the warm summer weather the roofing felt may have expanded and split, creating gaps for the rain to penetrate, so check for any signs of water-staining inside the hutch around the sides of the roof. If necessary, remove your pet temporarily and replace the roofing felt to keep the interior of its quarters as dry as possible.

Even if kept outdoors, a long-haired guinea-pig must be given a thorough grooming every day to remove any bedding that has become caught in the coat, and to deal with any tangles before they can turn into solid mats.

21

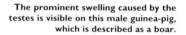

Breeding

As with any pet, breeding small mammals is something that you should take very seriously. The prolific nature of most of these animals means that, if you plan to breed from your pets, you must give proper thought to finding good homes for the offspring before arranging a mating. Do not simply assume that friends will want the young, or that a pet store will be interested in buying them from you.

The prominent swelling caused by the testes is visible on this male guinea-pig, which is described as a boar.

At one day old, a rabbit's ears are relatively small in comparison with its body size; note also the dark areas of skin, which reveal what a rabbit's patterning will be once its fur has grown.

At 13 days old, the same rabbit as shown above has a good covering of fur and its eyes are open.

SEXING

Sexing small mammals is a fairly straightforward task, as the gap between the anal and genital orifices is generally much smaller in a female than in a male. There are some other specific differences, but in the majority of cases this is the simplest guide when looking at a young small mammal at a stage before the testes of a male become clearly visible.

MATING

With the notable exception of hamsters, there is generally little difficulty in persuading small mammals to mate. Gerbils should be housed in groups in any event, while placing a male guinea-pig in the company of a female is likely to lead to her becoming pregnant within a month or so.

Unlike a rodent, a female rabbit will ovulate when a buck is introduced, rather than having a regular cycle, so she can be mated at any time (rodents ovulate very quickly in any case – approximately every four to five days – and so successful mating is unlikely to take very long).

If you put a male and female hamster together they are very likely to fight, so the mating should be carried out in a neutral cage with a partition. Place the male and then the female in the cage on either side of the partition, and then remove it. If fighting does break out, separate the animals again. Alternatively, you can place the female in

the male's cage, but never introduce the male into the female's quarters as she will almost inevitably attack him. Do not leave hamsters together unsupervised, as they may inflict severe injuries on each other. Once mating has taken place (within an hour or so), separate them again.

The age at which rodents are mated can be significant, particularly in the case of guinea-pigs. If a guinea-pig sow has not bred before, you should not allow her to mate after the age of 10 months because her pelvis will have become fused. This will increase the likelihood of birth difficulties, and may mean that your vet has to carry out a Caesarean section. Rabbits can be mated from about five months onwards, although the larger breeds are slower to mature than their smaller counterparts (see pages 38–9).

PREGNANCY

You should avoid handling a pregnant small mammal any more than is strictly necessary, particularly towards the end of the pregnancy, because you could injure it. If you do have to pick up a pregnant animal – especially a guinea-pig, which may become very large towards the end of pregnancy – be sure to provide adequate support with both hands.

There is a marked difference between the so-called myomorph rodents and members of the caviomorph group in terms of their reproductive biology. The myomorphs (rats, mice, hamsters and gerbils) have a relatively short pregnancy and their young are born naked and helpless. In contrast, the caviomorphs (guinea-pigs and chinchillas) have much longer gestation periods and produce fewer young on average, but these are born fully developed with open eyes and a full covering of fur. The lagomorphs (rabbits)

The female guinea-pig's teats can be clearly seen here; she is called a sow.

are more closely allied to the myomorphs, as their young are born undeveloped and with much smaller ears than those of adults.

Pregnancy toxaemia

Although young guinea-pigs can feed themselves from birth, it is important that they suckle from their mother as well. However, guinea-pig sows can sometimes develop the metabolic illness known as pregnancy toxaemia (this particularly affects obese animals). The illness is generally manifested by severe twitching and collapse. If you see these signs in your guinea-pig sow, seek veterinary treatment for her without delay.

REARING

In most cases a female rodent will rear her offspring with no problems, although small litters of just one or two young are occasionally neglected. This is because many rodents are able to mate again successfully almost immediately after they have given birth, and in survival terms it may be better for them to breed again rather than to expend a significant part of their brief lives in rearing just one or two offspring. This is an instinctive reaction, and does not mean that the female will not prove to be a model mother to her young in the future. It may be possible to improve litter sizes by adding more fresh items – such as small pieces of apple and raw carrot – to the diet (see pages 16–17); your vet will be able to give you further advice on this.

Rabbits can behave in a similar fashion, with any significant disturbance of the nest also resulting in a female abandoning her litter. It is therefore better to restrain your curiosity rather than poking around in the nest in the female's absence to see how many young have been born. Even if you cover them over again the female is very likely to detect your scent, and this will disturb her. If you do have to inspect the nest for any reason, wipe a pencil or similar instrument in the cage litter and use this so that you do not leave behind any unfamiliar scent.

Young rabbits will be fully weaned and ready to go to their new homes by the time they are six weeks old. Be careful at first to stick to the food that they are used to eating, as this will greatly reduce the likelihood of digestive upsets. Always make changes to the diet very gradually.

23

Before breeding your pet rodents, you must be sure that you will be able to find good homes for all the offspring.

Health care

Antibiotics have proved so valuable in treating many illnesses afflicting our pets that it is easy to forget that they can have harmful side-effects. This is certainly true within the small-mammal group, where these drugs are liable to disturb the beneficial bacterial lining of the gut, inducing a fatal diarrhoea. You must therefore take great care when giving antibiotics to small mammals, particularly in countries where they are available over the counter rather than on veterinary prescription. Always seek experienced professional advice before using treatment of this kind.

Small mammals may be affected by a number of health problems, such as those described here. Carry out regular health checks on your pet, so that you can spot possible problems and seek veterinary advice as necessary.

DIGESTIVE PROBLEMS

These are relatively common in small mammals. Sudden dietary changes can disrupt the bacterial flora critical for the proper digestion of food, so you must avoid these at all costs. Newly acquired pets are at greatest risk, and may benefit from having a probiotic (available from your vet or a pet store) added to their food to help stabilize the bacteria in the gut.

Rodents are also sometimes affected by the following serious enteric (gut) infections.

Tyzzer's disease

This is a bacterial illness which spreads through breeding colonies and is most likely to afflict young animals – including gerbils, which are fairly resistant to the majority of infectious illnesses. A small mammal that is affected by Tyzzer's disease will be inactive, with fluffed-up fur and a hunched posture. Treatment of this condition can be difficult.

'Wet tail'

Stress may trigger a number of diseases and is thought to be a factor in the illness known as 'wet tail', which affects hamsters. The condition is also called proliferative ileitis because of its effects in the ileum (the final part of the small intestine). The bacterium known as E. coli is implicated in this illness. Young animals are at greatest risk, and the outlook for an affected individual will unfortunately be poor.

PARASITES

Rodents have a reputation for carrying fleas, mites and ticks, but these parasites are actually very rarely encountered in domestic animals. Mites are most likely to be a problem, and should be suspected in cases of unexplained hair loss. Your vet will be able to confirm the diagnosis by taking and analysing a skin scraping, and will then prescribe suitable treatment. Guinea-pigs and hamsters are especially vulnerable to mites.

Rabbits are vulnerable to infestations of ear mites, which lead to the formation of thick brown scabs in the ear canals. Flowers of sulphur dusted into the ears is the traditional treatment. If the mites penetrate into the inner ear the prognosis will be poor, as they are likely to affect the rabbit's sense of balance.

In hot weather flies are likely to be attracted to a guinea-pig or rabbit suffering from diarrhoea, and will lay their eggs in the soiled fur around its vent. These will hatch rapidly into maggots, which will eat into the animal's flesh and produce toxins that can prove deadly in a short time. Prevention is obviously better than cure, but if you do encounter so-called 'fly strike', be sure to clean the affected area thoroughly and remove the maggots straight away.

Coccidiosis

This protozoal (one-celled, microscopic) parasitic disease is a particular problem in rabbits and strikes either the liver or the intestines, where it strips the gut lining. Drugs that will suppress the infection – known as coccidiostats – are regularly added to rabbit foods by manufacturers as a precautionary measure. Domestic rabbits can often be infected by eating green food contaminated by wild rabbits, and some rabbits can harbour the infection and represent a danger to others without actually displaying any signs of illness themselves.

Tapeworms

Other internal parasites that can be a problem in rabbits are tapeworms. If you have a dog, try to keep an area of the lawn protected for your rabbit, and be sure to de-worm the dog regularly and remove any faeces as soon as possible (see page 59), or your rabbit may pick up tapeworm eggs which have passed out of the dog's gut. The eggs will then develop in its own body, causing cysts containing immature tapeworms to form. These can arise under the skin, becoming as large as golf balls, and may require surgical removal.

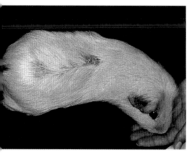

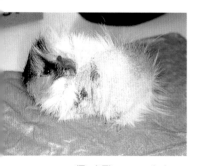

(Top) The crusty dark scabs in this rabbit's ears are a sign of canker caused by mites. This can be treated, but the rabbit must be kept away from others and its quarters disinfected thoroughly to prevent re-infection.

(Centre) Skin ailments are common in guinea-pigs. This one is thought to be suffering from scurvy, caused by a deficiency of vitamin C.

(Bottom) Here a severe mite infestation has resulted in hair loss; these mites also cause inflammation. Modern drugs can help, but the condition may recur. Contaminated bedding may be the source of an outbreak, although mites will also spread easily between guinea-pigs.

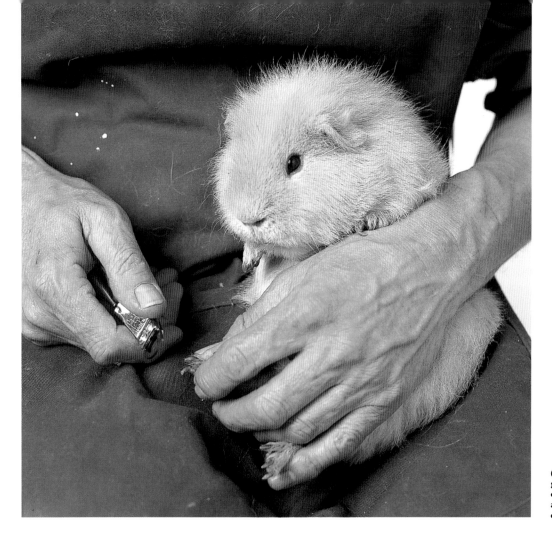

(Left) The claws of pet guinea-pigs and rabbits often become overgrown, and may need trimming every two months or so.

VIRUSES

A number of viruses have been identified in rodents, but these are of little concern to the pet owner. You are much more likely to encounter viruses affecting rabbits: these may well be fatal unless the animal is protected, so, if you have a rabbit, ask your vet's advice on vaccination.

Myxomatosis

When this disease was deliberately introduced into the UK in 1953 to curb the wild-rabbit population, it proved a devastating example of the power of germ warfare. The virus wiped out virtually all the rabbits exposed to it, leaving less than one in 10,000 survivors (according to early estimates) as the infection swept the country. A watery eye discharge is usually the first sign of the illness, starting after seven days. Soon afterwards the rabbit becomes blind, with pus-filled swellings forming around its eyes. It will become deaf and die within about a week, often from starvation.

The virus is spread in two main ways. It can be transmitted by rabbit fleas, which stick to the ears, feed on the blood of an infected rabbit and then transmit the illness when they move to a healthy individual; this is especially likely within the confines of a burrow. The second insect involved in the spread of myxomatosis is the mosquito, which transmits the virus via contaminated blood. Outbreaks of the disease tend to peak in the late summer, when mosquitoes are most prolific.

Pet rabbits are much more vulnerable to myxomatosis than their wild counterparts, because their body defences have not been triggered through exposure to the virus over many previous generations. If a pet rabbit develops signs of myxomatosis it will almost inevitably die (although it should be euthanased by a vet to prevent suffering), so vaccination is vital.

Viral haemorrhagic disease (VHD)

This virus, which only affects rabbits, has spread widely since being identified in 1984. It can be spread by contaminated food or on clothing, as well as between rabbits. Unvaccinated animals over eight weeks old are most at risk. Death usually occurs a day or so after infection, often with few signs except a bloody nasal discharge.

Guillotine clippers like these are the easiest to use, and will enable you to cut the claw precisely. It is very important that you position the animal firmly and locate the blood supply to the claw before cutting, as, if you cut too high, the claw will bleed. If you do not feel confident about cutting a guinea-pig's or rabbit's claws yourself, ask your vet to do it for you.

Hamsters

In 1930, a single Syrian hamster and her litter were discovered near Aleppo in Syria, and it is from this one family that almost all of today's pet Syrian hamsters are descended. The first progeny of this original stock were introduced to the UK in 1931, but it was not until after the Second World War that this creature's potential as a pet became recognized, whereupon breeding hamsters were established on a large scale to meet demand both in the UK and in countries throughout the world. The Syrian hamster is now one of the most popular smaller mammals, and many colour and coat variations have been developed.

CHARACTERISTICS OF THE SYRIAN HAMSTER

(Mesocricetus auratus)

An adult Syrian hamster is approximately 15 cm (6 in) long, and has glossy fur and rather loose skin. The paws are good at grasping, and the hamster uses them to hold food and branches (which it gnaws), and to groom itself. Its eyesight is fairly poor, but its hearing is acute.

The lifespan of the hamster is rather short, usually averaging 18–24 months, although many individuals live for less than a year. Cases of Syrian hamsters living for seven years – and in one case for 10 years – have been recorded, but these are exceptional.

Hamsters are nocturnal creatures in their habits, and so they make very good pets for owners who are out of the house during the day. They enjoy exercise and will constantly scamper around their cages, playing with any toys provided and carrying food back to their beds in their cheek pouches.

In spite of their appeal, however, Syrian hamsters are not recommended as pets for young children because they can be difficult to handle and have a tendency to bite. As adults, they must be housed individually or they will fight severely among themselves.

Variegated/Piebald hamster

Colour and coat variations

All adult Syrian hamsters are roughly the same size and shape, but many different-coloured varieties have been bred in captivity.

Golden: This is still the most common coat colour; the Syrian hamster is in fact sometimes known as the golden hamster. There are three variations: the normal golden (the coat is basically golden, with dark tips to the hairs and greyish roots; the abdomen is white and the ears dark grey); the dark golden (the coat has a reddish sheen and the black tips to the hairs are much more pronounced; the ears are black); and the light golden (there are no black tips to the hairs; the abdomen is white).

Cream: There are three different eye colours in this variation: red-eyed cream, ruby-eyed cream and black-eyed cream. The latter was one of the first colour forms to be bred in captivity; hamsters with this coloration tend to have a deeper-coloured coat than the other two varieties, as well as darker ears.

Grey: There are three shades of grey hamster, all of which are fairly new varieties: the dominant grey (the coat is dark grey overlaid with a flesh-coloured tint; the ears and eyes are black); the dark grey (dark grey overall, with black ears and eyes); and the light grey (this variety has a silvery tinge to the coat; its distinctive red eyes make it very easily recognizable).

White: There are three varieties that come under the heading of white: albino (completely white with pink eyes); the dark-eared albino (as the name suggests, this is the same as the albino but with dark ears); and the black-eyed white (the coat is white; the eyes are black and the ears are pink).

Cinnamon: This variety is the brightest-coloured of all, with a rich orange fur and lighter ears.

Yellow: This is similar to the black-eyed cream, but the fur is slightly darker with darker guard hairs.

Honey: This resembles the yellow, but has red eyes and lighter ears.

Rust: The fur of this hamster is darker than that of the cinnamon. The eyes are black and the ears brown.

Sepia: Although the sepia colouring is sometimes confused with the grey, it is in fact more beige than grey. The eyes of this hamster are black and the ears are grey.

Long-haired, black-eyed white hamster

Smoke pearl: The coat is completely pearl grey, with black eyes and dark grey ears.

Blond: As you would expect, here the fur is blond; the eyes are red.

Dove: The fur is medium grey with dark bases; the abdomen is white. The eyes are black and the ears dark grey.

Marked colours

As well as the 'self' (solid) colours already listed, the following are four possible variations of markings that may be found on the coat.

Banded: This hamster has an unbroken band of white circling the body (the remainder of the fur can be any colour).

Golden hamster (with full cheek pouches)

Variegated/Piebald: This has white and coloured areas (the markings can be very variable).

Dominant spot: This is similar to the piebald but with spotted markings.

Tortoiseshell and white: This is very similar in pattern to the tortoiseshell cat – the coat is overlaid with golden and white patches. There is also a banded variety of the tortoiseshell and white, as well as a cinnamon tortoiseshell and a grey tortoiseshell, but in these varieties the colour contrast is less obvious than in the white.

Coat varieties

The majority of hamsters are short-haired, but there are three additional main fur types.

Satin: This is very similar to the short-haired variety, but the coat has a glossy sheen which makes the colours look much richer.

Long-haired: This coat is long, fine and dense, and needs to be groomed regularly as it tends to become tangled. This coat type is known as the 'teddy' in the USA.

Rex: This coat is decidedly curly, as are the whiskers. Young rex hamsters have a wavy coat, which becomes curlier with age. In some instances the coat may be thinner than usual, which is undesirable.

Breeding data for the Syrian hamster

🌑 16 days   ⊞ 5–7 young   🛇 24 days

OTHER HAMSTERS

Some other hamsters are becoming more widely known and, as they are more sociable creatures than the Syrian hamster, their popularity is increasing. Most pet stores will keep the dwarf Russian, but you may need to go to a specialist supplier for a Chinese hamster.

Dwarf Russian (*Phodopus sungoris*) This hamster has recently become popular. It is smaller than the Syrian and, when young, may be able to escape through the mesh of a standard cage, so it is best housed in a covered aquarium. If a small group of these hamsters is kept together from weaning onwards they may live peaceably, although adding a new individual to an existing group will almost inevitably result in fighting.

There are two distinct subspecies of this hamster: Campbell's (*P.s. campbelli*) and the winter white dwarf Russian (*P.s. sungoris*), distinguishable by its change in coloration through the year. A second species, Roborovski's dwarf hamster (*P. roborovski*), is also sometimes available and needs similar care.

Pregnancy in dwarf hamsters is likely to last about 21 days. The young will be sexually mature at one to two months.

Chinese (*Cricetus griseus*) Also sometimes called the striped hamster, this variety may grow up to 12 cm (5 in) long and can be identified by the dark stripe running down its back. A white-spotted mutation of this species is also now established. Like the dwarf Russian, this hamster is relatively social with others of its kind.

Dove hamster

Gerbils

Gerbils originated in the desert regions of North Africa and Asia. It was only as recently as the early 1950s that they became generally available to buy in the USA, and they were unknown as pets in the UK until 1964. Now, however, they have become one of the most widely kept members of the small-mammal group, largely because of their very appealing natures.

KEEPING GERBILS

In many ways, gerbils make the ideal small pet. Unlike hamsters, which are nocturnal creatures, gerbils are active for short periods throughout the day. They are friendly, alert, curious and easy to tame. They are also odourless and, because they were originally desert animals, they conserve moisture by producing very little urine and hard, dry faeces, so that cleaning out their quarters is straightforward.

In the wild gerbils live in underground tunnels, and when kept as pets in the home they will also dig burrows in their quarters. They often balance themselves up on their hindlegs to examine their surroundings, and to free their front paws to hold food such as seeds. The long hindlegs enable them to leap away from enemies, although when running they normally drop down on to all fours. Gerbils make little – if any – noise but, when alarmed, they will drum on the ground with their hindlegs.

Argente gerbil

Males tend to be larger than females, with their average weights being 130 g (4½ oz) and 70 g (2½ oz) respectively. The lifespan of the gerbil is about three years, although, with careful attention on their owners' part to diet and general cleanliness, some may live for up to five years. Gerbils do not hibernate, although they will tend to sleep for long periods if the room temperature is too high.

Some strains of gerbil have a rather disturbing tendency to suffer from epilepsy. This is most likely to occur after a prolonged period of handling, particularly in the case of a gerbil which is unused to being picked up. Although worrying, this phase will pass quite rapidly if the gerbil is put back in its quarters and left to recover quietly.

Another aspect of care which must be borne in mind when handling gerbils is the fact that the skin covering on the tip of the tail is very thin and easily damaged, which will result in bleeding, so never restrain a gerbil by its tail.

MONGOLIAN GERBIL

(*Meriones unguiculatus*)
This gerbil is the type most commonly available. It is sandy brown with a black tipping to the fur; this colouring is known as 'agouti'. It also has whitish underparts and pale fur on the feet. The choice of colour forms is limited at present, possibly because this gerbil has only been domesticated for a fairly short time. Other colours are now more common, but if you wish to obtain a gerbil of a rarer colour you may need to seek out a specialist breeder.

The Canadian white spot was the first colour mutation to be recorded. This has a normal sandy-coloured coat, but with a white spot on the nose, forehead and neck; the feet and tail tip are also white. If the white areas are more extensive, the gerbil is described as 'patched'.

Other colours

Mongolian gerbils are also available in the following colours.

Pink-eyed white (albino): Pure-white coat, white whiskers and pink eyes. The ears are flesh-coloured with white hairs.

Dark-tailed white and agouti gerbils

Dark-tailed white: Until it is 13 weeks old, this variety resembles an albino; a dark ridge then appears on the tail.

Argente: This is golden all over without the usual longer, coarser hairs. The abdomen and feet are white, there are hairs on the ears and the eyes are red.

Black: The fur is jet black, and the eyes, whiskers and ears are also black.

Black gerbil

Egyptian (*Gerbillus gerbillus*)
This small gerbil is usually a light sandy brown, although some individuals have a tint of red in their coats. It is easy to tame, making it a good pet for children, and a group will live together happily.

Indian (*Tatera indica*)
Also known as the red-footed gerbil, this is small with no hair on the tail and feet, which are a deep pink colour. The Indian gerbil likes to live alone and, as it is difficult to tame, does not make a particularly friendly pet.

Jerusalem (*Meriones crassus*)
This species is much larger than the Mongolian gerbil, and the fur has a hint of red. It differs from other gerbils in that it is a solitary animal, and the males and females do not stay together after mating. It appears more rat-like than the Mongolian gerbil and is more likely to bite, so it is not a good pet.

Libyan (*Meriones libycus*)
This is the rarest gerbil to be kept as a pet. It is much larger than the Mongolian gerbil, growing up to 20 cm (8 in) in length, and has longer ears. It is more aggressive and is difficult to breed, as the females tend to eat their young.

Namib Paeba (*Gerbillus paeba*)
This gerbil – also called the snowshoe gerbil because of its foot shape – is less well known than the other species. It is reasonably friendly towards people, particularly if obtained as a youngster.

Grey agouti/Chinchilla: The fur has a very attractive grey tone.

Blue: A dark shade of grey.

Lilac: The body of the lilac gerbil is pale grey all over, and the eyes are a distinctive red.

Dove: The colouring is a slightly paler variant of the lilac.

Breeding data for the Mongolian gerbil

🌑 25 days   #️⃣ 4–6 young   🔔 21 days

OTHER GERBILS

As well as the Mongolian gerbil – which is generally very widely available from pet stores – a number of other gerbils are occasionally sold. These include the five following varieties.

Mice

Today's so-called 'fancy mice' are far removed from their wild ancestor, the house mouse (*Mus musculus*). The process of domestication began in the UK, well over a century ago, with many present-day varieties first appearing in the laboratories of that era, where the mice were kept and bred for medical experiments. Mice measure about 8 cm (3 in) on average, with a tail of similar length. The tail, like the ears, is hairless. There are now over 700 colour and coat variants, with fancy mice ranging in colour from pure white through fawn and red to black in the 'self' (solid) colours; combinations such as black and white or black and tan are also well established. You can even choose from short- or long-coated forms as well as sleek-coated satin strains or curly-coated races.

KEEPING MICE

Most mice live for less than three years, so it is important to start with young animals: ideally between five and six weeks of age. If you wish to keep more than one mouse, it is best to choose females. These will not fight – especially if you introduce them into their quarters at the same time – and will not have such a pungent odour as male mice. If you do have males and females, you should keep them apart unless you are planning to breed them.

For the purposes of breeding, a trio comprising two females and a male is often preferable. Mice reach sexual maturity quickly: certainly by 12 weeks old, and often earlier. Approximately nine offspring are normally produced, although this figure can be greater, and sometimes even doubled.

Handling a mouse is not difficult, but must always be done very gently. Having persuaded it to walk on to your hand, you can restrain it gently by holding the base of the tail. Never dangle a mouse by the tail, as you may well injure it.

EQUIPMENT

Mice are often rather shy and, although they can be safely kept in mesh-topped cages (see page 12), you must provide adequate retreats in which they are able to escape from human view. Tubes – such as the cardboard centres of kitchen rolls – are especially appreciated by mice for hiding inside, and they may enjoy gnawing them as well. When the tubes become soiled, simply replace them with fresh ones. You will also be able to buy various houses and similar items for the cage. Mice are far less enthusiastic than hamsters about using exercise wheels. If you do provide a wheel it must be of a 'closed' design so that there is no risk of your mouse becoming caught and injuring its long tail (see also page 13).

A GOOD DIET

Feeding mice is very straightforward. You can use pellets or cereal-based foods containing items such as barley, maize and rolled oats, all of which are widely available. A mouse will typically eat about 7 g (¼ oz) of a basic food mix every day. Supplement this food with other sources of fibre such as wholemeal bread, millet and dog biscuits, which will also help to keep its teeth in trim. If you are feeding cereals, give some additional protein occasionally, in the form of dry dog or cat food, or yolk from a hard-boiled egg.

You should also provide well-washed green food, fruit and vegetables two or three times a week. If any of this food remains uneaten, remove it from the cage daily to prevent it from turning mouldy, as this could present a hazard to your mouse's health. Check the bedding every day, too, as some food may be hidden away here.

SHOWING MICE

If you are interested in exhibiting your mice, you will need to start by joining a local club affiliated to the national body which draws up the judging rules and standards for competition. In the UK, the oldest organization of this type is the National Mouse Club, which was founded back in 1896.

Bear in mind that the appearance, or 'type' of mice sold in pet stores is likely

(Top) Self chocolate mouse
(Above) Dove tan mouse
(Opposite) Self fawn mouse

to be significantly different from those seen at shows, and by visiting such events, as well as exhibition breeders, you will soon gain a clear insight into what is required for showing success. Other factors – notably the condition of the mice – are also important.

Most exhibitors will take three boxes to a show: a carrying box, a separate container for grooming and the show cage itself. The grooming container is simple in design, and is merely an escape-proof box with a thick layer of hay into which the mouse can burrow. This helps to clean the fur, but the best way of imparting the necessary glossy sheen to the coat is by stroking the fur repeatedly with a silk cloth. Mice are still traditionally exhibited in standard Maxey cages, named after a prominent Victorian mouse fancier called Walter Maxey. These are a distinctive shade of green on the outside and red on the inside, and contain only one mouse each. The cages are available from specialist suppliers.

Breeding data

🕐 3 weeks   # 9 young   👤 3 weeks

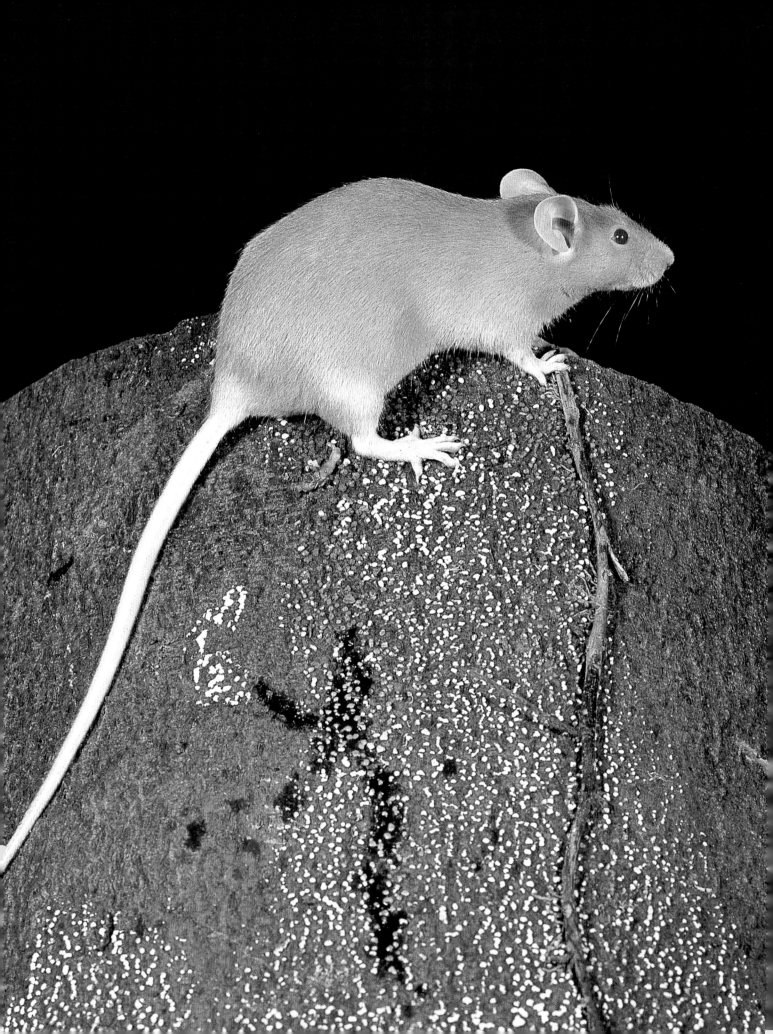

Rats

The keeping of rats has a rather chequered history. Interest first began in Victorian Britain, when professional rat-catchers worked in numerous cities around the country. Although these men were paid to trap rats, they did not always kill them – instead, they sold the rats caught in buildings (rather than sewer rats, which were more likely to be diseased) to owners of rat pits. These were often set up in pubs and provided a source of entertainment and gambling possibilities for the patrons. In this 'sport', terrier dogs were set loose among the rats in the pit and encouraged to kill them as quickly as possible.

THE FIRST PET RATS

Some rats were spared the fate of the pits. For instance, Jimmy Shaw, the proprietor of one of London's leading rat pits, became well known for his collection of unusually coloured rats. He apparently trapped his first white rat in a burial ground. Pied rats were also recorded during this period, and Jack Black – Queen Victoria's official rat- and mole-catcher – kept and bred these black-and-white animals, which he is said to have sold to young women who kept them as fashionable pets in squirrel cages. Among his customers may have been a young Beatrix Potter, who doted on her pet rat called Sammy. In 1908, when her story *Samuel Whiskers* was published, she dedicated it to her pet.

Interest in rats had apparently peaked by the end of the 1920s, and it was not until the founding of the National Fancy Rat Society in 1976 that interest in these intelligent rodents became widespread.

TYPES OF RAT

Today's fancy rats are all descendants of the ordinary brown rat (*Rattus norvegicus*), which, having displaced its small black relative (*R. rattus*), is now the most common species worldwide. However, for a period during the 1920s several colours of the black rat were

Mink rat

bred, of which the most unusual was a supposed greenish strain. Unfortunately, these colours have all disappeared.

Coat colours and types

While the albino form of the rat – pure white with reddish eyes – is still the most common, there are now roughly 25 different varieties recognized for show purposes. Recent introductions include the champagne (beige with pink eyes) and the pearl (predominantly white, but with dark tips to the hairs). The mink is a unique colour, with no counterpart at present in the mouse fancy, being a light coffee colour with

a bluish sheen. Darker colours – such as the self chocolate (which should be dark brown with no odd white hairs) – are also now established.

In addition, there are a number of patterned varieties. The most common of these is the hooded rat, which has a dark head and shoulders and a similarly coloured saddle area, offset against white on the flanks. The distribution of markings on this rat is important, as it is on the Berkshire rat, where light areas should be restricted to the underparts – excepting a white spot on the head.

A rex mutation has also emerged, resulting in a curly coat and curled whiskers. This feature can be combined with any of the colours or patterned variants, offering considerable scope for breeders. To date, however, neither long-coated nor satin-coated variants have been established.

CARING FOR RATS

Averaging at least 25 cm (10 in) in size with a tail of similar length, pet rats will obviously require more spacious surroundings than mice. They also have a longer lifespan, of up to four years in many cases. It is best to start with pups – as young rats are known – of about five weeks old, as they should be relatively easy to tame.

Rats are social creatures, and are happiest maintained in single-sex pairs rather than being housed on their own if they are not intended for breeding.

Cover the floor of the cage or converted aquarium (the latter must have a secure lid – see page 13) with a layer of woodshavings up to 5 cm (2 in) deep. Do not use sawdust as bedding for rats, as particles may irritate their prominent eyes. If you decide to breed your rats, you must provide bedding material – in addition to the normal woodshavings or other litter – so that the female can make a snug nest.

HANDLING

The correct way to pick up a rat is to place one hand over its back, with its nose towards your wrist. This will allow you to encircle the rat's body gently with your fingers, with your other hand supporting it from beneath. Alternatively, place a hand around the rat's shoulders, positioning your thumb under the lower jaw if necessary to avoid being bitten.

DIETARY REQUIREMENTS

The diet recommended for mice (see page 30) will also suit rats well, although, being larger, they will eat as much as 42 g (1½ oz) of food daily.

Breeding data

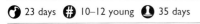 23 days 10–12 young 35 days

(Top) Albino rat
(Above) Cinnamon rat

Black-capped rat

Chinchillas

Baby chinchilla

Chinchillas are cute, cuddly and growing rapidly in popularity as pets, although they are considerably more expensive to buy than most other small mammals. Their clean habits and friendly nature have endeared them to many people who would never consider keeping better-known rodents – such as rats – in their homes.

THE CHINCHILLA'S HISTORY

Human interest in chinchillas has not always been as benign as it is today. These animals were hunted for their distinctive, beautifully soft fur, and by the early years of this century they were almost extinct. Instead of a single hair growing from a hair follicle in the skin, chinchillas can have as many as 80 hairs in each follicle, which produces a very dense pelt. This provides them with good protection against the cold in their homeland of the high Andes in South America. The coat is also so thick that parasites such as fleas cannot penetrate it. It was the Inca peoples who first hunted chinchillas for their fur, which was highly prized for making garments. The early Spanish explorers then took chinchilla fur back to Europe in the early 16th century, where, because of its exquisite softness and rarity, it was soon found decorating royal garments. In the late 19th century, more systematic hunting of chinchillas for their fur resulted in a dramatic decline in their numbers, and, worse still, attempts at farming them on a commercial basis in South America subsequently failed.

By the time an American mining engineer called M.F. Chapman saw his first live chinchilla in Chile in 1923, the species was already exceedingly scarce. However, Chapman was so fascinated that he decided to set up a breeding farm for chinchillas in the USA. He was quite undeterred by the fact that they were then on the very verge of extinction, and pressed on regardless, hiring 23 men to obtain stock for him. It took them three years to catch just 11 specimens, which were acclimatized to live at lower altitudes before starting the journey by sea to California. At this stage chinchillas – not surprisingly – sold for huge sums, but, as more became known about them and they started to breed freely in the USA, their price began to fall.

Until the 1960s, chinchillas were still kept almost exclusively for their fur. However, since that time and with the decline of the fur market, they have soared in popularity as pets around the world. Domestication has also seen the emergence of a range of colour forms. The traditional coloration of the chinchilla is slate blue-grey with a white belly (this is described as the 'standard' by breeders), but other colours now range from pure white through beige to charcoal and ebony, although some remain very expensive.

KEEPING CHINCHILLAS

Chinchillas will not thrive in damp surroundings, and so are usually kept indoors. They need to be housed in all-wire cages so that their droppings will fall through the mesh beneath them and not soil their coats.

They will also require a nest box, measuring approximately 50 cm (20 in) in length and 25 cm (10 in) in width and height; this should be placed on the

Fawn chinchilla

Black-velvet chinchilla

Pink-white chinchilla

floor of the cage to provide a secure sleeping place for the chinchillas.

A regular dust bath – using special dusting powder made of activated clay or volcanic ash – is also essential to keep the unique fur in good condition. This involves tipping a layer of powder about 5 cm (2 in) deep on to a metal tray, and placing this in the chinchillas' enclosure for about five minutes two or three times a week. The animals will roll around in the powder and so remove excessive grease from their coats. Special chinchilla combs are also available for grooming.

FOOD AND DRINK

A special pelleted food is available for chinchillas, and this – along with good-quality hay – will fulfil their dietary needs. Provide a constant supply of fresh water in a bottle with a metal spout – like other rodents, chinchillas have sharp, powerful incisor teeth which can crack plastic easily. The teeth will continue growing throughout the animals' lives and need constant wear if they are not to become too long. You should therefore supply wooden blocks for them to gnaw on, although they may also decide to attack their wooden nest box with their teeth.

BREEDING

You can safely keep a pair of chinchillas together, although on occasions a female may prove rather territorial and aggressive towards her intended mate. Chinchillas are generally bred from about six months of age. If a successful mating has taken place, you will see a so-called 'stopper' of whitish mucus on the floor of their cage, and about two months later, signs of mammary development will become apparent in the female. You should stop providing the dust bath just prior to the anticipated date of birth, as it could cause irritation at this stage; you can start this again after a week.

Young chinchillas are known as kits. While suckling her offspring the female will often lose the fur around her mammary glands. This is normal, and the fur will grow back in due course. Although the kits may start sampling solid food when they are only two weeks old, they will not be weaned for a further month or so. You can then offer them an infant food. The young chinchillas should soon grow used to being handled, and will become very tame. Chinchillas have been known to live for 20 years on rare occasions, making them among the longest-lived of all rodents, although the average lifespan is 10–12 years.

Breeding data

🕐 16 weeks   #️ 2–8 young   ⚊ 6 weeks

Standard/Agouti chinchilla

Guinea-pigs

Pet guinea-pigs, or cavies, are probably descended from the wild 'cui' kept 500 years ago by the Incas in South America. These creatures were smaller than the guinea-pigs of today, and were often eaten on special occasions. When the Spanish *conquistadores* landed in South America they noticed that the skinned animals looked like tiny pigs, and called them 'cochinillos das Indas' or 'little Indian pigs'. The prefix 'guinea' was probably added when the Spaniards took the animals to Guiana or even to Guinea in West Africa, on the long sea voyage to Europe. Guinea-pigs were first recorded in the UK in around 1750, although they were already popular in mainland Europe by this time. Today, many South American Indians still keep and breed the animals as a basic source of food.

KEEPING GUINEA-PIGS

A guinea-pig is a very easy pet to look after, either outdoors in a hutch or indoors in a suitable run, but you must ensure that it cannot be harmed by a dog or a cat, or even a fox if outdoors.

A special guinea food in the form of a cereal-based diet or pellets will be essential because of this animal's need for vitamin C (see page 16). You should also provide other food items – such as greenstuff and carrots – on a regular basis. Breeding guinea-pigs is not difficult.

GUINEA-PIG VARIETIES

Many different varieties of guinea-pig are now established and the list continues to grow, thanks in part to a keen interest among breeders in exhibiting their stock.

Pure-bred guinea pigs can be divided into four groups: smooth, short-haired English self guinea-pigs ('self' meaning solid colour); smooth, short-haired guinea-pigs with markings; rough-haired, or rosetted, guinea-pigs; and long-haired guinea pigs. Information on the different types is given here.

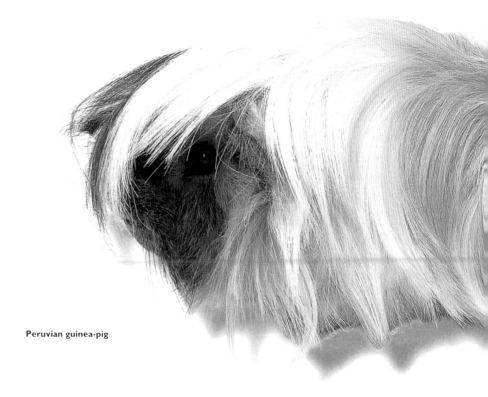

Peruvian guinea-pig

English self

These guinea-pigs are one colour all over. For showing purposes, the coat colour – which should be even and go right down to the skin – is the most important feature. However, 'type' (the overall body shape) is also important: an individual should have a broad head with a good width between the eyes, a short face with large, drooping ears and strong, high shoulders.

The most popular member of this group is probably the self black guinea-pig. A serious show fault in this variety is any trace of red or white hairs in the coat, but such animals will be ideal as pets. The pink-eyed white is also popular: this variety usually excels in type and should be spotless, although keeping any guinea-pig clean and free from staining is very difficult. There are also black-eyed whites, but these tend to have grey ears and feet, and are difficult to breed to show standard.

The self cream is often referred to as the 'champagne cavy'. It usually has very good type and is a beautiful pale cream with dark ruby eyes. A self golden can vary in colour, but should be a rich ginger with pink eyes; do not confuse this with the self red, which is a dark, rich mahogany and has black eyes.

Three other well-established English self guinea-pigs are the chocolate, beige and lilac. The chocolate should be the colour of dark (plain) chocolate with eyes to match, although these will have a ruby tinge. The beige should be a warm, pinky beige, while the lilac is a pale, even dove grey, again with a pink tinge. Both the beige and lilac varieties have pink eyes.

Smooth marked

These and all other breeds of guinea-pig are known as non-selfs. The smooth marked varieties include the agouti, Dutch, tortoiseshell and white, roan, Dalmatian and Himalayan.

Agouti: These are 'ticked' guinea-pigs, which means that they have two different-coloured bands on each hair in the coat, giving them a speckled look. The three main agouti colours are golden and silver (both with a black base colour), and cinnamon, which has a chocolate base colour.

any colour and even with long-haired forms (called texels). Young rexes have wavy coats which become woolly in texture as the animals grow older.

Long-haired

Although attractive, these guinea-pigs are not recommended as pets, because they require extensive grooming in order to prevent matting of the coat. The varieties in this category include the Peruvian, sheltie and coronet.

Peruvian: The hair on this guinea-pig lies towards its head, and therefore falls over its face and sides with a parting down the middle of the back.

Sheltie and coronet: These varieties differ from the Peruvian guinea-pig in that the coat flows backwards, leaving the head clear; the coronet also has a crest on its head. For show purposes the hair is not cut, but is rolled in small paper 'wrappers', each stiffened with a strip of balsa wood and then secured with an elastic band.

Breeding data

🌐 63 days   # 4 young   ⏳ 30 days

(Top) Rex guinea-pig
(Above) Tortoiseshell-and-white guinea-pig

Dutch: This guinea-pig has the same markings as the Dutch rabbit (see pages 38 and 39): the rear half of the animal is coloured with white socks on the hind feet, and the head markings should be round and even with a blaze of white extending up the middle of the face. It generally has red, chocolate or black markings with a white body colour.

Tortoiseshell and white: This is often described as the 'heartbreak breed', because it is extremely difficult to breed a show specimen. The ideal markings on this guinea-pig are considered to be square, equal patches of black, red and white, with straight demarcation lines down the back and stomach, and adjoining patches of different colours.

Roan: The roan guinea-pig has a solid-coloured head, feet and body, with an even intermixing of coloured and white hairs.

Dalmatian: This guinea-pig should not be confused with the roan. It has a spotted appearance and Dutch-type head markings.

Himalayan: This is marked like a Siamese cat, with a black or light brown nose and similar-coloured feet.

Rough-haired

This group includes the crested, the Abyssinian and the rex.

Crested: This guinea-pig is smooth and short-haired, with a crest or rosette on its head above the eyes and below the ears. Crested variations exist to all the previously mentioned breeds, along with the attractive American crested which has a white crest contrasting with a self-coloured body.

Abyssinian: This rosetted guinea-pig has a coat about 4 cm (1½ in) long that feels harsh to the touch. It should have four rosettes in a straight line across the middle and four around the rump, with well-defined ridges between them.

Rex: This has become very popular in recent years, and has a fluffy coat. This feature can be combined with

Rabbits

All pet breeds of rabbit are derived from the wild rabbit, which was introduced into Britain after the Norman Conquest in the 11th century. While it is unlikely that it was kept as a pet at that stage, its value as a food was certainly recognized, and throughout the Middle Ages artificial mounds or warrens were constructed to protect this important source of winter nourishment. Rabbits were first tamed and selectively bred in the monasteries, and they have been kept as popular domestic pets from the 19th century onwards.

KEEPING RABBITS

Pure-bred rabbits are divided into 'fancy breeds' and 'fur breeds', based on their origins. There are now over 200 breeds worldwide, and many more varieties.

When kept as pets, rabbits are responsive and very easily tamed, and they are ideal for children – especially for older ones who can take on the responsibility for their daily needs. Most rabbits are good-natured animals and will tolerate some mishandling by young children, but adult supervision is still important to prevent any injury – if a rabbit is dropped, for instance, it could suffer from damage to its back (see also page 18).

When buying a rabbit for a child, you must think ahead and choose a size that the child will be able to manage. For instance, dwarf rabbits weigh about 1 kg (2.2 lb) and can be handled easily by a young child, whereas most cross-bred rabbits will weigh about 2–3 kg (4–7 lb) as adults. Rabbits can live for up to 12 years, but this is unusual and most rabbits will show signs of senility from five to six years of age. The longer-lived individuals tend to be unmated females.

A rabbit can generally be kept safely together with a guinea-pig, although you should choose one of the smaller rabbit breeds if you have this in mind.

Dutch rabbit

DIETARY NEEDS

Feeding rabbits is quite straightforward, and prepared food rations are widely available for them from pet shops and other outlets. They will also enjoy various other foodstuffs, including grass, groundsel and dandelion leaves.

However, when you first acquire a rabbit – or at any other time – it is important that you do not suddenly change its diet. Keep to the food to which it has been accustomed (ask the breeder or pet store what has been fed, before you take the rabbit home) and introduce any changes gradually. This will help to prevent any digestive problems, to which rabbits are especially susceptible (see page 20).

Breeding data

 31 days   8 young   35 days

LARGER BREEDS

Some of the rabbits in this category can grow to a considerable size and weight. This should be a consideration if you are buying a pet for a small child, as rabbits are susceptible to injury if mishandled.

Belgian hare

☎ 3.5–4 kg (7–9 lb)

This resembles a hare in shape and size, but it is a rabbit and makes a good pet. It is chestnut with bold hazel eyes.

Beveren

☎ 3.5–4 kg (7–10 lb)

This rabbit is available in four colours, the oldest of which is the blue, which originated in the 1890s. The coat is dense, silky and lustrous.

British giant

☎ 5.5–7 kg (12–15 lb)

This is the largest of the British rabbits, and is available in a range of colours.

Californian

☎ 3.5–5 kg (7–11 lb)

This rabbit is bred mainly for meat, but it is a very docile creature and makes a good pet. The coat is white, with black or

38

chocolate-coloured markings (similar to those of a Siamese cat) on the nose, ears, feet and tail.

Lop

The lop-eared rabbit is the oldest of the fancy breeds. The ears appear normal until the rabbit is about 14 days old, when they begin to droop; on an adult they can measure up to 70 cm (28 in). A full range of colours has been bred. There are also several types of lop-eared rabbit, including the English lop: ⊗ 6.5–9 kg (14–20 lb); the French lop: ⊗ 4.5–5.5 kg (9–12 lb); and the dwarf lop: ⊗ 2 kg (4.5 lb). The latest addition to the group is the mini lop: ⊗ 1.5 kg (3½ lb), which was officially recognized as a breed in 1994.

Flemish giant

⊗ 5.5–10 kg (12–22 lb)

This is the largest of the domestic breeds, and is principally bred for meat. It needs a very large hutch. The coat is steel grey flecked with black.

New Zealand white

⊗ 4–5 kg (9–11 lb)

This rabbit is usually bred for meat or fur, but is docile and makes a good pet. It has a dense white coat and pink eyes.

MEDIUM-SIZED BREEDS

This group includes some very attractive rabbits that will make ideal pets.

Angora

⊗ 2.5–2.7 kg (5½–6 lb)

This is a wool-producing rabbit, and is available in several colours. The coat needs a lot of attention, so it is not suitable as a beginner's pet.

Netherland dwarf rabbits

Chinchilla

⊗ 2.5–3 kg (5½–6½ lb)

This was originally bred for its fine fur, which is a deep slate colour overlaid with bands of pearl white and tipped with black. This is a very attractive rabbit and makes an excellent pet.

Dutch

⊗ 2–2.5 kg (4½–5½ lb)

This well-known show breed makes an ideal pet. The coat is smooth and shiny. The basic colour is white combined with another colour (blue and grey are popular). There is usually a white blaze and shoulder, with a coloured abdomen, ears, cheeks and eyes.

English

⊗ 2.5–3.5 kg (5½–8 lb)

This popular breed is white with a coloured nose, ears and eyes, and chains of spots on the flanks.

Harlequin

⊗ 2.7–3.6 kg (7–8 lb)

This long-eared rabbit has attractive and unusual markings that are reminiscent of a chess board. Black and orange are the most popular colours; the black-and-white variety is called a magpie.

Rex

⊗ 2.5–3.6 kg (5½–8 lb)

This is a collective name for a range of rabbits, differing in colour patterns and eye colour. The coat resembles velvet and has no long guard (outer) hairs.

SMALL BREEDS

These rabbits are extremely appealing to look at. Their small size also makes them very manageable, particularly if they are to be kept indoors.

Himalayan

⊗ 2–2.5 kg (4½–5½ lb)

This very attractive rabbit, like the Californian, has the same colourpoints as a Siamese cat. The main colour is

(Top) Belgian hare
(Centre) Blue rex rabbit
(Bottom) Silver dwarf lop rabbit

white, with the nose, ears, tail and feet coloured black, blue, lilac or chocolate. The young are all white until they leave the nest, when colour starts to appear.

Netherland dwarf

⊗ 0.9 kg (2 lb)

When grown, this delightful rabbit will sit in the palm of a hand. Its ears are under 5 cm (2 in) long, and the eyes are large and bright. Many colours are bred.

Polish

⊗ 1 kg (2.2 lb)

This rabbit is small but more hare-like, with longer ears and limbs.

Other small mammals

Spiny mouse

The choice of more unusual small mammals sold as pets is growing, and those described here are among the animals that are being bred with increasing frequency. Availability will vary: for instance, you may well be able to buy a Siberian chipmunk from a pet store, but you would almost certainly need to go to a breeder for an African pygmy hedgehog unless you live in the USA, where this creature is better known. All the animals described here are rodents, except the African pygmy hedgehog which is classified as an insectivore.

SPINY MICE
(*Acomys* species)
Originating in parts of Africa and the Middle East, these lively rodents have unusual spiky fur. They have been kept and bred in the UK for over a decade, and are becoming a popular addition to the range of small mammals commonly kept as pets.

Multimammate mouse

Housing
The small size of spiny mice means that they may be able to slip through the bars of an ordinary cage, so an aquarium covered with a secure ventilated lid is the most suitable option for housing.

Although these mice are social animals, it is important to give them plenty of space or they are likely to start chewing their tails as a result of frustration.

Spiny mice have very fragile tails, so it is extremely important to handle them carefully when removing them from the aquarium. Never attempt to restrain one of these mice by the tail, as the tail may bleed; instead, let the mouse walk directly on to your hand or into a small box if required.

Feeding
A diet based on seeds and nuts, plus some greenstuff and the occasional mealworm, will keep spiny mice in good health. They will live for two to three years on average.

Breeding
Spiny mice differ in some respects from ordinary pet mice, particularly in terms of their breeding habits. A female gives birth to just two or three offspring after a long pregnancy of 38 days. However, the young are born fully developed and become active soon after birth. At this stage they have greyish fur, and will only acquire the sandy colour of adult mice when they moult at eight weeks of age.

To date, only one colour variant – mainly black, with a thin white stripe on the underparts – has occurred. Unfortunately this strain now appears to have died out, but it could crop up again in the future.

MULTIMAMMATE MICE
(*Praomys natalensis*)
These rather strange mice have been domesticated for over 50 years, but are not widely kept. They are found south of the Sahara in Africa. The unusual name of these rodents stems from the fact that females have a large number of teats – as many as 32 – although they only produce litters of eight offspring on average. The reason for this strange imbalance is unclear. Caring for these mice is generally straightforward, although females occasionally kill their offspring unexpectedly (this appears to be most common in the case of closely related stock).

Multimammate mice have a soft, greyish-black fur with lighter underparts, and grow to about 15 cm (6 in) in length. They were first kept in the UK in 1939, and a paler variant arose in this original laboratory strain. This was called the 'Bargawanath dilute', the name being taken from the spot close to Johannesburg where the original stock was obtained. A second pale variant came from Iscor, near Pretoria. There is now also a pure white, red-eyed albino and an attractive golden-yellow form of the multimammate mouse.

SIBERIAN CHIPMUNKS
(Eutamias sibiricus)
Friendly and cheerful, chipmunks are endearing rodents and are rapidly becoming popular pets. The Siberian chipmunk is the most widely bred species. It is usually brownish in colour with black stripes on each side and a white underside, but pure white albinos have now been bred. Its average size is about 10 cm (4 in) long with a 7 cm (3 in) tail. It is best to buy a pair of young chipmunks, as they are gregarious creatures and will be easier to tame from an early age. Once trained they will readily take food from your hand, but dislike being handled excessively.

Siberian chipmunk

Housing
You can keep chipmunks indoors or outdoors in a secure enclosure similar to an aviary, where they will spend their time busily scurrying about in search of seeds and nuts, which they normally hoard. If you wish to keep chipmunks indoors, you must position the cage in a room away from the television. This is because the noise can disturb their sensitive hearing, causing hyperactivity and stress, and sometimes even death. Chipmunks should also be kept well apart from other rodents – especially rats, which are their enemies in the wild.

Feeding
A prepared seed mixture, augmented with some fruit, nuts and vegetables, will make a good diet.

Breeding
Chipmunks start to breed when they are 12 months old. Pregnancy lasts about 31 days, and a litter consists of four to eight babies. The young emerge from the nest at about seven weeks old, and should be transferred to their own quarters after about a week. Chipmunks can live for up to 12 years.

AFRICAN PYGMY HEDGEHOGS
(Atelerix Albiventris)
This hedgehog is similar to the European hedgehog in general appearance, but it is significantly smaller. It is about the size of a grapefruit, and weighs about 0.5 kg (1 lb). Its quills are less ferocious than those of the European variety, being similar in texture to the bristles of a nylon brush and less sharp at the tips.

In the early 1980s a number of these hedgehogs were exported from Africa to the USA, where they were exhibited in zoos. At first their management proved difficult, but gradually, as more was discovered about them, breeding successes became more common. Youngsters bred in captivity proved very friendly, and many people fell under the charm of these small hedgehogs.

Housing
Caring for African pygmy hedgehogs is fairly easy, and they can be housed in a variety of enclosures. When kept in the home at room temperature, they display no tendency to hibernate. They soon become tame, and can be picked up without curling into a ball: in the USA, breeders offer their tame youngsters as 'roll-free stock'!

Feeding
The hedgehogs will readily eat cat and dog food, but may develop a taste for a particular brand. Offering a range of foods early in life appears to overcome this problem; special hedgehog foods are also available. Insects such as mealworms and crickets can also feature in the diet, as can the occasional helping of cottage cheese and hard-boiled egg. Provide constant fresh water, but do not offer milk as it may cause digestive upsets.

Breeding
For breeding purposes, keep a female in a box-type cage for greater privacy (an enclosed cage with a wire-mesh front is ideal), with a nest box inside. Put her in with her partner for two days, then transfer her back to her own quarters. Re-introduce the hedgehogs 10 days later, and for a third time after another 10 days. As female hedgehogs do not ovulate on a regular basis, putting the animals together repeatedly like this has proved the best way of ensuring success.

Pregnancy will last for 32–6 days, and you must leave the female undisturbed in the later stages or she may eat her offspring when they are born. If all goes well, remove the nest box when the hoglets are one month old. This will encourage them to start exploring their quarters, and they will soon begin feeding on their own. They should be fully weaned about two weeks later, and may go on to live for 10 or more years.

African pygmy hedgehog

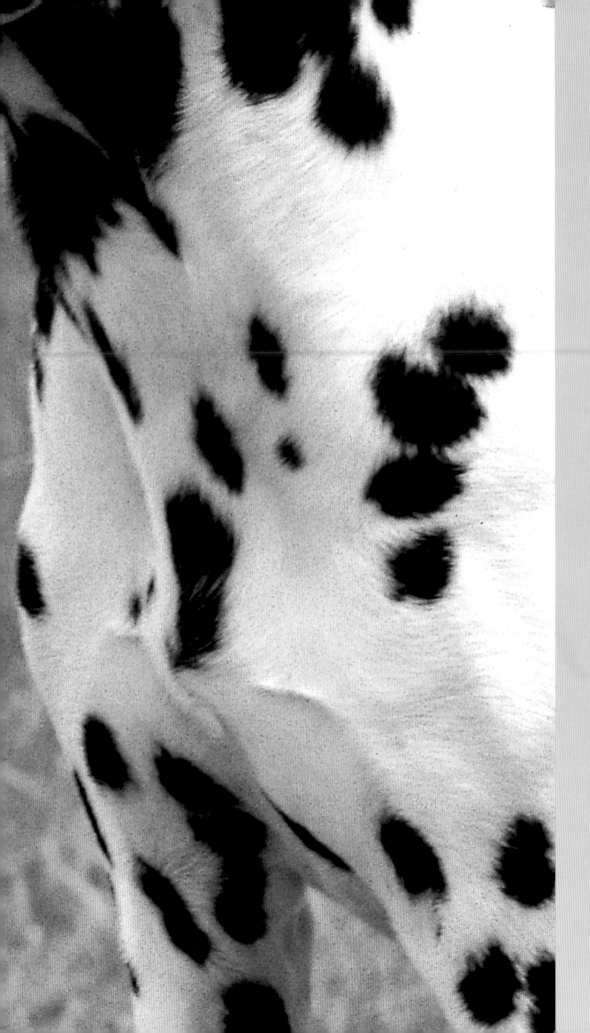

Dogs

There are now over 350 different breeds of domestic dog, ranging in size from the tiny Chihuahua – bred originally in the Mexican province of that name – to the Irish wolfhound, which stands over 91 cm (3 ft) tall at the shoulder. All dogs are descended from the grey wolf (*Canis lupus*), which was at one time the most widely distributed mammal in the Northern hemisphere.

2

THE DOG'S ANCESTOR

Perhaps surprisingly, the grey wolf itself showed great variation in size through its former range, the smallest member of the group being the Shamanu grey wolf, found in Japan, which was just 39 cm (15 in) tall. There was also considerable colour variation, not dissimilar to that of our domestic dogs. The Newfoundland grey wolf, for example, was in fact pure white; grey wolves from desert areas tended to have sandy-coloured coats; and elsewhere brown and even black wolf populations existed.

Today the close relationship between wolves and dogs remains more apparent in certain breeds of dog than in others, notably in the so-called Spitz group, which originates from the far north and includes the Siberian husky and other sled dogs. These have the typical upright ears, relatively long legs and slightly triangular-shaped face characteristic of the grey wolf; they also tend to howl rather than to bark.

DOMESTICATION

The origins of our dogs date back at least 12,000 years, with domestication probably occurring in different parts of the globe rather than in one place. It is likely that at least four different races of the grey wolf were involved in this process at various times in history. Archaeological evidence suggests that domestication began at an early stage in the Middle East, where the remains of a young boy buried with a puppy have been unearthed. The child's arm was carefully placed around the dog in an apparent gesture of affection. In the USA, evidence of the domestication process has been discovered in the Beaverhead mountains in the state of Idaho. About 9000 years ago, there were already two distinct types of dog in existence here. One of these was roughly the size of today's beagle, while a larger dog was as tall as a retriever.

It may have been orphaned wolf cubs brought back to villages and raised by children which began the domestication process. The advantages of having semi-tame wolves around human settlements would soon have become apparent – particularly at night, when their acute hearing would have warned of the approach of danger. They could also have been an asset for hunting,

driving quarry towards the hunters and then sharing in the kill as a reward. As life continued to become more settled and farming gradually took over from hunting as the major source of food production, so the role of the wolf-dog would have assumed that of protector, guarding flocks from attacks by wolves and other predators such as bears.

SELECTIVE BREEDING

Before long dogs were being bred selectively for a variety of purposes, and this trend has continued since the beginning of recorded history. In Roman times, for example, several distinctive types of dogs were kept throughout the Empire. Immensely powerful mastiff dogs – which probably arose in Asia – were used in battle and for hunting, where they were pitched against dangerous quarry such as wild boar, while the Roman forerunners of today's hounds were kept for hunting hare. Contemporary accounts describe these as being lemon and white in colour, and not dissimilar to greyhounds in shape. Called vertragus, it was probably this type of hound which evolved in the Middle East. There was, too, a smaller, shaggy coated hound which hunted by scent rather than sight.

Archaeological evidence has also revealed that there were types of small dog in existence by this stage, which were approximately the same size as today's toy breeds. This suggests that dogs were already being kept as companions and as house guardians. Unfortunately, however, it is almost impossible for us to piece together a detailed picture of what these dogs would have looked like, because the appearance of features such as the ears and coat cannot be gleaned from their skeletal remains.

FURTHER DEVELOPMENTS

Through the successive centuries dogs were essentially used as working animals, although the small breeds were kept as companions and were typically seen around the Royal courts of Europe and Asia. It was the rise of dog shows – pioneered by Charles Cruft in London in the late Victorian era, and gradually spreading to Europe and beyond – which did most to promote the development of the dog as a household companion.

Since that time its popularity as a pet has continued to grow enormously, although many dogs are of course still kept today for working purposes and their role in some areas has expanded. For instance, as well as carrying out more traditional tasks such as guarding livestock and herding sheep, some breeds of dog are widely used to assist people who have hearing and sight impediments, and also to seek out illegal drugs and explosives at airports.

43

Choosing and buying a dog

Before obtaining a dog you will need to make a number of decisions, including the breed or type of dog you would like. The options here will be a pure-bred (pedigree) dog, a cross-bred (a dog whose parents were pure-breds, but of different types) or a mongrel (a dog with one or both parents which were themselves cross-breds or mongrels). Cost may influence your choice, but do not imagine that pure-bred dogs are 'better' than cross-breds or mongrels – indeed in terms of health the reverse is generally true, as many pure-bred dogs are prone to problems less often seen in other types of dog. Additional important factors to think about when choosing your dog are discussed here.

SIZE

Bear in mind that a large dog will not only require more space, but will tend to need more exercise and will be more expensive to keep. The lifespan of a large dog is usually also shorter than that of a smaller dog. You should be particularly cautious if you are choosing a young mongrel because it may grow unexpectedly large, whereas the adult size of pedigree dogs is fairly standard and predictable. Most puppies are a similar size at birth, but large feet tend to suggest that a mongrel puppy will grow into a relatively big dog.

MALE OR FEMALE?

Male dogs are generally much more independent than bitches, and so are often more difficult to control. An intact (uncastrated) dog will also tend to wander, especially if there is a bitch in season nearby, although this problem can usually be overcome by having the dog neutered. Castration is a simple operation, carried out under a general anaesthetic, to remove the testicles of a male dog. The procedure is much more straightforward than a bitch spay (see below), and is therefore less expensive. As well as making the dog sterile, castration may lead to weight gain – especially from middle age onwards – so its food intake may need to be adjusted from time to time.

Bitches tend to be more popular as pets, as they are often considered to be more affectionate. However, the females of most breeds come into season twice a year, for about three weeks at a time, throughout their lives. Unless this is prevented with a contraceptive drug or by neutering (spaying), bitches must be kept under tight control during these periods to avoid unwanted pregnancies. Spaying is a major surgical procedure, carried out under a general anaesthetic, which involves removing the ovaries and womb through an incision made in the abdominal cavity. This can be done before a bitch reaches sexual maturity at about six months of age, although some vets advise that bitches should be allowed to have at least one season first (this is because early spaying may lead to incontinence later in life, although – on the plus side – it may also reduce the risk of mammary tumours). However, letting a bitch have a litter before neutering purely for this reason could lead to unwanted puppies, and is definitely not a good idea. Spayed bitches do have a tendency to put on weight, but careful attention to diet on the part of the owner, combined with adequate exercise, can control this.

If you go to a breeder for a pedigree puppy, you will probably need to make your choice and then wait until the puppy is old enough to come home with you; this will be at the age of eight weeks.

What to look for in a healthy dog

A healthy dog will look alert and be responsive to sounds.

The eyes should be clean and bright, not bloodshot; there should be no discharge or abnormal sensitivity to light.

Look inside the ears, which should be clean with no discharge. If the dog persistently scratches at its ears, there could be a problem.

Lift the lips gently and look at the teeth: these should be clean, and the gums pink with no signs of inflammation.

A cold and damp nose is a sign of good health (although not all dogs have cold, damp noses: if the dog appears to be normal in all other ways, a hot, dry nose may be normal for it). There should be no scabs on the nose, or discharge coming from it.

The dog's breathing should be quiet and even at rest, with no wheezing or coughing.

Look at all the claws in turn: they should be evenly worn and not overgrown, with none missing; check also for any cysts (swellings) between the toes.

44

BREED CHARACTERISTICS

Herding dogs
Responsive to training; very active by nature.

Hounds
Affectionate and friendly, but more difficult to train than dogs of other groups.

Gundogs
Popular as companions, being accustomed to working on an individual basis with their owners.

Terriers
Lively and tenacious; may be suspicious of strangers, and not always tolerant of children.

Working breeds
Temperament will be influenced largely by their upbringing and early environment.

Companion breeds
Small in size and generally friendly.

Part the fur in places and look at the skin, which should be clean and supple with no scurf, scabs or wounds. Check for any signs of parasites (see pages 59–60).

The coat should be glossy and clean, with no loose hair or dirt.

Check that the anus is clean – any fur-staining could indicate diarrhoea.

The abdomen should not be swollen or tender to touch.

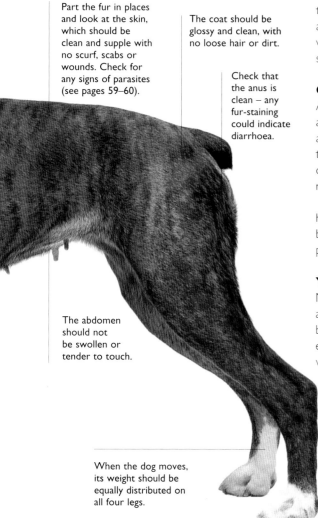

When the dog moves, its weight should be equally distributed on all four legs.

PUPPY OR ADULT DOG?

In common with the majority of would-be owners, you may wish to obtain your dog as a puppy. However, if you decide to take on a dog from an animal-welfare society you may end up with an older animal, which will need a different level of care and attention.

Selecting a puppy

Eight weeks is the ideal age to take on a puppy (moving it to a new home earlier than this may affect its future relationships with other dogs; leaving it with its mother and littermates for much longer may affect its behaviour towards people). If possible, select from a litter while the puppies are with their mother so that you can gain a good idea of her temperament, and only visit a litter bred by a reputable breeder or by a caring one-bitch owner so that you will get a sociable, healthy puppy that has had plenty of human contact during the important rearing period. Avoid a puppy which cowers at the back of the pen: choose a lively one which approaches you willingly.

You may be able to take your puppy away the same day, or you may need to make your choice and return when it is a little older. When you do take the puppy, ask the breeder for a diet sheet – including types of food, mealtimes and quantities being fed – as you should keep to these when the puppy first comes home with you. Ask for details of worming timings and treatments (see page 59), and for a vet's certificate showing any early vaccinations (see pages 58–9). If the puppy is a pure-bred, the breeder should also give you its pedigree registration papers.

Choosing an adult dog

Adult pure-bred dogs are available from breed-rescue organizations, and adult cross-bred dogs and mongrels (and sometimes pure-bred dogs) from animal-welfare societies. If you would like to obtain an adult dog you should think very carefully about it first as, unless you know with certainty the dog's origins, you may need to be prepared for possible problems such as soiling, nervousness or uncertain temperament.

It may also be best to avoid taking an adult dog of unknown origins if you have children, as the dog may prove less tolerant than a puppy and could become snappy. Most animal-welfare societies are aware of the difficulties in placing adult dogs, and match them as closely as possible with new owners.

YOUR DOG'S TEMPERAMENT

Many people looking for a pet dog choose a breed solely on the basis of appearance rather than considering its ancestry, which will have a great bearing on the dog's temperament and response to training. Hounds, for example, can be very difficult to train because they are highly independent, whereas many of the smaller breeds – which were developed to be companions – are relatively tolerant and make good pets in homes with children. How your dog looks will obviously influence your choice, but remember that its temperament is much more important in the long run.

A VETERINARY CHECK-UP

Whatever the age, breed or source of your dog, you must arrange for it to have a thorough veterinary examination as an urgent priority. You may already know of a good local veterinary centre; if not, ask dog-owning friends for recommendations. If the vet discovers any major defect or ailment, he or she may advise you to return the dog for a full refund; any good breeder will sell a dog subject to a veterinary examination.

Dogs

Settling in

You should transport a new puppy home with great care, preferably in a deep box lined with newspaper and a blanket, or in a special, secure pet carrier (this may also come in useful for carrying a small breed in the car when it is older). Carriers of various sizes are available from pet stores, and are advertised in dog magazines. If you wish, you could take the puppy for its initial veterinary check (see page 45) on the way home, or you may prefer to wait until it has had a chance to settle in with you.

FEEDING

At first, you should provide the same type of food and the same number of meals to which the puppy is accustomed (you can gradually

PUPPY FEEDING CHART

Under 8 weeks	5 meals daily: 3 milk/cereal; 2 meat/biscuit
8–12 weeks	4 meals daily: 2 milk/cereal; 2 meat/biscuit
12–16 weeks	3 meals daily: each meat/biscuit + drink of milk
16–20 weeks	2 meals daily: each meat/biscuit + drink of milk
20 weeks onwards	1 meal daily: meat/biscuit + drink of milk (optional)

change over to a different food later on; see pages 48–9 for more information on feeding). It must have its own feeding and drinking bowls for hygiene reasons. Make sure that fresh drinking water is available at all times.

Many dogs seem to prefer soft bedding or a bean bag – on which they can stretch out and sleep – to a traditional-style basket. Whatever bedding you choose, the cover must be easily removable for regular washing.

SOMEWHERE TO SLEEP

Give the puppy its own bed. A cardboard box will be ideal at first, and you can replace this as it becomes dirty or is gnawed. Cut away the side of the box so that the puppy can get into it easily, and provide some warm, woolly bedding.

Position the bed somewhere quiet and out of the way. All puppies enjoy periods of play and being stroked, but they must also be allowed to rest undisturbed when they wish. Teach the puppy to use its own bed from the start – do not encourage it to climb on to furniture or the family's beds, as this will be a hard habit to break.

A PLAYPEN

This is an excellent idea for the first few weeks, and you can easily make one or buy a ready-made pen from a pet store. Putting your puppy inside will prevent it from running out when you open the front door, or from disappearing when you are not there to watch over it. When in its playpen, the puppy should have access to bedding, water and toys. The floor covering should be non-absorbent, and you should line the bottom of the pen with old newspapers.

TRAINING

You can begin simple training, such as house training, straight away (see pages 50–1), although it will be some time before you can allow your puppy out into the neighbourhood on a lead (you must confine it to the house and garden until it has completed its primary vaccinations, or it could be at risk of contracting major infectious diseases – see pages 58–9).

Once the puppy is allowed to venture out with you, avoid very long walks as these can cause lasting joint damage. Regular, shorter walks are a much better way of exercising a puppy.

Extending lead

Dog toys and chew

SETTLING AN OLDER DOG

How quickly an older dog settles into your home will depend on its personality and upbringing. The process may be very easy, or considerably more difficult and frustrating. If you do have behavioural problems with an older dog, ask your vet for advice. He or she should be able to help, or, if necessary, may refer you to a canine behaviourist.

46

Plastic and earthenware food bowls

Equipment

You will need a number of basic items to look after your new dog. A huge range of dog-care equipment is available from pet stores and via mail order from magazines, but not all of this will be essential, especially for a puppy. Concentrate instead on the basic items, and buy any additional items if and when you need them.

A BED

Once your puppy's teething phase is past – after the age of about six months – you can replace its cardboard box with a proper bed. It is best to choose a plastic bed rather than a more traditional wicker design, so that you will be able to clean it thoroughly.

At some stage in your dog's life it will almost certainly suffer from fleas, which will also establish themselves in its environment (see pages 59–60). You should therefore choose washable bedding or a cushion with a cover that is removable for cleaning. Otherwise, as well as possibly harbouring fleas, the bedding will acquire a distinctly 'doggy' smell that will permeate the surrounding area. Some dogs like to sleep on a bean bag, and special designs for dogs are made in a range of sizes. Cleanliness here is also vital, and the outer cover of the bag must be removable for washing.

A COLLAR AND LEAD

It is a good idea to accustom a puppy to wearing a collar from an early age, but remember to check the collar regularly and let out the buckle as the puppy grows (you should be able to fit two fingers, on their sides, beneath it). An identity disc attached to the collar, or a barrel containing your address and telephone number, is essential in case your dog becomes lost – this is also a legal requirement in many countries. A harness may be more suitable for some breeds of dog – such as dachshunds (see page 67) – when they are being exercised on a lead.

A wide variety of leads is available, some of which are brightly coloured and can be co-ordinated with a collar. Choose a lead that feels comfortable in your hand, and is stoutly stitched. It should last a lifetime, so buy one that will still be strong enough for your dog when it is fully grown. Leads with metal links are popular because they are almost indestructible, even if they become wet. Long, retractable leads are also widely used, and can be very helpful for exercising in areas where there may be other dogs or traffic nearby, or for training young dogs (see pages 50–1).

You can also use a choke (check) chain for training, which works by tightening around the young dog's neck when it starts to pull ahead, causing an unpleasant feeling and teaching the dog to walk with you at the correct pace. However, take care with this type of chain or it could cause a neck injury, particularly if incorrectly fitted – the chain must loosen off when you relax your grip on it.

GROOMING TOOLS

All dogs, especially those with long or thick coats, should be groomed daily to minimize shedding of hair around the home and to prevent matting of the fur. A stiff brush is best for a short-coated dog, a similar brush and a hound glove (a silky glove used to give a gloss to the coat) are ideal for a medium coat, and a metal comb is essential to deal with tangles in a long coat. You are also likely to need other items such as thinning scissors and a fine-toothed flea comb on occasions.

Owners of breeds that need regular clipping sometimes invest in the tools needed to do this at home, rather than visiting a professional dog groomer every few weeks. This can be an economical option if you simply want to keep your pet's coat at a suitable length rather than having it styled for show purposes.

WATER AND FOOD BOWLS

A good range of water and food bowls is available for dogs, but be sure to choose designs that are heavy enough not to be tipped over easily. You may also want a special mat to stand the bowls on, which you can wipe over and disinfect as necessary. For safety, only use a veterinary disinfectant intended for this type for cleaning; most pet stores will stock a range of suitable products.

TOYS

You should select toys for your dog with care, avoiding any that could accidentally be swallowed. Young puppies often enjoy gnawing on chews to ease the discomfort of teething, and providing these may help to deter your pet from resorting to the furniture instead. Some toys – such as flying discs, which breeds such as the labrador retriever love to chase and bring back – are more suitable for older dogs, and provide a very good form of extra exercise on walks.

A KENNEL

Snug outdoor kennels – with a secure run attached, if required – are available from specialist manufacturers (look in dog magazines for advertisements), although you should beware of keeping your dog outside if its barking could become a nuisance to your neighbours. (See pages 54–5 for further details on outdoor kennels.)

Leather collar and nylon lead

A COAT

If you have an older dog, or one with only a small percentage of body fat – such as a greyhound – it will appreciate a coat when the weather is cold. When sizing your dog for this, you will need to measure the length of its body from the neck to the base of the tail (see also page 65). Check that the coat fits securely, or it could easily be lost during a walk.

Feeding

One of the main reasons why dogs have become so widely kept as pets is that feeding them is now so easy. In recent years, the major dog-food companies have invested heavily in research to produce complete foods containing all the necessary ingredients to meet canine nutritional requirements, and there are now even specific diets available for different stages of a dog's life, from puppyhood through to old age. Specially formulated vegetarian diets are also manufactured. Although dogs prefer to eat meat-based foods, they are omnivorous in their feeding habits and can be kept satisfactorily on such foods.

Feeding dogs today is straightforward. By using one of the good-quality prepared foods on the market, you can be sure that your pet is receiving all the nutrients it needs to stay fit and healthy.

WHAT TO FEED

Perhaps surprisingly, the least satisfactory diet for dogs is one consisting entirely of fresh meat, or of scraps left by the family. A dog's diet must provide a wide range of nutrients in the correct quantities, and getting this right is a complex task. If you do feed only meat, you must do so in conjunction with a vitamin-and-mineral supplement; you must also thoroughly cook the meat to avoid any risk of your dog developing any parasitic or bacterial ailments. A much easier and better option is to offer your dog one of the following complete prepared foods, each of which will satisfy all its nutritional requirements.

Dog biscuits can be fed alongside canned food. They consist mainly of carbohydrate, and have a crunchy texture that many dogs really enjoy.

Moist food

Proprietary canned food remains one of the most popular feeding options. The mixer and canned food should be given in roughly equal amounts by volume, not weight, so measure out the mixer using a washed and dried empty can. There is little to choose between the popular brand-name canned foods and mixers, although some have a firmer consistency than others. All the necessary vitamins and minerals are incorporated into this food, making the routine use of a supplement not only unnecessary but also undesirable; an excessive intake can actually be dangerous.

Most dogs generally bolt down their food as quickly as possible, so there should not be a problem with food left in the bowl attracting flies in hot weather. If you do not use up a whole can for one meal, store it in the refrigerator (special re-usable can caps are available, and will prevent unpleasant odours).

Dry food

This needs no special storage, provided that it is not kept in humid conditions or allowed to become damp. Advantages of dry food are that it is lighter to carry than cans, and you can simply tip it into your dog's bowl straight from the packet. As it is hard and crunchy in texture, it may also help to prevent a build-up of tartar on the teeth. Dogs fed on a dry diet usually drink more water to compensate for the deficiency of fluid, so, as always, make sure that plenty of fresh drinking water is available.

Semi-moist food

This third type of food is less widely used, and is only available in a few varieties. Like dry food it is packeted, but has a flexible texture. Semi-moist food has only a slight odour, and will dry out less quickly than moist food.

Dietary supplements

Dogs do not normally need supplements because of their generally balanced diets, but there are times when vitamin-and-mineral additives may be beneficial. For instance, bitches may require a supplement of this kind during pregnancy and lactation, as may fast-growing puppies of large breeds. Older dogs, or those recovering from illness, accidents or surgery, could also require specific supplements. In all these cases, your vet will be able to advise you.

Other food items

You can give your dog small amounts of your left-over cooked vegetables if you wish, although these may cause flatulence. If you offer any fish or meat, always be sure that you have removed any small bones.

WHEN TO FEED

An adult dog should normally be fed either one large meal in the evening or two smaller portions, morning and evening. Young puppies have small

stomachs, and need their food split into manageable portions. Three or four small meals a day until the puppy reaches half its expected adult weight, and then two meals a day, is normally recommended.

Never feed your dog and then take it straight out for exercise – this could lead to the condition known as gastric torsion (a twisted stomach), which is sudden in onset and often fatal.

HOW MUCH TO FEED

The amount of food that you offer will depend largely on the size of your dog and on the amount of energy it expends from day to day. You will find feeding advice on the packaging of proprietary foods, so follow this as a guide. If your dog puts on too much weight, cut back the food a little; if the dog is underweight, increase the quantity a little.

Regular weighing will enable you to spot any change quickly, and to take the appropriate action. If you are in doubt about any aspect of feeding your dog, ask your vet for advice.

Obesity

It is a sad fact today that over one-third of pet dogs are overweight. To prevent your dog from becoming obese, you should weigh it regularly (you can do this by standing on bathroom scales yourself, noting your weight, then standing on the scales with your dog and deducting your weight). You will also need to weigh your puppy or dog when deciding how much food to give initially (see right). If you have a pure-bred dog, compare the result with the figure specified in the breed standard, or consult your vet. Another indicator of obesity – applicable to all dogs – is if you cannot feel the ribs under a layer of fat.

Just as with humans, weight gain in dogs can be controlled by increasing exercise and reducing food intake. Curbing food intake to prevent obesity is also important for many dogs after neutering (see page 44). Always confine feeding to set mealtimes only. Never feed your dog from the table, or it will come to expect such attention and be a nuisance, as well as putting on weight. Nor should you give titbits between meals, the only exception here being rewards for obedience during training sessions, when you should provide healthy foods such as slices of carrot or apple (see page 50). Some human foods can even be poisonous to dogs if they are consumed in large quantities – notably chocolate

(although obviously not the type that is sold specifically for dogs).

If your dog is overweight, cut out most or all of the carbohydrate in its diet – this is usually predominant in mixer foods – and substitute green vegetables or bran. Special weight-loss diets are available to assist in slimming an overweight dog (your veterinary centre should stock a selection of these), but in many cases the problem relates essentially to a lack of exercise. If you are unsure whether your dog is overweight, or what you should do about it, ask your vet for further advice.

DAILY FOOD REQUIREMENTS

WEIGHT OF DOG	AMOUNT OF FOOD
2 kg (5 lb)	110–140 g (4–5 oz)
5 kg (10 lb)	200–280g (7–10 oz)
10 kg (25 lb)	400–570 g (14–20 oz)
20 kg (50 lb)	680–900 g (1.5–2 lb)
35 kg (75 lb)	900–1.1 kg (2–2½ lb)
45 kg (100 lb)	1.25–1.6 kg (2¾–3½ lb)
70 kg (150 lb)	1.7–2 kg (3¾–5½ lb)

Dry foods for dogs are becoming increasingly popular. They are very convenient to use, and can also help to keep a dog's teeth healthy.

49

Wipe-clean mats are sold in numerous bright colours and fun designs, and will help to keep your dog's feeding area clean.

Training

A well-trained and obedient dog is a delight to its owner and to other members of the public. It is also a much safer animal to exercise on or near roads as well as in the vicinity of livestock, where an instant response to commands is essential. Effective training involves carrying out regular sessions, with constant repetition of exercises and reward for the correct responses.

The basic principle of training is that, if a puppy or dog is immediately rewarded for performing the correct behaviour, it will be more likely to repeat that behaviour if the situation arises again. The reward may be your attention, or a non-fattening titbit such as a piece of carrot. You should give a reward every time at first, but, once the puppy has mastered an exercise, do so only occasionally. Given time, a dog will learn to respond to verbal commands and often to hand signals as well. However, some individuals do learn more quickly than others, so you must be patient.

BASIC TRAINING

The first word of instruction to teach is a stern 'No'. You must firmly establish this from the outset, and use it whenever your dog behaves disobediently. Similarly, you should give a few words of praise, spoken in a friendly manner, whenever the dog displays the correct behaviour. Dogs are extremely sensitive to the tone of voice that is used by their owners during training, and encouragement is very important.

House training

Start this on day one. Put the puppy out in the garden (choose an area that will be easy to clear up thoroughly and disinfect), or on newspaper, after each meal or drink and after waking up, when it is most likely to want to relieve itself. Always be sure to give the puppy plenty of praise when it performs as required.

If the puppy soils in the house, never admonish it if you do not catch it in the act, as the puppy will simply not comprehend what it has done wrong. Clean the area thoroughly, using a special repellent product (available from pet stores); avoid using a pine-based disinfectant, as this may attract the puppy back to the spot to soil again.

If you are with the puppy at the time, say a firm 'No', and put it out into the garden, or on to newspaper. It normally takes about six months before a puppy is able to 'ask' to go out when it wishes to relieve itself, but you will soon learn the telltale signs that your own puppy shows.

'Sit' and 'Down' (or 'Lie down')

You should begin teaching this in earnest when your puppy is about three months old, but there is no reason why, from the time you first bring it home, you cannot encourage it to sit before you place its food on the floor. Gentle pressure over the hindquarters will encourage the puppy to sit, while gently extending its forelegs once it is sitting will show it how to lie down on command. Give the command clearly at the same time. While praise and reward are particularly valuable with these exercises, never withhold your puppy's food if it fails to adopt the required position, as this is likely to upset it.

'Come'

Learning obedience to this command is essential for any dog which will be walked off the lead. It may take longer than with other commands to establish a quick and sure response to this instruction – which you should follow with the puppy's name – partly because the puppy will be at a distance from you, and because it may at first not differentiate the order from play.

Start the process with a young puppy simply by calling it and using its name regularly at every opportunity, so that it learns the sounds. The natural curiosity of a puppy will help to ensure its attention, and it will soon come on command for meals. For more specific training, put the puppy on a retractable lead. Ask it to come to you as usual, and reward it immediately. If the command is not obeyed promptly, gently tug the puppy towards you while repeating 'Come .....', and then repeat the exercise.

'Drop'

This is another important command, which you must teach from the outset. When the puppy is carrying an object in its mouth, gently remove it by holding the puppy's upper jaw across the nasal chambers and prizing down the lower jaw so that the object falls out on to the ground, while repeating the command 'Drop'. Give a reward immediately. By repeating this lesson a number of times, your puppy will soon come to realize what is required.

Young dogs in particular often jump up if allowed to do so, and may scratch you in the process with their claws; a large dog could even knock a child over and frighten him or her badly. To deter this unwanted behaviour, lift the dog's forelegs down on to the ground at once and make it sit, applying gentle pressure on the hindquarters if necessary.

'Stay'

You will need a retractable lead for this exercise. Ask the puppy to sit, and repeat the command 'Stay' as you back away, playing out the lead. If the puppy jumps up to follow you, ask it to sit once again and repeat the process. When you have reached the end of the lead, call the puppy to you and give a reward. Once it is familiar with the exercise, start to practise without the lead, walking further away on each occasion before calling the puppy to you.

Heel-work training

You can begin this when your puppy is three to four months old. The object is to teach it to walk close in to your left side, on or off the lead. You may find a check (choke) chain – rather than an ordinary collar – useful for this exercise, but make sure that it is fitted correctly (see page 47).

Walk at a slow pace with the puppy on the lead beside you. If it lags behind or pulls ahead, correct it by giving a sharp tug on the lead, commanding 'Heel' at the same time. Limit this exercise to 15-minute periods, allowing time for play and recreation off the lead so that the puppy does not become bored, and give a reward when it responds well. Walking with a wall or other barrier on the puppy's left side can be helpful in encouraging it to walk in a straight line rather than pulling out to the side.

ADVANCED TRAINING

Once your puppy has mastered the basics you may wish to progress to a higher level of training, which could ultimately lead to obedience competition. The purpose of advanced training – three examples of which are given here – is to build on the elements learned in basic training to produce a responsive, well-trained dog. You may find it very helpful to join a puppy-training class at this stage: look in a local library for details or ask your vet for recommendations.

The recall

Again, a retractable lead can be a useful training aid for this lesson. The dog, at heel, is placed in the 'Sit' or 'Down' position, and asked to 'Stay'. The handler walks away and turns to face the dog. On the command 'Come', the dog should move smartly to the handler and sit close to, and facing, him or her. The handler should then heel the dog to sit by his or her left leg.

The retrieve

The dog is sat to heel and asked to 'Stay', and the handler then throws an object (a wooden or plastic dumb-bell is often used). The dog awaits the command 'Fetch' to run and collect the object, returning quickly to the handler as in the recall. It should not try to chew the object, or drop it, but should allow the handler to take it from its mouth.

Scent discrimination

This exercise is based on the retrieve, and relies primarily on the dog's ability to detect and isolate a particular scent. The owner handles an object such as a rag or handkerchief and then places it among other, similar objects. On command, the dog will seek and retrieve the article.

Heel-work training: the puppy should walk beside you at your pace, even when the lead is slack (as shown in the first two pictures). At first, however, your puppy is likely to lag behind or to pull ahead if it detects an interesting scent (above), in which case you should correct it by giving a tug on the lead and repeating 'Heel'. Begin this training in home surroundings, as there are less likely to be distractions here. Once the puppy is obedient to your commands, you can start to practise without using the lead.

51

Always praise your dog when it responds well during training. A small treat such as a piece of carrot can be offered on occasions as an extra reward, but avoid giving fattening titbits.

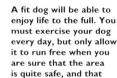

A fit dog will be able to enjoy life to the full. You must exercise your dog every day, but only allow it to run free when you are sure that the area is quite safe, and that it will not be a nuisance to other people.

General care

Hygiene is as important with a dog as with any other pet, and is generally based on common sense. For example, you should always wash your dog's food and water bowls separately from your own crockery, and strongly discourage it from climbing on to furniture or beds, not least because it could leave fleas behind (see pages 59–60). Children should be taught always to wash their hands after touching the dog and before eating (see page 59). Other basic aspects of routine care for your dog are as follows.

EXERCISE

You must maintain your dog's exercise at a consistent level: it can be harmful to walk a dog for only 30 minutes per day all week, and then for several hours at the weekend. The amount of exercise that your dog needs will depend on its breed or type, general level of fitness, age and the size of your garden. In general, larger or more active dogs require more exercise than toy dogs,

for whom a garden run may suffice. Terriers in particular have an enormous capacity for walking, whereas Great Danes can suffer from long walks. All puppies can easily be over-exercised up to the age of six months while they are still growing. The best policy with any dog is to give frequent short walks – once or twice a day is ideal.

HEALTH CHECKS

Carrying out a detailed weekly examination of your dog can be very useful in the early detection or avoidance of problems. If you obtain a young puppy, begin these checks straight away so that it becomes used to them and is easy to handle. The following are the basic points to look for.

Ears

Check the ears by sight and smell. Never probe into your dog's ears, although you can use a dampened cotton-wool bud gently to clean the outer areas and remove any slight build-up of wax. This is particularly important with spaniel breeds, which often develop ear ailments because of their long, heavy ear flaps.

You will need to groom your dog regularly, and this will include the following basic procedures:
(Top) If your dog's outer ears are dirty, gently clean them with a soft tissue or cotton wool, but never probe down the ear canal.
(Centre) Carefully wipe the area below the eyes if there are any signs of tear staining here.
(Bottom) Check the claws and trim them if necessary, or arrange for your vet to do this for you.

Eyes

Check that the eyes are not discharging and that there is no inflammation; bathe them gently with a special eye-wash if necessary.

Feet

Check the length of the claws, especially the dew claws (the canine equivalent of our thumbs or big toes). As these claws do not touch the ground they will not wear down, and, if neglected, could be torn or grow round into the pad. Trim the claws using special clippers, but be very careful not to cut into the pink 'quick' or you will cause bleeding. Ask your vet for a demonstration if you are in any doubt about what to do.

After a walk, check between your dog's pads for pieces of flint, glass or grass seeds. Carefully trim the fur here if necessary, so that foreign bodies will be less likely to become embedded.

Mouth

You can clean your dog's teeth gently using a special, non-foaming toothpaste and brush (kits are now available for this purpose – ask at your veterinary centre or at a pet store). Brushing the teeth for a few minutes once a week should be adequate, and is an effective way of removing the build-up of bacterial plaque before it can turn

Specially designed brushes and non-foaming toothpaste are now available to help you to keep your dog's teeth and gums in good condition.

into hard calculus, or tartar. If left unchecked, bacteria near the gum edges irritate the gum and, as the gum becomes more inflamed, other damaging bacteria become involved. Eventually the gum may begin to recede, and the tooth or teeth to become loose.

If your dog's teeth appear severely discoloured or the gums are inflamed, you may need to obtain veterinary treatment. Checking your dog's teeth regularly is especially important as it grows older (see page 65).

Skin and coat

Inspect the coat thoroughly for signs of insects – especially fleas (see pages 59–60) – and apply a veterinary insecticide if necessary (follow the instructions carefully, and consult your vet if you are in any doubt about which product to use or how to administer it). Part your dog's fur and examine the skin for any signs of wounds, irritation or missing patches of fur which may require attention from your vet.

Weighing

The weekly health check is a good time to weigh your dog to ensure that its weight is remaining steady (see page 49). Regular weighing will be particularly important if your dog has been castrated or spayed (see page 44).

BATHING

A bath every three months or so is adequate for most dogs. Do not wash your dog more frequently than this unless really necessary, or you will strip the coat of its natural oils. Wash your dog outdoors in a suitable tub – such as a baby bath – and rub it dry afterwards with a towel. If you use a hairdrier, keep your hand in the airflow to ensure that the air is never too hot

53

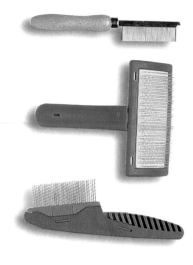

Your choice of grooming tools will be influenced by your dog's coat: for instance, a long-haired breed will need much more grooming than its short-haired counterpart. However, if you suspect that your dog has fleas, a flea comb with its very fine teeth (top) will be essential, whatever the dog's coat type (see also pages 59–60).

If a puppy becomes used to grooming early on, it will be easy to handle. Always keep a watch for parasites such as fleas in the fur (see pages 59–60).

against your dog's skin. Brush or comb a longer-coated dog after drying to remove any tangles.

Beware of exercising your dog soon after bathing it, because, deprived of its natural odour, it may seek out an alternative: for instance, rolling in cow pats is quite common behaviour. Keep your dog away from such opportunities for the first few days after giving it a bath, by which time the desire to roll should have passed.

Breeds that need regular clipping – such as poodles – are unlikely to need bathing at home if they are professionally groomed, as this will be carried out before each clip (about every six to eight weeks). You should only give additional baths if your dog's coat is excessively dirty; otherwise, leave any mud to dry and then simply brush it out.

If your dog suffers from a skin condition, your vet may recommend medicated skin baths. In this case, he or she will give you detailed instructions which you must carry out very carefully.

HOLIDAY CARE

Many owners like to take their dogs away with them on holiday, but whether you can do so will obviously depend on the type of holiday and the destination. A number of hotels will accept well-behaved dogs, but you must check this before making a booking.

If you cannot take your dog with you, a good option is to use a well-run boarding kennel. If you do not already know of a suitable kennel, you could ask your vet or other dog owners for recommendations, or arrange to visit two or three kennels (look in your local business telephone directory for details) and choose the best one. This is not just a question of facilities: kind, capable staff can be equally significant when settling your dog into strange surroundings. Most dogs do settle very quickly in kennels, and there are unlikely to be any problems in your absence. Remember to book well ahead as kennels often get very busy, especially during holiday periods.

You may be asked to pay for your dog in advance, and you will also need to show a

ROUTINE MONITORING

As you become familiar with your dog's normal habits and behaviour you will be able to spot any sudden changes, which could be signs of illness, at an early stage. This general monitoring should include keeping an eye on your dog's food and water intake (the latter is particularly important with an older dog – see page 65), as well as its toileting habits.

Behavioural changes can also be significant. For instance, if your dog starts to groom or scratch itself vigorously it may have a skin problem; while dullness and lethargy are often symptoms of illness. If you are concerned about any aspect of your dog's health or behaviour, ask your vet for advice.

vaccination certificate. It is a good idea to have the dog protected against kennel cough at least one month before kennelling, particularly if it is elderly. This ailment is not usually life-threatening, but is unpleasant and spreads very easily when dogs are housed in close proximity (see page 59). Having said this, a good kennel should take every precaution to avoid the spread of kennel cough by providing a fresh, airy environment and a separate exercise run for each dog. Leave the kennel staff with details of any special feeding or medical requirements for your dog, and with a contact number for your veterinary centre.

If you have an intact bitch which could come into season while at the kennel, do inform the staff beforehand as this can be very disruptive. It may be a good idea for your vet to give the bitch medication to prevent the season, so ask him or her for advice well in advance.

HOUSING

Pet dogs are not generally expected to sleep outside at night, especially in winter when it can become very cold. However, an outdoor kennel can sometimes be useful during the day, and will enable your dog to rest in comfort away from the hustle and bustle of life inside the house.

There are two types of kennel, the first of which is a simple design that can be positioned in a corner of an escape-proof garden. This should be in a sheltered spot out of the wind and direct sunlight, and preferably on a hard surface such as concrete paving slabs. The kennel should be raised off the ground to avoid damp getting in, and should have a pitched roof covered in roofing felt to allow rain to run off (the roof must overhang the walls slightly to prevent rain from running down them). A removable roof will allow easy access for cleaning. The kennel should ideally have two compartments. The first is for sleeping, and should contain adequate warm bedding, such as washable rugs and blankets or cushions on a layer of straw; the second should be large enough for the dog to stand up, lie down and turn around in.

Safe and secure in its own compartment, your dog should settle in the car without problems. Using a dog guard also protects the upholstery from claws and muddy paws, and ensures that you will not be distracted by your dog while driving.

The second type of kennel is a much more elaborate affair; this is larger and has an attached run to allow the dog free movement without being able to escape. This kind of kennel is only really suitable for a large dog, and will need a suitably spacious garden to accommodate it.

If your dog does not have a kennel, it must have its own special place in the house where its bed is kept and it can sleep in peace. The most usual place for this is in the kitchen or in a utility room, where there is a door to the garden and an easily cleaned floor.

TRAVELLING

Most dogs enjoy travelling in cars, but there are various points to remember before embarking on a journey with your dog for the first time. Put it in the rear of the car where it cannot jump about and distract the driver – the boot of an estate car is ideal. If the dog will not stay there of its own accord, you should use a car cage or dog guard (these are sold in pet stores, and can be fitted in estate or hatchback cars) to keep both dog and passengers safe.

Good ventilation is essential, as dogs are badly affected by the build-up of heat in cars and will quickly become uncomfortable if they do not have a supply of fresh air. Make frequent stops during a long journey to give your dog time to stretch its legs, relieve itself and have a drink of water; you should always keep a bowl and a supply of water in the car.

AVOIDING HEATSTROKE

Never leave your dog in a parked car for a long period – even in the shade on a sunny day, as the sun may move around while you are gone. Cars can heat up extremely quickly, and your dog could suffer from heatstroke which may develop into a potentially fatal condition in minutes.

If you do need to leave your dog for a short period, choose an underground car-park, or a space in a multi-storey complex that will not be affected by sunlight, and leave the windows slightly open.

Breeding

Breeding dogs is a great responsibility, and is something that you should only embark upon after careful consideration so as not to add to the yearly toll of unwanted puppies. If you have a bitch and you wish to breed from her, try to find homes for the puppies well in advance of the mating. If you do not plan to breed from your dog – whether male or female – you should have it neutered at the age of six months (see page 44).

From birth until the start of weaning towards the end of the fourth week, puppies depend entirely on their mother's milk; this also supplies them with antibodies which will protect them from disease in the first weeks.

All puppies are a similar size at birth, but from weaning onwards those of larger breeds will start to grow more quickly than their smaller cousins; this will be reflected in their food requirements.

SCREENING A BITCH

Before mating a bitch, you should arrange for her to be screened for potential hereditary weaknesses which could be passed on to her puppies; these include various eye conditions and other problems which occur more commonly in some breeds. Screening should be carried out well in advance of the mating; your vet will tell you how to organize this.

Bitches can be mated at their second or at a subsequent season, although it is inadvisable for a bitch to have a first litter when over five years old. Most bitches come into season for three weeks roughly every six months; the most fertile period for mating is nine to 12 days after the start of the season.

CHOOSING A STUD DOG

If you have a pure-bred bitch, you will need to find a suitable stud dog and make the necessary arrangements before the bitch's next season is due. Choose a male dog which has a good temperament and complements your bitch's appearance if possible, so that hopefully some of the puppies will be of better 'type' than their parents. The dog should preferably not be closely related to the bitch and, like her, should have been screened for potential hereditary weaknesses. It also helps if the dog is relatively close to where you live, because you will have to take the bitch to the stud for mating, although if the best dog is a little further away from your home you should be prepared to make the extra effort to get there.

PREGNANCY

The gestation period in the dog is about 63 days, although there are unlikely to be any changes in your bitch's appearance until at least five weeks after mating, when her abdomen will swell and her nipples will start to become more prominent. However, your vet may well be able to confirm the pregnancy earlier on (this can often be done just a month or so after the mating). The vet will also advise you on reducing your bitch's exercise, increasing her food ration as necessary, and adding any vitamin-and-mineral supplements to her diet.

As the time for the birth approaches, you will need to provide a suitable whelping box. This should have bars around the inside, as these will help to prevent your bitch from rolling on to her puppies. You may be able to borrow or hire a whelping box from a breeder. Line it with old newspapers and a blanket, position it in a quiet spot and encourage the bitch to use it prior to whelping.

Pseudo-pregnancy

Even if a bitch is not mated successfully while in season, she may develop all the physical signs of pregnancy. She may also behave as if she were soon to give birth to a litter of puppies and may become very protective towards her toys, regarding these as surrogate puppies and snapping if they are taken away.

This fairly common condition, which may be linked with pyometra (see box opposite), is known as pseudo-pregnancy. If your bitch shows these tendencies on one occasion, she is quite likely to do so after each season, in which case your vet may well recommend spaying her to resolve the problem.

BIRTH

When the birth is imminent, the bitch's vulval area will swell up and she will become distressed and very restless. Anywhere between one and

Young puppies can be allowed to roam outside in the garden, but they must not be taken out to public places such as parks until they have completed their course of primary vaccinations at about 12 weeks of age (see overleaf).

14 puppies may be born in due course (larger breeds tend to produce bigger litters). When each puppy appears, the bitch will chew away the membrane covering it, lick it into life and then push it towards her nipples for food and warmth.

Most bitches whelp without any problems, but it is important to recognize when things could be going wrong so that you can seek veterinary assistance promptly. Puppies are normally born within 30 minutes of one another, although this interval can be up to an hour. The puppies generally come out head first, and any malpresentation such as a breech birth (when the hind end comes out first) could indicate a problem. Some breeds – notably those with large heads, such as bulldogs – are more likely to have

difficulty giving birth, in which case your vet may need to carry out a Caesarean section to save both the bitch and her puppies. Once a litter is born, most bitches prove to be very good natural mothers, and will feed, clean and care for their offspring with no assistance.

WEANING

Puppies are able to start lapping from about four weeks of age, and will begin to take solid food when they are five to six weeks old. By the age of seven or eight weeks they will be fully weaned off their mother's milk and able to go safely to their new homes. For the next four months or so they will need to be fed on a special food formulated to meet all the nutritional requirements of growing puppies (see also pages 48–9).

ACCIDENTAL MATING

If your bitch is accidentally mated by a dog, the result is likely to be an unwanted litter. However, if you are aware of the mating your vet will be able to give your bitch an injection to prevent pregnancy, which should be administered as soon as possible – preferably within 24 hours. This treatment will prevent the fertilized eggs from implanting in the wall of the uterus, and will not affect any subsequent matings and pregnancies. However, if the bitch is mated again in the same season the injection should not be repeated because it could cause pyometra, an infection of the uterus which often manifests itelf by a sudden increase in thirst, and which could require surgery.

Health care

A great many of our dogs today are living longer than ever, usually for over 10 years and often well into their teens. This is largely thanks to our increased understanding of their nutritional needs, and also to the development of reliable vaccines to protect them against a number of killer diseases. However, these diseases have not actually been eliminated, merely controlled, and if dogs are not vaccinated they will be just as susceptible to the infections as were their ancestors. It is therefore vital to ensure not only that your puppy (or older dog) is protected, but that the necessary annual boosters are administered to maintain its level of immunity.

GIVING YOUR DOG A TABLET

Most dogs are reasonably tolerant of this procedure, although you may find it useful to have an assistant to help you restrain your dog, particularly if it is large.

To give a tablet, place the palm of one hand on the dog's muzzle, with your thumb and index finger on either side. Gently turn your dog's face upwards, and the lower jaw should start to open. Take the tablet between the thumb and index finger of your other hand, and use the remaining fingers of this hand to open the mouth further by pulling down on the teeth. Drop the tablet on to the back of the tongue, in the centre, and then quickly close your dog's mouth. Support its chin to keep it looking upwards, and gently rub down the throat with two or three fingers to encourage swallowing.

VACCINATION

Most of the vaccines now in use offer protection against several diseases in a single shot, and side-effects are very rare. Ask your vet for the latest information about the vaccinations that your puppy or dog will need (this may depend on where you live), and when they should be given. You must keep a puppy away from public places and from other dogs for at least seven to 10 days after it has completed its primary vaccinations at the age of about 12 weeks.

The following are the major infectious diseases affecting dogs for which vaccinations are available and routinely given by vets.

Distemper

This is a viral infection spread by close contact between dogs (an infected dog will often pass the virus in its urine). Early signs are a sudden rise in body temperature, diarrhoea and vomiting, with the dog becoming very sick. More than half of the dogs that survive this stage will go on to develop neurological symptoms in later life, ranging from facial twitches to fits. Thickening of the footpads is another indication of a distemper sufferer, and is the reason why this disease is sometimes known as 'hardpad'.

Infectious canine hepatitis

This disease is caused by a virus called canine adenovirus type 1 (CAV-1). Infection is usually through contact with an infected dog's urine, hence the term 'lamp-post disease' which is often given to the condition. An affected dog will show symptoms such as jaundice (most obvious as a yellowing of the mucous membranes inside the lips, and of the 'whites' of the eyes), abdominal pain and bloody diarrhoea, or it may die very rapidly. In some instances where a dog does survive, a blue opacity over the cornea of one or both eyes will become visible for a period. CAV-1 infection also leads to long-term kidney damage. An infected dog will remain a danger to others for perhaps months after recovery.

Canine leptospirosis

This is a bacterial rather than a viral ailment. One form is spread by rats (this also gives rise to Weil's disease in people), so terriers and other rat-catching dogs are most at risk of contracting it. There is also a canine variant which threatens all dogs, causing infectious jaundice. Antibiotics may help, although the prognosis will be poor.

Canine parvovirus

This is a relatively new viral ailment to be recognized in dogs, and was first identified in the 1970s. It is transmitted via exposure to an infected dog, or through contact with its faeces. The virus can attack the heart muscle, causing sudden death in young puppies. It can also affect the digestive tract of susceptible older dogs, resulting in blood-stained diarrhoea, vomiting and permanent damage to the intestinal lining; if the dog survives, this damage will restrict the absorption of nutrients in the longer term.

Rabies

In parts of the world in which rabies is endemic, it may be a legal requirement for owners to have their dogs vaccinated against the virus, which can be deadly for dogs and people alike. In any event, if you live in an area in which rabies is prevalent (at present, only islands such as Australia, Hawaii, Iceland, the UK and the Irish Republic are free from the disease) you should have your dog vaccinated. Transmission between dogs and from dogs to people is via saliva, either through a bite, or – less commonly – through an existing open skin wound such as a cut.

Contagious respiratory disease ('Kennel cough')

This is a much less serious disease than those already described, but it can still be seriously debilitating, especially in older dogs. There is no single cause of this ailment, although the bacterium *Bordetella bronchiseptica* and the virus canine adenovirus type 2 (CAV-2) are frequently isolated.

Kennel cough is an airborne infection – easily spread within the confines of a boarding kennel or show hall where many dogs are present – and results in a dry, hacking cough that is triggered by placing a hand on the dog's windpipe. An unpleasant discharge from the nostrils is also often apparent. A vaccine administered as a nasal spray will afford a good level of protection against this disease, which, although it normally resolves itself in about three weeks, may occasionally lead to life-threatening pneumonia.

INTERNAL PARASITES

All dogs are at risk from common internal parasites such as roundworms and tapeworms, and you must carry out routine preventive treatment to deal with them.

Roundworms

There are a number of types of roundworm, but perhaps the most common type to affect dogs is *Toxocara canis*, which can grow up to 15 cm (6 in) long and has a cream-coloured body that is pointed at both ends.

Routine treatment of puppies and dogs against roundworms is essential – especially when they are kept in households alongside young children – because, in rare circumstances, *Toxocara* larvae may migrate to a person's eye. Children aged between 18 months and three years old are most vulnerable, with worm eggs often being swallowed from dirty fingers.

Your vet will be able to advise you on a suitable de-worming regime for your dog, and will provide you with tablets or powders. Puppies need more frequent de-worming than older

dogs, as they are often born already infested with roundworms passed via their mothers' milk. In severe cases, this can result in diarrhoea and a pot-bellied appearance. You must also thoroughly clean up your dog's faeces in the garden, because roundworm eggs passed out in the faeces can remain viable in the environment for long periods (particularly in soil) and will still be hazardous if they are ingested at this stage.

Tapeworms

These are flat and ribbon-like in shape. A dog suffering from fleas (see below) will be most at risk of a tapeworm infestation, because immature tapeworms can develop in the fleas' bodies and then infest the dog if it swallows them while grooming itself. A dog can also become infested with tapeworms by eating small rodents and contaminated uncooked offal. Special tablets will deal with these parasites, and your vet will advise you on the timings of treatments.

Other worms

Other parasitic worms may be more common in certain breeds, or can be more localized in their distribution. For example, heartworms are spread by mosquitoes and so are a problem in many tropical areas, including parts of Australia, and regular medication to guard against their development in a dog's circulatory system is important. Hookworms, also present in tropical areas, can be a danger; these enter the body through the dog's feet and then migrate to the intestines. Lungworm infestations are most commonly associated with greyhounds, and can result in severe coughing after exercise.

EXTERNAL PARASITES

Fleas are by far the most common and most troublesome external parasites to affect dogs, and can cause severe skin irritation. Now that so many homes have central heating, fleas have become a year-round rather than just a summer problem; they can also spread from cats to dogs and vice versa. Other common external parasites include lice, ticks and mites.

Fleas

You will need to use a special fine-toothed flea comb to confirm the presence of fleas on your dog. Carry out this grooming outdoors, as any fleas which jump off will be less of a hazard here. They often tend to congregate on a dog's back, close to the tail. Another technique is to brush

Fleas can strike at any time of year, although they are more prevalent in the summer. If your dog is scratching more than usual, and biting at its fur to relieve the irritation, it will almost certainly be infested by fleas and you must take action accordingly.

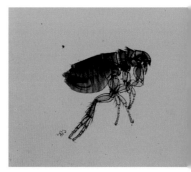

The culprit is the dog flea (*Ctenocephalides canis*). The long front legs of this parasite allow it to leap considerable distances – and, if it is lucky, on to a passing dog for a meal.

debris from your dog's coat on to white paper, then to mop it up with damp cotton wool or blotting paper; any flea droppings will show up as reddish stains as the dried blood inside them starts to dissolve.

Special powders and sprays will help to eliminate fleas. Always read the instructions carefully, and ask your vet's advice if necessary (for example, not all products are suitable for puppies). As well as treating your dog, you must vacuum around its bed and wash the bedding regularly to remove any eggs or immature fleas here, thus reducing the risk of re-infection. If you have a cat, you will need to treat it as well.

Lice
These parasites are more common on puppies than on adult dogs. They cling on to the coat, producing eggs which attach to the hairs. Flea treatments will also kill lice, although you may need to apply these repeatedly to kill off new adult lice as they hatch from their egg cases.

Mites
These are microscopic, but their presence is made obvious by areas of hair loss and intense, persistent itching. Seek veterinary advice if you suspect that your dog has mites (other causes of hair loss include the fungal ailment ringworm, which usually results in circular patches and can spread to people).

Ticks
Ticks are a particular problem in heathland and sheep-grazing areas, where there is good cover for them to survive. They are potentially dangerous parasites, as they can transmit various blood-borne diseases.

One of the most serious tick-borne diseases which can affect dogs is known as Lyme fever. This is now found in many parts of the world, including areas of Europe, the USA and Australia. Even immature stages in the tick's lifecycle can transmit this disease, which causes fever and arthritis, usually affecting the main limb joints.

Once Lyme fever is diagnosed with certainty in a dog, treatment with specific antibiotics will help to prevent any long-term damage. The risk of acquiring this infection (which can also be transmitted by the ticks to people) will be reduced by avoiding walking your dog in areas of heathland where ticks are most likely to be numerous. Your vet will probably be able to advise you of the risk factor in the area where you live, but take particular care over where you exercise your pet if you go away on holiday.

Ticks attach themselves to a dog – usually around the head or shoulders – and swell in size as they suck its blood. If you see a tick on your dog, do not pull it off as this will leave the mouthparts embedded in the skin. Instead, smear the tick with petroleum jelly, which will block its breathing hole and cause it to relinquish its grip. Wait a few minutes, then grasp it with tweezers, rotate it through a quarter turn and remove it.

INTERNAL AILMENTS
Dogs may be affected by a number of internal conditions, of which three common examples are included here. Kidney disease is another fairly widespread problem, but is generally only seen in older dogs (see page 65). If at any time you are concerned about your dog, go to your vet.

Stomach upsets
Vomiting and diarrhoea are very common in dogs, and are often caused by the scavenging of contaminated food. Home treatment usually consists of withholding food for 24 hours and then giving bland foods such as chicken or white fish with rice or pasta, but you may need to obtain medication from your vet as well. Do not delay seeking advice if you are concerned, particularly if you have a young puppy, as it could quickly become dehydrated. If you see any blood in your dog's faeces, go to your vet immediately.

After a digestive disturbance it is a good idea to give a probiotic product (available from your vet or pet store) to re-establish the beneficial bacterial lining in the gut.

Cystitis
Inflammation of the bladder is more common in bitches than in male dogs because they have a shorter urethra (the tube through which urine exits the body from the bladder). An affected dog will show signs of pain when urinating; it may also pass small volumes of urine more frequently, have 'accidents' indoors and have blood-tinged urine. Often the result of a bacterial infection, cystitis needs veterinary treatment with antibiotics.

Heart disease
This is more commonly seen in older dogs, but can also strike younger ones. A dry cough and reluctance to exercise are typical signs. Regular medication will alleviate the symptoms of heart disease, while other steps – such as reducing the dog's weight – may also help. Regular screening should help to detect this and other chronic ailments in older dogs at an early stage, so that the condition can be stabilized as far as possible.

EXTERNAL AILMENTS

Dogs are also liable to suffer from the following external problems. You should only attempt to treat very minor conditions yourself. If you do so and the condition does not quickly improve, or if you are at all worried about your dog, always contact your vet as soon as possible for further advice and specific treatment.

Ear problems

Breeds with long, heavy ear flaps – such as spaniels – are at greatest risk of suffering from ear problems, which can be a source of great discomfort. Do not try to treat your dog yourself, as the cause of irritation will have to be identified correctly by your vet if any treatment is to be successful. Ear mites, fungi and bacteria can all be involved in infections of this type, which will cause the dog to scratch its ear repeatedly. Seek treatment before the condition worsens, and before your dog can damage its ear flap through excessive scratching.

Eye problems

These are often revealed by persistent watering of the eyes, usually due to irritation or to a scratch. Bathe the eye gently with a special eye-wash, and consult your vet if there is no improvement.

Eye irritation could also be due to the eyelid turned inwards and rubbing against the eyeball. In this case, surgery to correct the condition – which is known as entropion – will be required.

Anal-gland disorders

The two small anal sacs are located inside the anus and produce a secretion which marks the dog's faeces. If the sacs become blocked, impaction will occur and your vet will need to empty them. Typical symptoms are persistent licking and 'scooting' as the dog drags itself along on its hindquarters.

Regularly adding a little bran to your dog's food may help to prevent recurrences, although if it repeatedly suffers from overful and impacted anal sacs your vet may well recommend surgery to remove them.

Cuts and abrasions

If a cut or abrasion is only minor, bathing it gently with a veterinary antiseptic solution and bandaging where possible will promote healing in a few days. A more severe injury may need to be stitched by your vet. When out walking your dog, beware of barbed wire, which can cause severe lacerations.

Poisoning

A dog can be poisoned through ingesting a wide range of chemicals and other substances; these can also contaminate a dog's coat, and be ingested as it tries to lick itself clean.

If you know or suspect that your dog has swallowed poison, you must contact your vet urgently; take any container or package with you to help the vet to identify the poison.

Accidents and emergencies

If your dog is involved in an accident, take it to the nearest veterinary centre as quickly as possible, where all facilities to identify the damage will be to hand. If necessary, you can improvise a stretcher using a towel or blanket, or slide the dog on to a flat object such as a tray or board. If the dog is aggressive when you try to handle it – and remember that even the gentlest dog may react like this when in pain – muzzle it with a length of bandage, a tie or even a pair of tights to protect yourself from being bitten. Give the dog nothing by mouth in case it requires surgery, and carry out first aid if necessary (see below).

Even if your dog appears relatively unhurt after an accident such as a collision with a car, you should still take it to your vet for a check-up as there could be unseen internal bleeding, which could prove fatal if not investigated and treated.

FIRST AID FOR AN INJURED DOG

If your dog is not breathing, open its mouth and check that the airway is clear, removing any obstruction. Lift up the dog's chin to extend the neck and then, holding the mouth closed, breathe into the nose at about 30 breaths per minute.

Check for a heartbeat by holding your fingers firmly against your dog's chest just behind the left elbow. If you cannot feel a heartbeat, begin chest compressions at a rate of two per second: with a small dog, place one hand on either side of the chest behind the elbows, and squeeze your hands together to compress the chest; position a larger dog on its side and use your hands on top of each other to apply pressure in a 'cough-like' manner to the chest wall. Every four compressions, breathe into the nostrils for two breaths.

Continue compressing the chest in this way until you can feel a consistent heartbeat, or until veterinary help arrives.

Dogs

Canine behaviour

A dog's character starts to develop at birth, and will be greatly affected by its experiences during the first weeks of life. These are especially important during the so-called 'socialization period', lasting from the age of four to 12 weeks, when all puppies must be introduced to a range of different people, objects and other animals if they are to develop into confident and sociable family pets.

As a puppy grows older, good training should serve to correct or control most of the unwanted behaviours that can arise, such as persistent barking. However, if you encounter a particular problem in training your dog, or an aspect of its behaviour concerns you, ask your vet for advice.

BEHAVIOURAL PROBLEMS

If you do come across a behavioural problem with your dog, do not just sit back and hope it will improve. Instead, seek help early, as this should help to overcome the problem more easily and before it has become an established part of your dog's behaviour pattern. There could be a medical reason for the problem – for instance, a urinary disorder such as cystitis could be responsible for incontinence (see page 60) – so your vet will begin by giving your dog a thorough check-up. If all seems to be well physically, he or she may refer you to a canine behaviourist, who can work with you and your dog to overcome the problem. Having a clear insight into its onset can be very important, so write down any information you think may be relevant before your initial consultation so that no possible cause is overlooked.

It is conceivable that the cause of the problem may rest with you, as inconsistencies in training will confuse your dog. For instance, if you do not want it to lie on your chairs, do not encourage it

to sit there with you as a puppy and then simply expect it to stay off the furniture once it is older. Lack of exercise, leading to boredom, can also cause behavioural problems. Certain breeds and individual dogs have almost unlimited energy which can be wrongly channelled into vices such as aggression, barking, destructiveness or running away. In this case you may well need to review your dog's lifestyle.

INTRODUCING A NEW DOG

Many behavioural patterns that you see in your dog will be linked with its sexuality and territorial instincts. For example, adult male dogs will mark their presence in an area by cocking a leg and depositing drops of their urine – which has a distinctive scent – on fence-posts and other objects; and, when meeting for the first time, dogs of both sexes identify each other by sniffing at the jowls and at the scent glands under the tail.

Introducing a young dog to the household can give a new lease of life to an older one; it can also help to ease the inevitable sense of loss and

Scent plays an important part in all aspects of canine communication. Sniffing nose-to-nose is a typical greeting when two dogs meet for the first time.

emptiness caused by the death of a much-loved pet. Domestic dogs are fairly social animals, but introducing one dog either temporarily or permanently into the home of another needs to be carried out carefully. The likelihood of problems will be greatest if you acquire a young male dog and already own an intact (unneutered) older male. For instance, there may be an apparent breakdown in the house training of your established pet, but it will in fact simply be seeking to assert its position by scent-marking in the home. In contrast, bitches tend to be far more amenable to the company of younger companions.

This puppy is in trouble! Note how its tail is firmly tucked down between its legs, and the way its ears are flattened against the side of the head. A puppy will often respond in this way when being scolded by its owner.

It is a good idea to introduce the dogs on neutral ground to minimize the risk of conflict, and then to walk them home together. Feed the new dog separately so that there will be no dispute over food, and alter both dogs' sleeping arrangements if necessary to prevent disagreements. Do not scold your dog if it growls at the newcomer, as it will simply be asserting its dominance and this will hopefully not lead on to conflict. It is vital not to show favouritism to the new arrival, as this will be a challenge to your established dog. Instead, keep to the normal routine. The time needed for the dogs to settle together will depend largely on the individuals concerned. You cannot rush this, so be patient.

BODY LANGUAGE

Dogs have evolved a complex series of gestures to communicate with one another, and use their body language to express and interpret a range of emotions and behaviours.

For instance, if your dog encounters a strange dog it will not just suddenly attack but, if it is uncertain, will sniff or move forward cautiously, with its tail kept low. Raising the hackles along the back at the base of the neck serves as a warning gesture, effectively appearing to increase body size. The lips will be drawn back, exposing the front teeth, and the dog may also snarl or growl loudly while staring hard at its opponent.

If the other dog is willing to back down it will retreat, showing its submission by crouching with its ears lowered. If cornered, it will roll over on to its back. The other dog will recognize this as a gesture of appeasement and will then not attack. In some cases it may chase the other dog away, but again serious physical conflict is unlikely. Only if neither dog backs down will combat ensue and, even then, once one dog breaks away the victor will not pursue it for any distance.

When meeting another dog or a person it knows well and is pleased to see, a dog will wag its tail in greeting, with its ears raised and pointing forward. If it is hoping for attention, it may sit with one of its forelegs raised off the ground. Barking can also sometimes be used as a means of attracting attention. Dogs will keep in touch with one another by barking; they may also bark as a deterrent, which makes them valuable as guardians warning of possible danger.

Here the dog on the right is trying to encourage its companion to join in a game. A dog will adopt a characteristic position – known as the 'play bow' – when in playful mood. This involves placing the forelegs horizontally on the ground while keeping the hindquarters raised, and then springing up excitedly, as this young dog is doing in its bid to provoke a game.

Caring for the older dog

Signs of old age in dogs are not difficult to spot, especially in the case of black-coated individuals, which will develop grey areas around the muzzle and sometimes close to the eyes, although the overall body coloration will be unaffected. Once your dog reaches the age of seven (or five if it is a giant breed) you should take it for twice-yearly check-ups with your vet, so that any problems can be diagnosed and treated at an early stage.

FAILING SIGHT

An old dog's eyes may start to look slightly cloudy, which can be evidence of cataracts (opacity of the lenses). However, declining vision is not necessarily a major handicap for dogs, as they rely much more heavily on their sense of smell than on sight. Even a puppy will tend instinctively to search for a titbit dropped on the ground using its nose rather than its eyes.

DEAFNESS

A dog may also be afflicted by deafness as a result of advancing years. This is difficult to recognize with certainty, although you are likely to find that your dog does not respond in certain situations – perhaps when you call it from some distance away – whereas in the past it would

have shown some recognition of your call. Cases of deafness increase dramatically from the age of about 10 years onwards, when perhaps one in 10 dogs suffers from the condition; the figure rises six-fold in dogs of 14 years old and above. Your vet will be able to carry out certain hearing tests on your dog, but little can be done to treat deafness at present.

MENTAL PROBLEMS

There is now growing recognition among vets and canine behaviourists of declining mental faculties in old dogs, even to the extent of identifying a canine equivalent of Alzehimer's syndrome. Like their owners, dogs are now tending to live longer than in the past, and so such ailments are becoming more commonplace.

One of the most frequently seen problems in older dogs has been dubbed 'geriatric separation anxiety', signs of which usually become apparent at night when the household is asleep. The dog wakes up, and feels disorientated. It starts barking and panting, showing signs of obvious distress; in an extreme case, it may even soil its surroundings. If this happens with your dog, you must give reassurance rather than reacting crossly – not least so that everyone can go back to sleep. You should then arrange a veterinary check-up as a matter of urgency, in case there is an underlying medical reason – such as a tumour – for your dog's behaviour. In cases where there appears to be no physical reason for the condition, drugs can be given to treat the dog's anxiety and so help to resolve the problem. Interestingly, dogs which tended to be nervous when they were younger appear to be most vulnerable to this condition.

TUMOURS

Advances in veterinary care are now helping to treat a number of the ailments of old age. For example, instead of having to rely largely on surgery to treat tumours in dogs, a vet may be able to use chemotherapy or radiotherapy.

Cryosurgery can also be useful in situations in which conventional surgery could be dangerous because of the blood flow to an area, or because of an underlying risk of infection. This technique uses a special probe to apply freezing liquid nitrogen to a tumour, to mask it off from the surrounding healthy tissue. There is no need for a scalpel. By freezing the cells comprising the tumour, the liquid nitrogen should kill them so that in due course they slough away, hopefully to be replaced by healthy cells.

Signs of advancing years are visible on this boxer's face, particularly in the greying of the hair around its muzzle. Boxers are susceptible to tumours, which are most likely to crop up from middle age onwards. Always be alert to the appearance of any unusual lumps on your dog, which will need to be checked as soon as possible by your vet.

64

KIDNEY FAILURE

Failing kidneys are one of the major reasons for the death of elderly dogs and, although actual treatment of damaged kidneys is not yet possible, feeding a diet consisting of protein of high biological value (in limited amounts) will help to stabilize the condition in many cases, often for years.

A dog's kidneys have an amazing excess capacity, and it is not until their level of function has declined by at least two-thirds that signs of illness become apparent. The most obvious of these is likely to be a significant increase in the dog's fluid consumption, and a corresponding increase in its urinary output.

You should keep an eye on the amount of water your older dog is drinking to alert you to this problem at an early stage. Doing this can be harder than it sounds, because the volume of water that any dog drinks will be affected both by the temperature and by the type of food that it eats: for example, a spell of hot weather combined with a dry-food diet (see page 48) is likely to raise its water consumption. Another complication is that dogs often choose to drink from muddy pools and puddles when out on walks, so establishing a volume measurement can be difficult. However, you will know what is normal for your dog and so should quickly spot any obvious change.

With the increasing throughput of water resulting from kidney disease, other essential compounds – such as B vitamins – are likely to be lost, leading to a deficiency. Absorption of calcium into the body may also be affected, because of the lack of a hormone produced in the kidneys which normally stimulates this process from the gut. Once again, however, adjusting the diet can help to overcome these problems.

Another obvious sign of kidney failure in the older dog is likely to be bad breath, although this can be due to dental disease.

An older dog will benefit from greater protection against the elements, so a warm coat is a good idea in cold weather. To establish the size of coat you will need, measure from the bottom of your dog's neck to the base of its tail in a straight line.

DENTAL DISEASE

Dental problems can affect a dog of any age, but are more commonly seen in older individuals, particularly if they are fed on a diet of soft food. Certain smaller breeds – such as toy poodles – also seem to suffer more from dental disease than others. If tartar is allowed to accumulate on your dog's teeth the gums are soon likely to become inflamed, and the attachments of the affected teeth will become weak. As the gum line becomes eroded, so bacteria

can gain easier access to the roots of the teeth, possibly causing an abscess to form. Your dog will then suffer from raging toothache and may well have difficulty in eating.

Your vet will examine your dog's teeth at its twice-yearly check-ups and, if necessary, will strip off the hard calculus, or tartar, before it can cause any serious harm. Feeding dry foods and certain types of chew (ask your vet for advice) will help naturally to prevent accumulations of tartar on the teeth, as will regular tooth-brushing with a special canine toothpaste (see page 53).

Your vet will check your dog's teeth at its twice-yearly examinations, but you should also look for any problems during your weekly health checks, as unhealthy gums and loose teeth will combine to make eating a painful experience. Bad breath is often indicative of a dental problem, although it can also be a sign of kidney failure.

Major dog groups

The different breeds of dog are divided into specific categories for show purposes. There is no universal method for this, and the precise arrangement will depend on the canine governing body in the country concerned. Furthermore, not all breeds are recognized for show purposes in all countries and, while some breeds have established a strong international following, others remain very localized and so are unlikely to be seen outside the region in which they were originally developed.

Fashion does undeniably play a part in this process, although there is a growing appreciation of the need to preserve rarer breeds. The shar pei is one of the most recent beneficiaries of this approach. The breed was on the verge of extinction in southern China and Hong Kong by the 1970s, but enthusiasts in the USA mounted a determined campaign to save it. Today the shar pei is widely kept, and its future now seems to be assured.

The dogs included here are grouped according to their general functions, rather than on a show basis, and descriptions are given of the appearance and characteristics of breeds found within each category. Note that the heights given for dogs are measured at the shoulder, according to the standard procedure.

HERDING DOGS

In general, the herding dogs are easily trained and intelligent. Some of them were originally used solely for herding livestock, whereas the larger herding breeds also served as flock guardians, driving off wolves. Members of this group are very loyal to their owners. They are extremely active dogs, and need plenty of exercise as well as mental stimulation if they are not to become bored and destructive around the home.

Rough collie

⬙ 61 cm (24 in)   ☗ 30 kg (65 lb)

The rough collie was originally kept as a working sheepdog in Scotland, and has since become well known for its starring role in the *Lassie* films. It is a handsome dog with a long coat that is usually merle (a combination of black and white hairs, giving a greyish-blue appearance), sable or tri-colour; each of these colours is marked with white.

The smooth collie is a similar, short-coated version of the breed, which requires less in the way of grooming.

Shetland sheepdog

Shetland sheepdog

⬙ 35 cm (14 in)   ☗ 7.5 kg (16 lb)

This small version of the rough collie, which is often affectionately described as the 'sheltie', comes from the Shetland Isles off the north-east coast of Scotland. The breed's long coat is usually sable, tri-colour or merle, but both pure black and black-and-white individuals are sometimes seen.

The sheltie is an extremely good-natured dog and makes an excellent family pet. However, it does require thorough daily grooming to keep its long coat in top condition, which is a consideration when choosing this breed.

German shepherd dog

⬙ 65 cm (25 in)   ☗ 38 kg (84 lb)

Also known formerly as the Alsatian, this breed was developed in its present form about 100 years ago, and has since become the best known of the European shepherd dogs. Its natural intelligence and ability to respond well to commands when properly trained has made it a frequent choice for police and guide-dog work. The coat is usually short and dense in texture, although long-haired individuals do occasionally crop up in litters.

For many years white individuals were not encouraged, but they now form a breed on their own and are increasingly popular dogs.

German shepherd dog

HOUNDS

The dogs in this group were originally developed to hunt game, working alone or in packs. Anyone contemplating buying a hound as a pet should be aware that they are strong-willed and single-minded in pursuit of potential quarry, and are correspondingly difficult to train. They can be broadly split into two groups: the sight hounds and the scent hounds.

Sight hounds – such as the Afghan – have evolved to hunt in relatively open countryside, pursuing their quarry by sight. The eyes are positioned on the sides of the head to give wide-ranging vision, and the nose is tapering and fairly slender. A deep chest provides good lung capacity, while a curved or 'roach' back – connected to powerful hind limbs – enables the dog to run fast over considerable distances when hunting. The sight hounds are very much the athletes of the dog world.

In contrast, scent hounds – such as the bloodhound – have broad noses for detecting scents easily. Stamina rather than pace is a feature of these hounds, which are frequently hunted in packs. They are powerfully built and often hunt in wooded terrain, keeping in touch with other pack members by means of their distinctive baying calls.

Hounds in general are friendly dogs with excellent dispositions. They are also less susceptible to the breed weaknesses that can afflict some pure-bred dogs (such as progressive retinal atrophy in sheepdogs and gundogs, hip dysplasia in retrievers and patellar luxation in toy breeds – see page 71). Smooth-coated hounds need little in the way of grooming, although long-haired breeds, such as the Afghan, need daily coat care. Hounds are very active dogs, and will not adapt well to city life – they need space and plenty of exercise.

Afghan hound

Afghan hound

⬦ 74 cm (29 in)   ☒ 27 kg (60 lb)

The Afghan has become one of the most popular and fashionable of all the hounds. It was first imported into the UK in the 1880s by British Army officers, but subsequently died out and was not re-introduced until 1920; it first arrived in the USA in the 1920s. The Afghan hound was originally used to hunt gazelle and mountain deer, and is said to be the fastest hurdler among the hounds. In recent years it has been developed into an excellent and very popular show dog.

Beagle

⬦ 33–41 cm (13–16 in)   ☒ 14 kg (30 lb)

This small hound was originally bred to hunt hares in packs, but is now widely kept as a pet. The coat of the beagle is short and smooth, and is typically either lemon and white or tri-coloured (black, reddish-brown and white), with these combinations found predominantly in hound breeds. Although an affectionate and very lively dog, the beagle does tend to display the slightly obstinate temperament associated with the hound group.

Beagle

Dachshunds

Standard ⬦ 23 cm (9 in)   ☒ 11.5 kg (25 lb)
Miniature ⬦ 13 cm (5 in)   ☒ 4.5 kg (10 lb)

There are six breeds of dachshund: three different coat types, with a standard and a miniature form of each. The dachshund originated in Germany and was bred to hunt badgers, as its name reveals (in German, 'dachs' means 'badger'; 'hund' means 'dog'). Its long body and short legs allowed it to go underground into narrow passages, while its large paws were ideal for digging. It is still used in Germany as a hunting dog.

Although the dachshund's diminutive size makes it a good choice for a smaller home – where it will act as an alert guardian – its elongated body puts it at risk of suffering from an intervertebral-disc prolapse (a condition often referred to as a 'slipped disc'). As a precaution, it is safer to exercise a dachshund on a harness rather than with a collar, as this exerts less pressure on the vulnerable part of the neck. Never encourage a dachshund to jump on to chairs or to climb stairs, as these activities may also predispose it to a slipped disc.

Long-haired: This dachshund can be recognized by its soft, wavy and shiny coat. The hair should lie flat on the body, being longer under the neck and body with feathering (long hair) on the ears, on the underside of the tail and down the backs of the legs. The coat must be groomed daily to keep it in good condition, and the hair between the toes needs occasional trimming as it may be uncomfortable if left too long.

Smooth-haired: This is the oldest of the six dachshund breeds, and makes a good family pet and watchdog. Any of the usual colours are acceptable (except white), with the three most popular colours being black and tan, chocolate and tan, and red. The coat has an attractive gloss to it.

Wire-haired: This dachshund was bred in Germany in the 18th century. It can be distinguished by its thick, wiry coat, complete with bushy eyebrows and a beard of longer hair under the chin.

(Top) Golden retriever
(Above) Cocker spaniel

GUNDOGS

The spaniels and setters are the oldest members of this group, with retrievers only coming to prominence with the advent of shooting in the 18th century. Pointers are also included in this category. The tasks of gundogs are to locate and indicate the position of game birds and waterfowl, and then to retrieve them after they have been shot. Many gundogs can swim well, and also have highly developed scenting skills for use on land. As a group, they are responsive to training, frequently working on a one-to-one basis with their owners. They can make good pets, but must have plenty of exercise.

Labrador retriever

⬆ 56 cm (22 in) ⚖ 27–34 kg (60–75 lb)

This is one of the most widely kept of all gundogs, and is popular as a working dog, in the show ring and as a pet. The labrador has a short, glossy, water-resistant coat that is able to withstand cold and wet conditions. It is usually black or yellow in colour, but chocolate is also acceptable for showing. This breed is susceptible to obesity, so adequate exercise combined with a sensible diet is vital.

Golden retriever

⬆ 61 cm (24 in) ⚖ 27–36 kg (60–80 lb)

Like other gundogs, this breed is usually calm and good-natured. The coat is wavy, and longer than that of the labrador. The coloration of individuals can vary from a pale cream through to rich gold, but must not be reddish if the dog is to be shown.

Cocker spaniel

⬆ 41 cm (16 in) ⚖ 15 kg (32 lb)

One of the smallest of the gundogs, the cocker spaniel is bred in a wide range of colours including black, golden, red, blue, roan, black and tan, and tri-colour. The coat is very silky and needs regular grooming. The ears can prove troublesome throughout a dog's life, and must be cleaned as necessary. In the USA, this breed was used in the 1800s

to develop the American cocker spaniel, which has a more profuse coat trailing to the ground.

Springer spaniel

⬆ 50 cm (20 in) ⚖ 23 kg (50 lb)

This breed has only existed for about 180 years, although the name 'springer' has been known since Elizabethan times when these dogs were used to 'spring' – or flush out – game birds from the undergrowth. The coat is usually liver and white, but can also be black and white or tri-coloured.

English setter

⬆ 61–68 cm (24–27 in) ⚖ 25–30 kg (55–65 lb)

With its 200-year history, this is the oldest of the setter breeds. The coat is long and slightly wavy; it is usually white with flecks of black, creating a mottled appearance. The name 'setter' refers to the traditional way in which these dogs would 'set', or sit, to show that they had detected game nearby.

Irish setter

⬆ 68 cm (27 in) ⚖ 32 kg (70 lb)

The Irish setter is often popularly known as the red setter because of its rich mahogany colouring. Over 100 years ago the coat was red and white, but pure-red individuals subsequently became favoured. The traditional red-and-white form was almost lost, but has been revived in recent years and is now recognized as a separate breed called the Irish red-and-white setter.

Irish setter

TERRIERS

Members of this group were originally bred to keep down pests such as rats, mice and foxes, and were also used for the 'sports' of bull- and bear-baiting. Their name comes from the Latin *terra* ('earth'). Terriers are alert, hardy and energetic working dogs, whose innate desire to investigate any hole in the ground may render them less easy to train than other small breeds. Some individuals can be fairly noisy, while a possible tendency to be snappy (this is most often seen in young puppies) can make them unsuitable as pets for families with young children.

All the terriers will need careful handling during their formative months and, although they are generally small dogs, will enjoy and require plenty of exercise if they are not to become too mischievous.

The vast majority of breeds in this group are of British origin.

Staffordshire bull terrier

⬡ 41 cm (16 in) ⬤ 17 kg (37 lb)

This is a descendant of the bull terriers that were formerly used for dog fighting. The Staffordshire bull terrier has been known in the USA since the 1870s, but in the UK it did not become officially recognized as a breed in its own right until the 1930s.

Staffordshire bull terriers tend to be hostile towards one another as well as towards other types of dogs, which can be a disadvantage for some owners, but they are friendly with people. They are available in a fairly wide range of colours, which include white, black, blue, red and fawn, and in any of these colours combined with white.

Bull terrier

Standard ⬡ 56 cm (22 in) ⬤ 24 kg (52 lb)
Miniature ⬡ 35 cm (14 in) ⬤ 11 kg (24 lb)

This breed was developed from crosses between bulldogs and terriers in the 19th century, and has a distinctively broad, tapering face. The coat can be white, white with colours on the head, or 'coloured' (black or brindle being the main colour). The earliest examples of the breed were probably brindle-coloured. A miniature form is also now established.

Airedale terrier

⬡ 61 cm (24 in) ⬤ 22 kg (48 lb)

The largest of the terrier breeds, the Airedale is named after the River Aire which flows through its Yorkshire homeland. It served as a messenger in the trenches in the First World War, and has been trained for police work. The Airedale's loyal nature makes it a good guard dog. It has a hard, wiry coat which is black or dark grizzle and tan in colour, and which requires considerable preparation for the show ring.

Cairn terrier

⬡ 25 cm (10 in) ⬤ 7 kg (15 lb)

This small dog came originally from Skye and the Western Isles of Scotland, where it was used to drive out foxes from their hiding places. The name comes from the Gaelic for 'a pile of stones', reflecting the areas frequented by the breed. The coat is rough, and can be any colour except white.

West Highland white terrier

⬡ 28 cm (11 in) ⬤ 7 kg (15 lb)

One of the best-known terriers, this dog first appeared about 100 years ago when white pups were produced in litters of Cairn terriers. Initially these were often destroyed at birth, but in time they became accepted and evolved into a separate breed. The 'Westie', as it is popularly known, has a coarse coat which needs very little trimming and is easy to keep clean, as any dirt brushes out of it readily.

Border terrier

⬡ 25 cm (10 in) ⬤ 7 kg (15 lb)

This small dog came originally from the Border region between England and Scotland, where it was bred to rout foxes from their underground earths for waiting foxhounds.

The border terrier has a less excitable temperament than some of the other terrier breeds; it is also very responsive to training, making it a more suitable pet for a family with young children. The short and wiry coat – which needs very little in the way of grooming – can be red, wheaten or grizzle in colour, and sometimes also has tan markings.

Scottish terrier

⬡ 25 cm (10 in) ⬤ 10 kg (22 lb)

Affectionately known as the 'Scottie', this breed was formerly called the Aberdeen terrier after its home town. It was first introduced to the USA in 1884, where it has remained popular as a family pet ever since.

The Scottie is wary of strange people, and is not especially well disposed towards other dogs. Its coat needs a great deal of attention and trimming, particularly for showing purposes. The most common coat colour is black, but Scotties can also be brindle- or wheaten-coloured.

West Highland white terrier

WORKING BREEDS

These have been kept for a range of purposes over the years, and include dogs that are quite variable both in size and in their general characteristics. Working dogs also differ significantly in temperament: for example, those bred primarily for guarding are usually fairly slow to learn and may become naturally aggressive as they develop.

For this reason, if you would like to obtain a puppy from this group it is worthwhile seeking out an experienced breeder who specializes in show stock. Such dogs are much less likely to be instinctively aggressive, because this behaviour is very heavily penalized in the show ring.

Dalmatian

🔺 61 cm (24 in) ⬛ 25 kg (55 lb)

A well-known breed, the Dalmatian's coat has either black or chocolate spotting on a white background (the puppies are actually pure white at birth). The patterning on individuals is highly variable, but in a good show dog the spots should be round and even, and must not overlap. Originally bred as a carriage dog, the Dalmatian is elegant, alert and active.

Dobermann pinscher

🔺 68 cm (27 in) ⬛ 40 kg (88 lb)

Created by a German tax collector called Ludwig Dobermann to protect him as he carried out his duties, the breed that he inspired has since built up an international following. The short, sleek coat is usually black and tan.

The Dobermann pinscher needs firm training from an early age, and so will be more suited to an experienced owner. It is not recommended for a home with young children, as it is not particularly tolerant by nature.

Rottweiler

🔺 70 cm (27 in) ⬛ 40.5–50 kg (90–110 lb)

Originating in Germany and initially used for driving cattle, this breed is now frequently chosen for police and guard work. The short coat is black with distinctive tan markings. This is a powerful, muscular dog which tends to have a dominant personality.

Boxer

🔺 63 cm (25 in) ⬛ 32 kg (70 lb)

Bred in Germany in the 19th century, the boxer first appeared in the USA in 1904 and in the UK in the 1930s. Friendly and exuberant by nature, the only significant drawback of the breed is its susceptibility to tumours.

The boxer's short, shiny coat is usually either brindle or fawn, with some white markings and a black mask.

Miniature poodles

Poodles

Standard 🔺 38 cm (15 in) ⬛ 21–32 kg (45–70 lb)
Miniature 🔺 28–38 cm (11–15 in) ⬛ 12–14 kg (26–30 lb)
Toy 🔺 25–28 cm (10–11 in) ⬛ 7 kg (15 lb)

The name 'poodle' comes from the German word 'puddeln' ('to splash in water'), and the breed is so called because it was originally used to retrieve game from water. It has quite a harsh-textured coat that comes in a range of colours, including brown, black, white, cream, silver, blue and apricot. The miniature poodle was developed as a companion breed from the original standard form in the 1890s, and the smaller toy poodle subsequently came to prominence in the 1950s.

The poodle's coat is very dense and is not moulted, which can be an advantage both for the house-proud and for those who are allergic to dog hair. Clipping was traditionally carried out to assist the poodle's swimming abilities; hair was left on the joints to give protection from the cold. Several styles of clip are now recognized, and grooming can be carried out at specialist parlours.

Chow chow

🔺 45 cm (18 in) ⬛ 28 kg (62 lb)

This breed originally came from China, where it was bred for its fur and for meat. It has also been used for hunting and guarding, and as a sled dog. The thick, dense coat is often red, but may also be black or blue. One unusual characteristic of this dog is its blackish-blue tongue. Rather strong-willed by nature, the chow chow is not an easy breed to train. It is available in both rough- and smooth-coated forms.

Dalmatian

Cavalier King Charles spaniel

Smooth-coated chihuahua

Long-haired chihuahua

Chinese crested

COMPANION BREEDS

As you might expect, most of these dogs are small in stature, often being described as 'toys' (some are scaled-down versions of larger breeds). Unfortunately, soundness is not always a feature of these diminutive dogs. They can be susceptible to a number of congenital problems – especially patellar luxation, a condition affecting one or both kneecaps which can result in serious hind-limb weakness and is likely to require surgical correction. Members of this group require only limited amounts of exercise and so are often quite well suited to living in urban surroundings, although some can be rather excitable by nature. They are popular as pets, particularly in homes with children.

Yorkshire terrier

⬗ 23 cm (9 in)　☒ 3 kg (7 lb)

Over 50 years ago, when this breed was significantly larger than it is today, it was kept by Yorkshire miners and used mainly for ratting. The 'Yorkie' still retains its ratting instincts and, despite its delicate appearance, is a very game little dog with plenty of character. The coat coloration is a distinctive combination of steely blue and tan.

Cavalier King Charles spaniel

⬗ 33 cm (13 in)　☒ 8 kg (18 lb)

One of the larger toy dogs, this breed was popular in England in Tudor times and was a favourite of King Charles II, after whom it was named (although today's Cavalier is in fact a modern re-creation). It has a fairly long, silky coat that may be coloured black and

tan, tri-colour, ruby (rich ruby red) or Blenheim (white with chestnut patches), the last coloration being named after the strain of dogs bred at Blenheim Palace in Oxfordshire by the Duke and Duchess of Marlborough.

The Cavalier King Charles has a flatter skull and a longer muzzle than the King Charles spaniel, which is classified as a separate breed.

Chihuahua

⬗ 15–23 cm (6–9 in)　☒ 1–1.5 kg (2–4 lb)

Originating in Mexico, there are two separate varieties of the Chihuahua – smooth-coated and long-haired – both of which can appear in the same litter of puppies. The breed is available in a wide range of colours. Unlike most dogs, the Chihuahua can prove to be rather fussy about its food.

Pekingese

⬗ 23 cm (9 in)　☒ 6 kg (12 lb)

This small dog first appeared in the courts of the Chinese Emperors and was taken to England in 1860, when one was presented to Queen Victoria as a gift. A distinguishing feature of the Pekingese is its long, thick coat, which may be any colour. Its prominent eyes can be susceptible to injury.

Lhasa apso

⬗ 28 cm (11 in)　☒ 7 kg (15 lb)

Also called the Tibetan apso or, rather confusingly, the Lhasa terrier, this breed makes a good watchdog. Its long, coarse coat is often golden and white in colour. A parting runs down the back, with the coat itself trailing down to the ground.

Shih tzu

⬗ 25 cm (10 in)　☒ 7 kg (15 lb)

This breed originated in the Far East and has a lengthy history, having been taken from its Tibetan homeland to China in the 1600s. It reached the West in the 1930s, but did not become popular here until the 1950s.

The Shih tzu is related to the Lhasa apso. Its unusual name translates as 'lion dog', describing its rather leonine appearance. The dense, long coat makes this dog look larger than it is in reality.

Pomeranian

⬗ 20–28 cm (8–11 in)　☒ 2.5 kg (5 lb)

The early Pomeranians were much larger than the dogs we know today – weighing up to 14 kg (30 lb) – but selective breeding with the smaller individuals in litters has led to a great reduction in size of this Spitz breed.

The Pomeranian is available in a wide range of colours, with the orange variety being particularly popular.

Chinese crested

⬗ 23–33 cm (9–13 in)　☒ 2–5.5kg (4½–12 lb)

This ancient breed occurs in two forms: the normal powder-puff form, which has a coat of long, soft hair; and the unusual 'hairless' form, which in fact has plumes of hair present on the head, tail and lower parts of the legs.

The bare skin of the hairless Chinese crested dog can be prone to sunburn – particularly if the skin is pinkish rather than dark in colour – so care should be taken not to allow this type of dog out for long periods in hot weather.

Cats

The relationship between people and cats began about 5000 years ago in Ancient Egypt. African wild cats (*Felis lybica*) were probably first drawn to human settlements by the presence of rodents. These often decimated human food stores at that time, bringing widespread starvation, so anything offering help from the menace was to be welcomed. Some young kittens may have been reared by hand and subsequently started to catch rodents, fending for themselves and serving a useful purpose as they grew older.

3

EGYPT AND BEYOND

Cats were ultimately to have a major impact on Egyptian society, even achieving divine status. The cat goddess was given a variety of names, including Pasht, which may have led to the affectionate term 'puss' that we use today. When a cat died, its body was embalmed like that of a ruling Pharaoh, and a period of mourning followed. However, there was also a much more sinister side to this cult, with many millions of cats deliberately sacrificed and buried in huge tombs.

Merchant ships sailing around the Mediterranean region carried cats from Egypt to Europe. The Greeks did not show great enthusiasm for them – possibly because they already used weasels to kill their vermin – but they kept cats as pets and took them out on leads for exercise, rather like dogs. The Romans in turn viewed cats as companions, and introduced them to a wider area of the Continent.

Cats were also transported east along the trade routes into Asia at an early stage in history. As in Egypt, they acquired a religious association here, and many of today's popular breeds were kept and worshipped as sacred temple pets. These included the Birman, which originated in Burma (now Myanmar), and the Siamese, which came from the country formerly called Siam (now Thailand).

DEVELOPMENTS IN EUROPE

By the Middle Ages, cats faced a troubled future in Europe. They were seen as creatures of the night and linked with witches, and were soon suffering from intense persecution. This mood appears to have been triggered by the rise of pagan religions, which often regarded the cat as a fertility symbol. Black cats were especially feared, and were popularly believed to be witches' familiars, providing a direct link to the devil and also possessing mysterious powers.

However, in the 17th century cats were given grudging acceptance once again, largely because of their ability to control rodents. Ships' cats were vital in protecting food stores from rats, and their presence on board also helped to enliven long voyages for the sailors. A subtle

but significant shift also occurred in the way writers began to portray cats: for instance, in Charles Perrault's well-known story *Puss-in-Boots*. He based this character on matagots – cats with supposed magical powers – but portrayed Puss not as the devil's agent but as a cat which helped to ensure that his owner became wealthy and was lucky in love.

Artists such as Manet also helped to rehabilitate the cat in the public's mind, and the widespread interest in competing and selective breeding that arose in Victorian Britain saw cats becoming highly prized among the wealthier section of society. The world's first major cat show took place in London in July 1871, and was followed in 1895 by the first major event of this kind in the USA. Rather ironically, an Englishman called Charles Cruft tried his hand at promoting cat shows, but lost money and was forced to concentrate instead on an annual dog show which today is internationally famous. The story could therefore have been very different, particularly as Cruft himself was more of a cat-lover and did not even keep a dog!

THE SEPARATION OF BREEDS

The trend towards establishing different cat breeds began in earnest this century, and there are now over 50 distinctive breeds and countless hundreds of colour varieties. However, the cat-owning public at large has shown little enthusiasm for pure-bred cats, preferring instead to stick with non-pedigree cats (commonly known as 'moggies' in the UK), which have no distinct lineage. This is particularly surprising, because pedigree cats show very few of the hereditary weaknesses so prevalent within pure-bred dogs.

With modern standards of care, cats usually live for 12 to 16 years, or even longer. They are naturally self-reliant animals, although thought needs to be given to protecting them in urban areas where they are especially vulnerable to passing traffic. Cats retain a more independent side to their nature than dogs, but they can prove to be very loyal and rewarding companions, and will ask for little in return except food, shelter and affection.

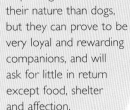

Cats

Choosing and buying a cat

You will be able to obtain a new cat or kitten from a number of sources, including breeders, pet stores and animal-welfare organizations. Alternatively, you may perhaps know of a friend or neighbour whose cat has recently given birth and who is looking for homes for the kittens – this can be a good option, as you will already be familiar with the mother cat and know whether she has a good temperament. Another possibility is to visit your local veterinary centre, which may well have a noticeboard advertising kittens.

If you are looking for a particular breed of kitten, you will almost certainly need to track down a breeder (look at the advertisement columns in cat magazines or contact a national cat organization for names and addresses). You may have to be patient in your search: kittens are not always available all year round, because fewer are born in the late winter than during the spring and summer months.

SELECTING A KITTEN

Eight weeks is the ideal age for a non-pedigree kitten to go to its new home. By this time it should have had contact with a wide range of people and other animals, particularly during the fourth to seventh weeks (the so-called 'socialization period'), when a kitten's experiences will have lasting effects on its personality and on the way it reacts to people and

other animals in later life. In the UK, pedigree kittens are often kept by their breeders for 12 weeks, so that they have had their initial vaccinations (see page 88) and are litter-trained before going out into the world; this usually varies in other countries.

When choosing a kitten, you should aim to select from a whole litter if possible. The appearance of the young cats will obviously influence you, but so too should their behaviour and health. Choose a friendly, frisky kitten that is quite happy and confident about approaching you, rather than a shy one which tends to hang back. If any of the kittens appears to be unwell – sneezing, with runny eyes or nose, soiled fur under the tail, flea-bitten, with a poor coat or excessive wax in its ears – it will be best to take none of them, and to look elsewhere.

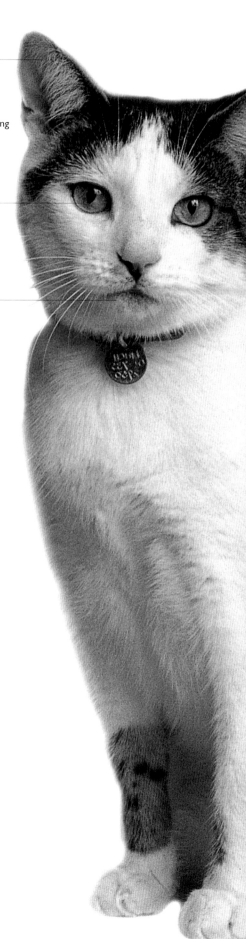

The ears should be clean with no unpleasant smells. White, blue-eyed cats are prone to deafness, so test a pure-white kitten's hearing by making sounds from a point outside its field of vision (all kittens' eyes are blue at this stage).

The eyes should be clear and bright, with no signs of 'weeping'.

Gently lift the lips and look at the gums: they should be pink (not red), and the teeth should be white.

74

Non-pedigree kittens are often much more popular with pet seekers than their pure-bred relatives, and there are usually many looking for good homes.

What to look for in a healthy cat

The coat should be clean and unmatted. Check for fleas (tell-tale signs are the tiny black dots they leave in the fur), and for bald patches or flaking skin which could indicate a skin disorder.

Check for signs of diarrhoea under the tail – in a healthy cat this area should be spotless.

A VETERINARY CHECK-UP

Soon after acquiring your kitten, you should arrange to have it checked over by a vet to ensure that it is fit and healthy, and is not suffering from any obvious developmental problems. If the vet does detect any signs of serious ill-health in your kitten at this consultation, he or she will help you to decide what to do. All good breeders should sell their kittens subject to veterinary approval, and will refund your money if there is a problem. If you collect your kitten at eight weeks, it will need another appointment at 12 weeks for its first vaccination, plus a second round of general checking.

If you do not already know of a good local veterinary centre, look in your local business telephone directory or ask cat-owning friends for recommendations. Choosing a centre that is fairly close to your home is a good idea, in case you ever need to get there quickly with your cat in an emergency.

TAKING ON AN ADULT CAT

Opting for an older cat can be a good idea if you do not have the time to spend training a kitten, particularly if you are offered a well-behaved animal by a friend. Other sources may be a

There are many older cats in need of good homes. They can settle well, although much will depend on an individual cat's background and personality.

75

breeder who has no further use for a particular cat, or an animal-welfare organization. Sometimes a cat simply moves into a home where it finds a welcome, and, if this happens to you, it is quite possible that you may never find out where your cat originally came from.

If the cat is from an animal shelter, find out as much as you can from the staff at the shelter about its background. Some cats, for instance, may not be properly house-trained if they have spent much of their lives roaming about on their own, and may not integrate well into a domestic environment. If a cat's age is unknown, there are really no reliable indicators you can use to determine whether it is relatively young or not. Even when an older cat has been fully vaccinated you will need to keep it indoors for at least two weeks – complete with a litter tray – before allowing it outdoors. Otherwise it is likely to stray, possibly back to its former haunts if these are nearby.

Settling in

When you bring a new kitten home, it is very important that you introduce any children – and other pets – to it gently and quietly. Show your children how to handle the kitten safely, as cats will often bite or scratch if they are teased or inadvertently hurt.

Your kitten will soon settle down with you, although it will miss its mother and littermates at first. You must therefore take care to prepare for its arrival, and make it welcome. If the kitten is a present for a child, Christmas and birthdays can be noisy times and it will be much better for the kitten if you bring it home a few days later, once things have returned to normal. Aim to collect the new kitten when you have some free time so that you can give it as much attention as possible, and make the appointment with your vet for the kitten's initial health check (see page 75).

TRAVELLING HOME

Your kitten will probably not have been in a vehicle before, and is likely to be nervous about travelling. If you simply restrain it on your lap it

may try to bite or scratch you, so you should invest in a proper carrier. You could buy a cardboard pet carrier, although this may not be secure – particularly if the base becomes wet. An ordinary cardboard box with its lid taped down is even less adequate, especially for an adult cat which will be able to push its way out through the flaps quite easily. A wicker basket is another option, but be sure to line the base with a thick layer of newspaper as the wicker will be awkward to clean if it becomes dirtied.

The ideal carrier is a plastic container with a wire-mesh front and air holes around the sides. This is easily cleaned and will give more privacy to your kitten than an all-mesh container. It will obviously cost you more than a cardboard box, but you will be able to use the carrier whenever you take your cat to the vet or to a boarding cattery, so it will be money well spent.

Be prepared for your new pet to start howling and sounding distressed during the journey. This is usually nothing to worry about, however, and you should just concentrate instead on getting home safely and quickly.

AT HOME

Allow your kitten or cat to come out of the carrier in its own time, as if you try to lift it out you could end up being badly scratched or bitten. Remember that it will need time to settle down, so put out out fresh drinking water and a little food, make sure that the kitten knows where to find its bed and litter tray, and then leave it by itself for a little while.

Keep the kitten confined to one room until it gets used to being there, and make sure that children behave gently and quietly around it. The kitten needs time to sleep in peace as well as to play – if woken suddenly, it could react by scratching. Children must also learn to handle it correctly. A mother cat carries her kittens safely by the scruff of the neck, but, when you lift your kitten, be sure to provide more support by holding its tail end with one hand and its chest with the other.

Introducing other pets

A new cat – especially a kitten – will integrate well with other animals in the household, given a little time. If you have a dog, shut it in a separate room when the kitten

FEEDING YOUR NEW KITTEN

Before you go to collect your kitten, ask the breeder or owner for a diet sheet so that you can buy a supply of the same food items; the diet sheet should also include details of mealtimes and how much food is given. This will reduce the risk of you overfeeding your kitten or supplying too rich a menu, either of which could lead to a stomach upset.

arrives. After an hour or so you can let the dog into the kitten's room while holding the kitten in your hand, and stay with the animals so that you can supervise the whole introduction period. This may be fairly brief – in most cases, once a dog has seen a kitten it will soon lose interest.

Introducing a cat may need to be a more gradual process. Always supervise the initial meetings, and never try to force cats of any age together – they will adjust to each other at their own pace. When meeting for the first time, the the kitten and cat will probably investigate each other nose-to-nose. Depending on your kitten's personality, it may become frightened and arch its back to show some bravado, and may even hiss; the older cat may ignore the kitten, sniff at it or become threatening, in which case you may need to intervene. However, if all goes well the cats will soon grow bored of each other.

Be sure to keep your kitten well away from pet birds or small mammals, which may be severely frightened – even if they are not harmed directly – if it attempts to catch them. You will not be able to prevent this instinctive behaviour in your cat, so the answer is to keep the animals apart.

Confining your kitten

You should keep your new kitten in the same room – many owners choose the kitchen – for about a week, making a 'pen' if necessary to prevent it from running out. Even when its vaccinations are complete, at about 12 weeks of age (see page 88), it will still be a good idea to keep your kitten indoors for a few weeks as it becomes established in its new home. All young kittens are inquisitive, and yours will soon learn its way about. Once it has overcome its initial fears, it will amuse itself for hours with very simple, cheap toys such as ping-pong balls, cardboard tubes and woolly stuffed toys.

At this stage, you can accompany your kitten on its first trip outside and back again. Continue to go with it for the next few outings, as this will give the kitten a sense of security, and encourage it to come when you call.

HOME SAFETY

You will need to make some adjustments at home before you collect your new kitten. Shut all windows and doors, and ensure that the house is safe for a young, inquisitive animal. Block off any spaces under furniture which could become traps, cover fireplaces and do not leave clothes hanging to dry in front of an open fire. Keep all appliance doors shut, including those of the refrigerator, the washing machine and the tumble drier, and put electrical flexes out of reach. Never leave elastic bands, buttons, pins, needles or other small objects in places where your kitten could play with and possibly swallow them.

Equipment

You will not need a great deal of equipment to care for your new kitten or cat, but the basics are included here; you will also need to buy suitable food and water bowls for it (see page 81). As time goes on, you may of course wish to buy additional items, such as more toys. A huge range of these is now sold in pet stores, from rubber balls to elaborate climbing frames, but your cat will probably be just as happy to play with a ball of paper or with a length of string pulled across the floor.

Training your cat to walk on a lead may be useful if you live in an urban area and it will not be allowed to roam freely outdoors.

Many cats will appreciate a covered bed like this one, as it will give them a greater sense of privacy and security, particularly in a very busy household. Whatever type of bed you choose for your cat, it must be fully washable.

A BED

Provide a special bed for your kitten, and train it to sleep there right from the start. Tempting though it may seem, you should discourage the kitten from sleeping on your own beds, or you may end up with fleas in the bedding. A small cardboard box with a side cut down for easy access will make an ideal bed at first. Place this in a warm, draught-free spot, and add a soft lining – such as a blanket or a cushion – on top of a layer of old newspapers.

As the kitten grows older you could make a more permanent bed yourself from wood, or buy one made of wicker, fibreglass or fabric. The simplest type of bed is open-topped, with a step in the side for an entrance. Alternatively, you could buy or build a covered bed – complete with its own hood – which may give your cat greater privacy if there is no convenient niche (such as under a table or the stairs) to cover its sleeping quarters.

GROOMING TOOLS

A fairly stiff brush (preferably one with natural bristles) is very useful for grooming any cat; for a longhair you will also need a metal comb with wide spacing between the teeth and a pair of round-ended scissors to cut through tangled fur. A fine-toothed flea comb is helpful when checking for fleas and for more thorough grooming. You can use cotton buds for gently cleaning the outer part of your cat's ears, but never poke these down the ear canals. A pair of special claw clippers completes the essential feline manicure set.

Stuffed toys and rubber balls are always popular with cats of all ages.

A COLLAR OR HARNESS

Your cat should wear a collar fitted with an identification disc or tube, but the collar must be elasticated in case it should become caught: for example, on a branch when the cat is climbing a tree. Some owners train their cats to go for walks on a harness and lead – Siamese cats in particular often take readily to the experience. If you wish to do this, go out only in your garden at first until your cat is familiar with the harness. Never exercise it in places where dogs may be about because they may be tempted to chase it, and trying to restrain a frightened cat under these circumstances will be very difficult.

TOYS

There is now a vast range of toys for cats, making play even more fun and providing exercise and stimulation, which are especially important for a cat kept indoors most of or all the time. Many stuffed toys contain catnip (*Nepeta cataria*). This herb – also called catmint – appeals to many cats, inducing an apparent sense of well-being. You can also grow it in the garden, where your cat will often visit the plant and sniff at the leaves. The effects are temporary, and wear off within 15 minutes or so. Young kittens are less affected by the scent of catnip than other cats.

A SCRATCHING POST

Every cat has a biological need to scratch, which helps to keep the claws in trim. It also serves to delineate a cat's territory: other cats will see the marks, and will also detect the scent – produced by glands between the toes – that is deposited through scratching.

However, the value of a scratching post will be limited unless you make a determined effort right from the start to train your cat to scratch on the post and nowhere else in the home (many cats will also do all the scratching they wish on trees and fence-posts outdoors). If your cat takes to scratching a particular piece of furniture, one way to deter it is to fix a plastic sheet over the area. Cats do not like the feel of plastic, and so will tend to leave the furniture alone. Rubbing the scratching post with catnip may also encourage the cat to use it instead. Avoid using a carpet-covered post (the ready-made types are often wound with sisal), or your kitten may see your household carpet as a convenient extension of it.

A LITTER TRAY AND LITTER

You will need a litter tray when your kitten first comes to live with you, and on any other occasion when it is confined indoors: for example, if you keep it in at night. Choose a tray that is deep enough to hold several inches of litter and sufficiently roomy for your cat to turn around in easily. Position the tray in a quiet place, and well away from your cat's food and water bowls.

Various types of litter – including wood- and clay-based materials – are now widely available. Avoid using garden soil because, although it is cheap, it will stain your cat's fur and is likely to re-appear in the form of muddy paw marks all the way across your floor. Line the base of the tray with sheets of old newspaper before pouring the litter on top, as this will make the tray much easier for you to clean out.

Some cats are reluctant to go back to a used tray, but you can remove just the soiled litter (special scoops are available for this) rather than tipping away the entire contents each time. You should completely empty the tray and clean it with hot water and veterinary disinfectant at least once a week. Leave the tray to dry thoroughly before re-filling it with clean litter. Dispose of soiled litter with your own garbage – not down the toilet, as it could cause a blockage.

A CAT FLAP

Many cat owners fit a cat flap to an outside door or window. Doing this will allow the cat to go in and out whenever it wishes, but take care because some designs will also let other cats in. The flap must obviously be low enough for your cat to use comfortably, and far enough from the door or window handle to prevent a burglar from reaching inside and letting himself in.

A number of designs of cat flap are available. One type only swings outwards and will not let the cat in again unless you train it to open the flap by lifting it with a paw. Another has a ring of flexible plastic triangles, with their points meeting at the centre, fixed around the rim of the hole; in this case the cat simply has to part the triangles and push through them. Electromagnetic and electronically operated cat flaps are also available for a reasonable price. These will open only to the cat carrying a special device attached to its collar, and are useful for preventing unwanted visits from other cats in the neighbourhood.

Training a cat to use a cat flap is usually fairly straightforward. Prop the flap open at first, using a pencil or piece of adhesive tape, and call your cat through the opening, first from one side and then from the other. When it is accustomed to this, gradually lower the door until you can remove the prop altogether.

A hooded litter tray will help to prevent spillage of the litter. A cat can feel very vulnerable while toileting, and a tray of this type will give it greater privacy.

Using a cat flap for the first time can be a rather unnerving experience for a young kitten. Prop the flap open to begin with, so that the kitten can look through it and see what is on the other side.

Use a toy or some tasty food to encourage the kitten to walk through the flap, and repeat this on either side of the door. Once the kitten is confident, remove the prop and encourage the kitten through again. It will soon start to use the flap on its own.

Feeding

Cats are what are known as obligate carnivores: in other words, they depend on meat and other, similar items such as fish as a source of vital nutrients. This is not to say that cats will not eat plant matter, as they will often eat a little grass when outdoors, or if it is grown for them indoors. However, this is to aid digestion (grass is often used as an emetic for cats suffering from intestinal worms) rather than being of nutritional importance.

TYPES OF CAT FOOD

Good-quality proprietary foods make by far the simplest feline diet from the owner's point of view. As long as you follow the manufacturer's instructions about how much and how often to feed, this type of food is very reliable. It will contain all the required nutrients in the correct proportions, including vitamins and minerals, which could be lacking in a diet of fresh meat or scrap foods. Cat foods are available in three forms: moist, semi-moist and dry.

Moist food

Canned foods have a relatively high water content. They are available in a wide range of flavours, and are usually the preferred choice of most cats. However, these foods will deteriorate quite rapidly, and once you have opened a can you must store it in a refrigerator and use it within 24 hours (special plastic lids to fit over the top of open cans are available, and will prevent the odour from tainting other foods). After storing the food like this you should allow it to warm up a little before using, as cats generally dislike eating cold foods.

Note that although dog foods may well be more economical to buy, it is dangerous to feed a cat on these for any length of time because they do not contain all the necessary ingredients for feline requirements – such as the amino acid taurine – in the correct proportions.

Semi-moist food

These foods are supplied in sachets and often contain some vegetable protein such as soya. They keep well in a bowl without drying out or losing texture, and they taste good to cats. Fold over an opened packet to prevent moisture loss.

Cats generally prefer canned food, because it closely resembles fresh meat in smell and taste. Unlike dogs – which can exist on a vegetarian regime – cats must have at least some meat in their diet to stay healthy.

80

Try to establish a routine when feeding your cat, offering food at the same times each day. Moist food will dry out quickly, so do not leave it out for long periods if uneaten.

Dry food

These foods had a bad press when they first came on to the market, as they were linked to a condition known as feline urological syndrome (FUS), in which crystals in the urine could cause a partial or total blockage of the urethra, leading from the bladder. Urination would then be very painful for an affected cat, shown by a hunched appearance. However, the formula of dry foods was altered, and today they are widely used.

Dry food contains very little moisture, so your cat will also need at least one large cupful of fluid (water, gravy or milk) each day. Special 'cat milk' (sold in pet stores and supermarkets) is better than cow's milk, as some cats (especially Siamese and other oriental breeds) cannot digest the milk sugar called lactose, and are liable to suffer from diarrhoea after drinking cow's milk.

If you offer dry food, check that your cat is drinking properly; always provide fresh water.

two meals from 16 weeks.
Special kitten diets make a
good choice at this stage,
although variety is important
to introduce the kitten to
the different types of food;
otherwise you may have
difficulty in persuading an
older cat that has been fed
entirely on moist food, for
example, to eat dry food
later in life.

Adult cats are generally fed
twice a day; the total daily
ration should be approximately
150–250g (5–8 oz). You will
need to increase this daily
amount for a pregnant female or for a mother
suckling a litter of kittens; ask your vet for more
detailed advice.

FOOD AND WATER BOWLS

Your cat should have its own food and
water bowls, which cannot be tipped over:
the earthenware type is ideal. Include a
spoon and a can opener with your cat's
special equipment, and wash all these items
separately from your own utensils. Certain
household disinfectants and antiseptics are
liable to be harmful to cats, so use only
products stated to be safe for them
on the packaging.

Provide fresh water for your cat daily;
many owners find that their cats prefer
this to be some distance away from the
food bowl. Place the feeding bowl on a
mat or on newspaper to make cleaning
easier, as cats often lift the food to eat
it outside the bowl. You may find an
automatic cat feeder useful: this stores one
or more meals and has lids that will open at
pre-set times, enabling the cat to reach the food.
This keeps the food fresh and protected from
flies in hot weather.

WHEN TO FEED

Try to encourage your cat to eat its food at
a single sitting rather than leaving it out all day,
unless you are providing dry food which will not
deteriorate significantly. Constant access may
also encourage your cat to pick at its food, which
could contribute to obesity unless you strictly
ration the amount of food offered according to
the manufacturer's instructions.

RULES FOR FEEDING
- **Feed your cat at the same time and in the same place every day.**
- **Place newspaper or a mat under the bowl, as many cats will drag out their food and eat it on the floor.**
- **Leave the cat to eat undisturbed.**
- **Leave food out for at least an hour, as most cats eat their meals slowly.**
- **Avoid sudden changes to the diet.**
- **Never give your cat spiced food.**
- **Always remove bones from fish or chicken, as these could become stuck in the cat's throat and cause it to choke.**

Whether you choose earthenware or plastic food and water bowls for your cat, they should have non-slip bases and be sturdy enough not to be tipped over easily.

Other foods

Many cats appreciate fresh foods occasionally,
but basing an entire, balanced diet around these
will be very difficult; a vitamin-and-mineral
supplement will almost certainly be needed as
well. If you do give this type of food, you must
cook it and then allow it to cool before using.
However, if a cat has been unwell and lost its
appetite, giving fresh foods may encourage it to
start eating again. Items such as cooked rabbit,
chicken or fish are often appreciated, although
you must be sure to remove any bones.

HOW MUCH TO FEED

In general, very young kittens are best left to their
mother's care, and it is dangerous to interfere
in any way until they are weaned. Kittens stop
drinking their mother's milk by the age of eight
weeks, although they may begin the process
of weaning gradually from four to five weeks.

From weaning to 12 weeks, kittens should
have a minimum of four small meals daily, each
of approximately 25 g (1 oz). From 12 to
16 weeks give three meals daily, dropping to

General care

Most cats enjoy being groomed, especially if accustomed to it from kittenhood. A long-haired cat must be groomed daily, or its coat is likely to become matted; a special cat comb with swivelling teeth may help to break down minor tangles without hurting your cat by pulling its fur. Grooming also lessens the risk of a cat suffering from fur balls ingested through licking its fur.

Many owners worry about their cats settling in new homes, but remember that cats attach themselves to humans, not to property. However, to be safe, keep your cat confined to the house (with a litter tray always accessible) for the first two weeks. After this you can allow it to go outside – preferably with you – for short periods which you can gradually increase. Most cats will not run off, but gradually move further afield, exploring their new environment and often pausing to sniff cautiously. Do not allow a kitten outside until its vaccinations are complete, normally at about 12 weeks (see page 88).

YOUR CAT AND CHILDREN

Children of three years old or less cannot be expected to know how to handle a cat correctly, so close supervision is the best way to prevent them being scratched. It is surprising just how tolerant some kittens can be with babies, but this is not something that you should put to the test. As has been mentioned earlier, you must teach young children not to disturb the cat – especially by grabbing at it – when it is resting in its bed, or

VACCINATING AN INDOOR CAT

Even if your cat lives permanently indoors, you must not neglect its initial vaccinations and regular boosters (see page 88). You never know when you might need to leave your cat at a cattery in an emergency, and it is even possible that you could bring some viruses indoors on the soles of your shoes.

they may be rewarded with a scratch. Your cat may sleep for up to two-thirds of the day, which is quite normal behaviour.

There is a common misconception that a cat may try to sleep in a baby's cot or pram and may smother the baby in doing so, but this is highly unlikely to happen. However, to put your mind at rest if you have a baby, it is sensible to use a special net (available from child-care stores) as a precaution, and to shut your cat out of a room in which a baby is sleeping.

DAILY ROUTINE

In comparison with some other household pets, the domestic cat needs relatively little in the way of care, although you should make every effort to integrate your cat into the household. For example, call it to you for feeding at the same times each day – cats are generally creatures of routine, and will soon get into the habit of responding if conditioned to do so from kittenhood, although it can be harder to form a bond of this type with an adult cat.

Grooming

Whatever type of cat you have, you should brush it daily to keep its coat in prime condition. This is essential for a longhair, which will need help with its very thick coat: you must comb this daily to remove any tangles before they can develop into solid mats, which would need to be cut out of the coat. Check too for any signs of flea dirt – which is often more conspicuous to the naked eye than the fleas themselves – in the coat, and take action if necessary by treating your cat and its environment (see page 87).

Cats are generally fastidious about grooming and washing themselves, so bathing is not normally necessary unless you are showing your cat or your vet recommends a medicated bath to treat parasites or a skin condition.

AN OUTDOOR RUN

Living in urban environments is becoming increasingly dangerous for cats, thanks to the growth of traffic on most roads in recent years, and the free-ranging lifestyle of many individuals leaves them at risk of being killed or at least badly injured by passing vehicles. While you can try to encourage your cat to stay indoors, or even design your home with special activity centres and similar items to occupy a house-kept cat, another good option is to provide a spacious run – not unlike an aviary in design – in your garden.

Your cat will be able to exercise and play safely during the day in this type of run, as well as getting plenty of fresh air, and you can then bring it indoors to join you at night. Suitable ready-made runs and other equipment, such as safe heaters, are sold by cattery manufacturers (look in cat magazines for advertisements). If possible, you should put down a solid concrete base for the run so that you can easily clean and disinfect the area.

INDOOR LIVING

In many towns and cities owners keep their cats entirely indoors, and they do not to appear to suffer from this restriction. The major problem can be boredom, which may lead to behavioural difficulties such as furniture scratching. One of the best ways to prevent a cat from becoming bored at home without human company all day is to provide a companion pet. If this is to be another cat, you should ideally start out with two kittens together as they will settle down and remain friendly, whereas an older and a younger individual may get on less well together.

If you do not plan to breed from your kitten and it lives indoors, you must have it neutered when it reaches sexual maturity at about five months. Confining an entire (unneutered) tom or queen will result in unpleasant odours because the urine of these cats is very pungent, while the calls of a female in season (often made at night) can be very disturbing.

(Above) If you live in an urban area, it may be a good idea to invest in an outdoor run and shelter for your cat, rather than letting it roam free; this will provide it with plenty of fresh air and exercise in a safe environment.

83

HOLIDAY CARE

You should make arrangements well in advance for your cat's care during holiday times. Cats often cannot be taken abroad on holiday (as an anti-rabies precaution), and few hotels are geared to feline guests. In any case, most cats – apart from show cats, which become used to travelling from an early age – are poor travellers. In an unfamiliar environment your cat could even go missing, which would certainly spoil your holiday. Nor will it always be possible or desirable for a neighbour to drop in to feed a cat left at home.

The best option when you go away is to take your cat to a good boarding cattery. There are many excellent establishments about, but standards can vary considerably, so it is worth spending some time investigating the alternatives. Ask friends or your vet for recommendations, and visit all the catteries in your area before deciding which one to use. Remember to book in your cat well ahead because good catteries often get extremely busy, especially during the peak holiday periods.

Whenever you need to transport your cat in the car – when visiting your vet, for example – always do so with the cat in a proper carrier. Secure the carrier on the back seat using a seatbelt, or place it in a footwell so that it cannot slide about.

Breeding

Far too many unplanned and unwanted kittens are produced each year and are then abandoned or destroyed. Avoid adding to their numbers by only mating your cat if you can be quite certain beforehand of finding good homes for all the kittens, or if you are prepared to keep them yourself.

If you do not intend to breed from your cat – whether male or female – you should have it neutered by your vet at about five months of age to prevent unwanted pregnancies.

MATING

If you wish to mate a pedigree female cat, you will need to take her by prior arrangement to a suitable tom (stud) cat when she is in season, or 'calling' (see below). Matings are carefully supervised, and the female (queen) will usually stay for about three days. She will need to be fully vaccinated, and you will be asked to show the certificates to the stud cat's owner. You may also need to arrange for certain blood tests to be carried out in advance to ensure that your cat is free from infections such as feline AIDS (see page 88).

A queen does not undergo spontaneous ovulation – the act of mating itself triggers the release of eggs from her ovary. However, a number of signs will indicate when the queen is ready to mate, starting with the 'pro-oestrus' phase of the cycle when she will become overtly friendly, rolling on the floor. She will also howl, or 'call', frequently to attract tom cats in the area. Soiling around the home is common, as an unneutered queen's urine contains chemicals called pheromones; these will be wafted on the wind and detected by other cats, again indicating her readiness to mate.

Repeated matings with the stud cat will give the greatest chances of pregnancy. Once the queen returns home to you, keep her inside for about 10 days or she could slip out and mate with another tom cat; this would result in the litter having two sires.

PREGNANCY

Pregnancy lasts for approximately nine weeks, although it will only be in the later stages that the cat will show a noticeable increase in weight. While your queen is pregnant you must handle her with great care and provide an increasing amount of food, together with any supplements prescribed by your vet. A queen is generally checked by a vet about four weeks after mating and one week before kittening.

BIRTH

Your cat will seek a quiet place to give birth. Provide a bed in a secluded spot and encourage her to use it beforehand, or she may disappear out of the door and give birth away from your home, where it will be much harder for you to keep an eye on her and the kittens.

Cats normally give birth without assistance, but you should inspect the nesting place occasionally in case your queen seems to be having problems and you need to seek veterinary help. Once she has produced the kittens, avoid disturbing her in any way or she may move them – carrying each one in turn by the scruff of its neck – to a quieter spot. Kittens are born with their eyes sealed; these will open when they are a few days old.

EARLY LIFE

From the start, you should handle all the kittens gently every day to accustom them to human contact. Kittens are taught by their mothers to lap at four to five weeks, and will start eating solid food (known as weaning) soon afterwards.

Kittens become sexually mature when they are about five or six months old, but it is unwise to breed them until they are 12 months old. If you are particularly keen to breed from your female kittens and do not wish to have them neutered,

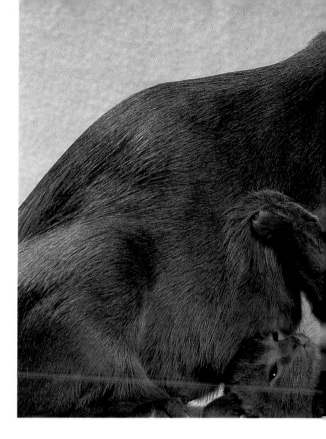

84

Sexing kittens: in the male (top), the distance between the ano-genital opening is greater than in the female (above).

A queen will take charge of every aspect of her kittens' care and hygiene in the early weeks, including washing them and even cleaning under their tails.

How much to feed

Feed every two hours for the first week, giving 5 ml (1 tsp) per feed. Gradually increase the quantity of each feed and work down to four feeds per day.

Milk formula for hand-rearing

In an emergency situation, you can use either human baby milk food at double the normal strength, or a mixture of the following:

• 200 ml (1 cup) fresh milk (ideally this should be the milk produced specifically for cats – see page 80).
• 50 ml (¼ teacup) single cream.
• ¼ egg yolk.
• 1 drop cod-liver oil.
• 1.25 ml (¼ tsp) sterilized bonemeal (sold in pet stores).

Stir the mixture until it has a uniform consistency, and serve it at body temperature. Ideally you should make up a fresh mixture for each feed, but you can store any unused mixture in the refrigerator for a few hours as long as you allow it to warm up again to body temperature before giving it to the kitten.

HAND-WEANING

Once the hand-reared kitten has survived its first four or five weeks and is doing well, you will need to wean it off the milk formula and gradually introduce kitten food (this is the stage at which a queen would naturally be weaning her kittens on to solid foods).

Milk formula for weaning

Any of the following will be suitable for feeding a kitten of this age:

• Either of the preparations described above for hand-weaning.
• Proprietary powdered formula (available from pet stores).
• Milk mixed with raw egg yolk.
• Puppy biscuit simmered in milk.

MASTITIS

A queen will usually take full care of her litter, and will show a natural and well-developed maternal instinct.

The problem that you are most likely to encounter with your queen is mastitis, when one or more of the mammary glands becomes reddened and swollen due to infection. As a result the kittens will be unable to feed here and will appear restless, crying out repeatedly (healthy, well-fed kittens are normally quiet). If you suspect mastitis, seek veterinary help for your cat without delay.

your vet will be able to give them tablets or an injection to stop them coming into season, which can occur every three to four weeks.

HAND-REARING KITTENS

If one or more kittens is abandoned or orphaned, you may need to take over its care. Hand-rearing is a difficult task, not only because of the time involved and the need to give frequent feeds, but also because such kittens are often more susceptible to illness. If possible, try to foster the kittens to a queen who is producing milk but has only a few kittens of her own: your vet may be able to put you in touch with a fellow breeder who can help. The following are guidelines of what to do if you have to rear kittens yourself.

Hygiene

When hand-rearing a kitten, it is crucial to observe strict rules of hygiene and to sterilize all your equipment very carefully. The mother's milk gives a kitten valuable antibodies which will protect it in the first weeks; without these a kitten may easily die if it catches an infection.

Equipment

The equipment needed for hand-rearing is simple. To place drops of milk formula in the kitten's mouth you can use an eye dropper (available from pharmacists), a medical syringe with the needle replaced by a length of fine tubing, or a special kitten-feeding bottle from a pet store.

Health care

You should carry out a weekly health check on your cat. This will only take a few minutes, and should enable you to spot any signs of illness early so that you can take appropriate action. While grooming your cat, check for any unusual lumps or bumps under the skin. Keep an eye on its daily intake of food and water, on the appearance of its urine and faeces (if it uses a litter tray), and also on its general behaviour and appearance. By learning what is normal for your cat, you will quickly become aware of potential problems.

SIMPLE HEALTH CHECKS

Ideally, you should begin routine health checks from an early age so that the kitten becomes familiar with the experience and easy to handle. If at any time you are concerned about your cat's health, ask your vet for advice. The following should all be part of your routine checks.

Mouth

Gently lift the lips and inspect the teeth and gums, making sure that there are no excessive tartar deposits on the outside of the cheek teeth and that the gums are a healthy pink colour.

Eyes

Check the eyelids for evidence of tears; if the lid-linings are red, bathe them with a special eye-wash from your vet and seek help within 48 hours unless they become clear.

Ears

Gently clean away any extra wax in the outer ears using a cotton bud moistened in olive oil (if the wax is copious or smelly, you should take the cat for a check-up with your vet). Never poke a cotton bud into the ear.

Claws

Check that the claws are not torn or overgrown; if so, you will need to trim them (ask your vet's advice if you are unsure of what to do).

Skin

Look at the skin for bare patches or sores. Early treatment of skin disease is especially important, and often leads to rapid recovery rather than the development of a chronic problem.

GENERAL SYMPTOMS OF ILLNESS

Identifying a sick cat is usually easy. It will be lethargic and, if fevered, may feel hot to the touch. It may show signs of pain – especially if handled – and its breathing may be fast or laboured when it is at rest. Even a healthy cat may refuse food for a day or so after an experience such as moving home or being badly frightened, but if your cat does not eat for a longer period you must take it to your vet.

One awkward problem is that when a cat is ill or injured it may well go off by itself and hide, perhaps in a shed or in some bushes. This behaviour is thought to originate from life in the wild, where cats too weak to defend themselves had to hide from predators such as jackals.

The following are some of the ailments that most commonly affect cats.

Urinary disease

This is a common problem in cats. If your cat shows any signs of a great increase in thirst, has difficulty in passing urine or passes discoloured urine, seek veterinary treatment urgently.

Vomiting

Cats vomit quite frequently, particularly after eating grass. Fur balls are also often regurgitated, and this is the normal way for cats to expel fur swallowed while grooming themselves. However, persistent vomiting needs urgent investigation, as it could be caused by an obstruction such as a bone, or may even be linked with a tumour (especially in an older cat).

Abscesses

These usually result from injuries sustained in fights with other cats, and may need lancing by your vet followed by a course of antibiotics. An abscess will swell up very quickly, often on the head (an early sign may be that your cat is sensitive to being touched here). If you examine the area closely, you may be able to see the puncture wound caused by the opponent's teeth. Unneutered toms are particularly likely to become involved in fights with others in the neighbourhood, especially at dawn and dusk, so keeping your cat in at these times is a good idea.

Vaccinations can now protect against most of the serious viral illnesses likely to be encountered by a cat. However, as pet cats live at relatively high densities, the risk of the spread of infection is higher than would be the case in the wild, which is why routine vaccination is so important.

86

Skin problems

An allergic skin condition caused by flea bites is fairly common in cats; the reaction is to the saliva injected by fleas as they bite. Subsequently, just a single bite can cause a severe reaction, so you must make every effort to keep your cat free of fleas. Veterinary treatment is essential for an allergy, and you will need to be vigilant to prevent exposure to fleas in the future as far as you can.

If your cat's allergy is severe your vet will recommend a long-acting anti-flea treatment, or will advise you on what other treatment to use. You must also treat your house with an appropriate product, and vacuum and wash your cat's bedding regularly, as fleas will spend more time here than on the cat itself. Fleas are also hazardous to cats because they can spread tapeworms (see overleaf).

In addition, cats can suffer from ringworm, a fungal ailment which can spread to people and gives rise to red, circular patches on the skin. Slight hair loss may be a symptom of ringworm, and your vet can carry out tests to confirm the infection. It is treatable, but wear disposable gloves when handling your cat and keep it indoors until it is no longer infectious (your vet will advise you).

Eye conditions

A cat's eye may be injured in a fight, or be scratched by undergrowth; runny eyes may also be linked with various infections, including cat 'flu. The appearance of the third eyelid at the corner of each eye, protruding partially across the eyeball, may be another sign of illness. In each case, you must take your cat to the vet for a check-up.

Tear staining around the eyes is common in Persians and similar flat-faced breeds, but gently bathing the area with a special eye-wash and cotton wool should help to resolve the problem.

Ear conditions

These are indicated by excessive build-up of wax, pain on touching, or any unpleasant smell. Do not be tempted to treat such conditions yourself, but go to your vet as soon as possible.

(Above) Repeated and persistent scratching is often indicative of skin parasites – notably fleas.

(Left) Adult female fleas lay their eggs on a cat, but these will then fall off in the cat's bedding or on carpeting, where they will hatch into larvae. To control fleas, you must therefore also treat your cat's environment, not just your cat. Vacuum frequently to remove immature fleas before they can bite, and wash the bedding regularly.

Worms

Kittens most commonly become infected by roundworm eggs present in their mothers' milk, and must be de-wormed regularly. This is often carried out along with the primary vaccinations at about 12 weeks (see below), and must be repeated on a regular basis (the frequency will depend on the product used; your vet will give you specific advice).

Tapeworms are most likely to be found in cats which hunt regularly, as the immature parasites are present in the bodies of prey such as mice. When eaten by a cat, the tapeworms will then go on to develop in its gut. Fleas can also spread tapeworms, as the worm eggs may be present in their bodies and be swallowed by a cat while grooming itself. Tapeworm infestations are not serious, but you should worm your cat at least every six months. Again, your vet will advise you.

Diarrhoea

Cats suffer from diarrhoea quite frequently, although their outdoor toileting habits mean that the condition often goes unnoticed by owners. In the vast majority of cases, diarrhoea is caused by the food that a cat has eaten – possibly cow's milk (see page 80) or scavenged food that is contaminated. Diarrhoea normally clears up by itself, but if you are concerned – particularly if your cat is young or old – consult your vet, as the cat could become dehydrated. Giving a probiotic (available from pet stores or from your vet) will also help to re-establish the beneficial bacteria in the gut, aiding recovery and reducing the risk of further problems.

HEALTH CARE (URBAN LIVING)

Having your cat vaccinated against serious feline viral diseases such as cat 'flu is vital, as there is no treatment for these illnesses. Vaccinations are currently available to protect your cat against the killer disease feline panleucopaenia (feline infectious enteritis), and against the two forms of cat 'flu (feline viral rhinotracheitis and calicivirus).

After an initial course, which should be completed by the time a kitten is about 12 weeks old, annual boosters are usually recommended. Always keep your cat's vaccination certificate in a safe place, as you will need to show it when you take the cat to a boarding cattery.

FELINE DISEASES

In recent years, considerable publicity has been given to feline leukaemia virus (FeLV) and so-called feline AIDS, or feline immunodeficiency virus. Both illnesses can be fatal, although it is now possible to protect cats against FeLV by vaccination. Unfortunately, one result of cats becoming increasingly popular as pets is that viruses are able to spread more easily, especially in urban areas where cats often live at high densities. This is another reason why protective vaccination is so important. Neither FeLV nor FIV can be spread to people, so there is no risk of you developing leukaemia or AIDS through contact with an infected cat.

Feline leukaemia virus

FeLV will not survive for long outside a cat's body. The virus is present in saliva, so a cat may be infected by a bite sustained in a fight; it can also be transmitted to kittens before birth by their mothers. However, even once the virus is detected a cat will not inevitably develop leukaemia or the other symptoms of illness linked with the virus, and this is where blood testing is important. Although an initial test may be positive, a second test carried out three months later could reveal that the cat has produced antibodies and overcome the infection, indicating that it has recovered and poses no threat to other cats (once a positive test for the virus is confirmed, a cat must be kept isolated until a negative result is obtained).

However, in other cases the virus overwhelms the cat's body defences. It will lose weight, may show other signs such as vomiting, and will become a persistent carrier of the virus. The cat will then represent a threat to others, and is also likely to develop clinical signs of the illness. Cancer of the white blood cells (leukaemia) and of the lymphatic system (lymphosarcoma) are typical and, sadly, euthanasia will be necessary.

Feline AIDS

This disease is caused by the feline immune deficiency virus (FIV), which attacks the immune system. Like FeLV, the infection is spread via saliva, not by sexual contact. General malaise linked with anaemia (a lack of red blood cells) is a feature of this illness, which can be confirmed by a simple blood test.

Feline infectious peritonitis

FIP is another viral ailment which has become more significant in recent years. It strikes younger cats, typically those under three years of age. The virus attacks the peritoneum (the lining of the abdomen), causing swelling. The body organs may also be affected, and the cat's general condition will tend to deteriorate. Once again, no treatment is possible for this disease.

This kitten is obviously unwell, with the so-called 'third eyelid', or haws, clearly visible. This is not a symptom of a specific illness, but simply reflects a cat's loss of condition. As its health improves, the haws will recede to the corner of each eye.

88

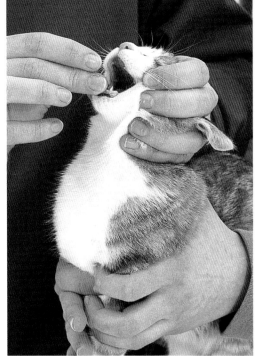
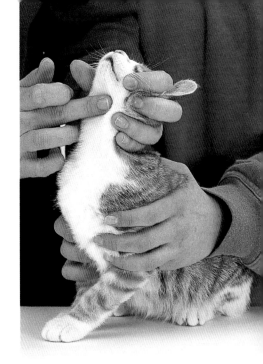

If you need to give your cat a tablet, it will help to have an assistant: if he or she holds the cat across the shoulders, it should not be able to lift its forelegs to scratch you. Hold the cat's head, and gently open its mouth.

With the cat's head tilted upwards, and using the fingers of your first hand to 'anchor' the upper jaw, drop the tablet as far back as you can on to the centre of the tongue; this will make it more difficult for the cat to spit out.

Allow the cat to close its jaws. Still holding the head in the same position, use a finger to rub very gently down the cat's throat to encourage it to swallow the tablet. Only release it when you are sure it has done so.

ACCIDENTS

As well as disease, cats living in towns face additional dangers, with many sadly being killed on the roads. The speed of traffic often gives them little hope of escape, while after dark they may be momentarily 'blinded' by headlights. However, you should not always fear the worst after an accident – if a cat does not move after a collision, it may simply be unconscious. Before rushing to rescue it, you must check that there are no oncoming vehicles or you could end up on the casualty list as well.

What to do after a road accident

Do not try to attend to the cat in the road, but move it to safety without delay. One of the most common road-accident injuries in cats is a ruptured diaphragm. This sheet of tissue acts as a divider between the chest and abdomen, and, if it is torn, the body organs may move internally. When picking up an injured cat, you must therefore lift it with both hands under its body (or, ideally, carefully slide it on to a makeshift stretcher such as a board) to keep it in a horizontal position.

The cat will be suffering from shock after an accident and is likely to be in considerable pain. Even if it is normally a very gentle-natured cat, it may therefore try to bite and scratch, so

wrap it carefully in a towel or blanket if possible. Carry the cat indoors, place it in a quiet, warm spot away from other pets and seek veterinary advice without delay.

Even if your cat appears to be relatively unhurt following a road accident, a thorough veterinary check-up is extremely important. This is because there could be unseen internal haemorrhaging, which could become life-threatening if not detected and treated.

Other injuries

Friction burns on the skin and severe grazes are often apparent after a collision with a vehicle. These will heal in due course but your vet may need to treat them in the short term, particularly if a large area of the cat's skin has been affected. The hair may never grow back completely in a case like this.

Fractured limbs are another very common consequence of road accidents, and the cost of delicate orthopaedic repair work on the broken bones is unlikely to be cheap. It is partly for this reason that many cat owners now insure their pets to cover themselves against unexpected large bills of this kind, as well as for the cost of other veterinary treatment for illness. Look in cat magazines or ask your vet for details of insurance companies willing to insure pets.

Feline behaviour

Watching a cat's behaviour can be fascinating, particularly because our domestic cats mimic the behaviour of their larger wild counterparts. All cats are active hunters, and are especially well suited to catching their prey from dusk until dawn using a combination of stealth and subterfuge. Their very highly developed sense of hearing enables them to detect prey well before seeing it, and they are also assisted by certain physical traits: for example, tabby stripes on the coat help to break up a cat's outline, a characteristic that is sometimes described as 'disruptive camouflage'. In addition, cats have refined senses of both smell and taste, which probably accounts for their reluctance to eat food unless it is fresh and may also help to protect them from swallowing poisonous substances.

All kittens are playful by nature. This behaviour may appear to be just fun, but in fact it has a definite purpose, in helping the kittens to develop their hunting skills. Although a cat will instinctively catch prey, the hunting technique itself has to be learned.

Some play bouts between kittens may look like fights, but they usually end amicably. Kittens will be most actively involved in this so-called 'social play' from about nine to 14 weeks; play with objects reaches its peak at about 16 weeks.

HUNTING BEHAVIOUR

A cat can stalk its prey unseen and unheard for long periods at a time, and its claws and teeth, together with a supple and muscular body, underline its success as a predator. A cat does not fully know how to catch prey by instinct alone – its hunting technique develops through learned behaviour as a kitten, by watching and imitating the actions of its mother.

However, as a result of domestication and having food constantly available at home, some cats have lost much of their enthusiasm for hunting. If a kitten has not been taught these skills by its mother, it may later on in life catch a bird or a mouse but not instinctively know how to kill it (this is normally carried out by a bite to the neck). In this case you may have to step in to save the quarry from further suffering, although your cat is likely to be very reluctant to give it up.

If you have a young cat which is an avid hunter, you may actually be able to train it not to catch birds. To do this, make a 'lure' with the feathers of a bird that the cat has killed, and tie this to the end of a long thread or string. Hide yourself in a suitable place and let the cat find the lure in the garden, and then, whenever it attacks the lure, direct a well-aimed shot at it with a water pistol. Regular sessions of this type of training may deter your cat from stalking birds, yet without associating the punishment with you.

TREE-CLIMBING

Most members of the cat family use trees as vantage points for eating and resting, and as hiding places from which to leap down and attack unsuspecting prey below. This is how the domestic cat has acquired its well-known ability both to climb and to land on its feet if it loses its grip by swivelling its body around in the air and landing upright, usually without suffering any serious injury.

Owners sometimes under-estimate their cats' skill in tree-climbing, and raise the alarm when they see them apparently stuck in a tree. However, experience has shown that a cat will almost always work out a way of getting down within 24 hours. Indeed, the folklore about cats having nine lives may derive from their innate sense of balance and remarkable ability to get out of tricky situations of this kind.

If your cat is up a tree, try encouraging it to come down by placing some food at the foot of the tree – this should bring the cat home without the need for the fire brigade!

TERRITORIES AND 'CALLING'

Domestic cats are strongly territorial creatures. An unneutered tom reaches sexual maturity at six to eight months, and will then begin to establish his own territory. He will mark out this area using drops of urine – a behaviour known as 'spraying' – and will battle fiercely with other male cats to defend or increase his domain. In an urban environment a tom will go for the biggest area he can lay claim to and defend, which may extend across several gardens; in country districts, he may take 1.5 sq km (one square mile) or more.

Female cats also hold territories, although these are smaller than those of toms. An unneutered female will start to 'call' early in the first spring after she has reached the age of five months, as she actively seeks potential mates; pheromones in her urine will also attract them (see page 84). Siamese cats are known to be especially vocal. If you have an unneutered female, visiting toms will loiter around her territory and you will have to put up with their spraying. There may be fights in the vicinity, as well as loud, persistent caterwauling during the night.

(Left) Cats find descending from trees much harder than climbing up, because if they come down head-first their claws give them little support. As a result, they will often back down part of the way before turning and leaping to the ground.

THE BEHAVIOUR OF NEUTERED CATS

If they are neutered as kittens, the behaviour of male and female cats will be almost the same – at least from the practical point of view of an owner. Their territories are much smaller than those of unneutered individuals, the males do not spray and females do not call. Territorial fights may still occur, but they will be much less of a problem. Neutered male cats tend to grow larger than females (just as when they are unneutered), and females are generally more dainty, but both are affectionate and amenable. They will also spend more of their time at home.

There is some truth in the observation that all neutered cats become more inactive than entire animals when they grow older, although their life expectancy will be greater. To prevent your cat from putting on too much weight you may need to adjust its diet; you can also help by playing with your cat every day and encouraging it to exercise in order to keep its weight down and maintain its level of fitness.

Cats are able to express a wide range of emotions through their use of body language. Here, the cat on the left is feeling threatened: with its ears flattened tightly against its head and hissing loudly, it may decide to attack – or simply to look for an escape route – if the other cat continues to advance towards it.

(Below) A schematic view of feline territories. Toms range over a wider area than females or neutered cats. Various factors will influence the size of the territories, and, in areas with many cats, toms will evolve a network of paths crossing one another's territories to avoid conflict in most cases.

91

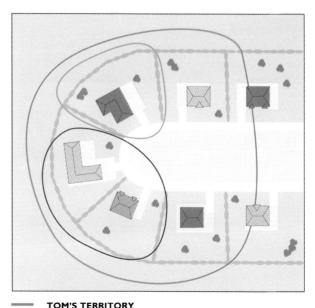

— **TOM'S TERRITORY**
— **NEUTERED CAT'S TERRITORY**
— **FEMALE CAT'S TERRITORY**

Caring for the older cat

Cats show few of the obvious signs of ageing associated with dogs, such as greying of the fur in the case of black cats. As a result it is often harder to detect signs of ageing, but you must keep a close eye on your cat as it grows older. While it will probably not be possible to reverse the symptoms of old age, much can be done to offset the worse effects and allow a cat to maintain a fairly active life. Recent advances in feline geriatric medicine are confirmed by the fact that nearly 30 of every 200 cats in the USA are now at least 15 years old. Once your cat reaches the age of eight, take it for a twice-yearly check-up with your vet, who will be able to detect any problems at an early stage.

DENTAL PROBLEMS
Older cats are naturally less active than kittens and their metabolism also slows down, leaving them at greater risk of obesity. If, in contrast, your cat is proving to be rather a finicky eater, this may not even be linked with its food but could well be the result of a dental problem. Your vet will examine your cat's teeth at its regular check-ups, and will de-scale them and give treatment for gum disease if necessary.

KIDNEY DISEASE
Bad breath is often linked with tooth decay, but it can also be a sign of kidney disease. This will affect all older cats to some extent, but only once the functioning capacity of the kidneys falls significantly will signs of illness become apparent. The kidneys will then be unable to concentrate the urine as much as when the cat was younger, so the cat is likely to produce larger volumes of urine.

This increased output will also affect the cat's water intake because it will require more fluid, so if you feed your cat on dry food it may be better to switch to a canned food containing a higher percentage of water. Special foods are also now available to meet the changing nutritional needs of older cats. A cat with failing kidneys is likely to be at greater risk of suffering a deficiency of water-soluble vitamins, which are lost through the kidneys, so giving a vitamin B supplement in particular is likely to be useful (ask your vet for further advice on this).

Bad teeth and inflamed gums are not uncommon in older cats. If you feed your cat on a dry food and it loses some of its teeth, you may need to change at this stage to offering canned food, which is softer and will be easier to eat.

FUR BALLS
Older cats are probably at the greatest risk of suffering from fur balls because their digestive systems are less efficient, so you must groom your cat regularly to remove loose hair from the coat before it can be swallowed and form a solid mat in the stomach. An affected cat will only eat small quantities of food because of the obstruction, while still appearing to be hungry

and returning to its food. Your vet will prescribe a laxative to overcome the blockage, although surgery will be necessary in a serious case.

OVERGROWN CLAWS

Your older cat is likely to be less active and will not climb trees as it used to do, so its claws may become overgrown. A typical sign of this is if the cat appears to experience difficulty in freeing

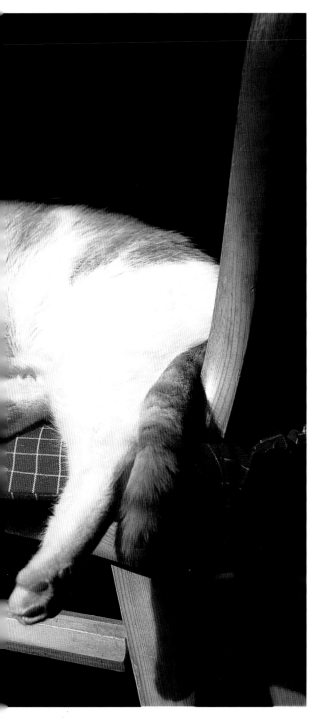

itself from the fabric in its bed, indicating that the claws may have become slightly hooked at their tips (this is seen more frequently with the front claws).

If your cat's claws are overgrown they will need to be trimmed with special clippers (ordinary scissors may split the claws rather than cutting cleanly through them). If you do this yourself, be sure to cut beyond the point at which the pinkish streak in the claw disappears towards its tip, or it will bleed. If you are not confident about cutting your cat's claws, ask your vet to do it for you.

LEAVING YOUR OLDER CAT

An older cat can present a problem at holiday times, as it may not settle well at a cattery. You may be able to persuade a friend or neighbour to keep an eye on your pet and to provide food and water in your absence. This will avoid any major disruptions to the cat's lifestyle, but is not the same as having company at home; and visiting care will only work if your cat is used to letting itself in and out via a cat flap.

A very good option, especially if you have a number of pets, may be to arrange for a home-sitter to stay in your house while you are away. However, be sure to use only a reputable agency – ideally, one recommended by word of mouth – which chooses staff carefully and offers insurance in case of any mishaps.

An older cat may often be reluctant to venture far outside when the weather is wet or cold, preferring instead to pass its time sleeping.

One of the pleasures of owning a cat is that it will remain playful and active right up until the end of its life. Be sure to keep your cat's vaccinations up to date as it grows older, because its immune system may be less able to resist infections at this stage of life.

93

HYPERTENSION

There is now a growing awareness among vets of the significance of blood-pressure readings taken from older cats suffering from organ damage. Raised blood pressure occurs in approximately two-thirds of all cats with kidney failure, and can result in other symptoms such as hypertensive retinopathy (a degeneration of the retina at the back of the eye on which the image falls, caused by high blood pressure).

Treatment of hypertension in cats is not yet particularly advanced, but drugs such as beta blockers – which are used for the same condition in humans – can help to alleviate the symptoms. These are frequently used in conjunction with a low-sodium diet, which is also recommended to support the failing kidneys.

Long-haired cats

Maine coon

Cats vary far less in size and shape than dogs, but, as with their canine cousins, each of the pedigree cat breeds has its own special personality and physical characteristics.

The registration process for pure-bred cats is similar to that used for dogs, and most countries have one or more organizations responsible for registering breeds and setting show standards. When pedigree kittens are born, the breeder or owner registers them with the relevant organization and receives in return a certificate confirming the breed and the ancestry of the kitten. This will show its parents, grandparents and often earlier generations as well, so it will be an important document if you plan to breed from your kitten in the future.

Turkish Angora

Long hair appeared as a mutation among cats in central Turkey centuries ago, and this ancient breed is named after the Turkish city of Angora (now Ankara). By the 16th century travellers had taken Angoras to France, from where they spread to the rest of Europe. However, after playing an important part in the development of the Persian breed (see opposite), these cats gradually became scarce and were only saved from extinction by a breeding programme based at Ankara zoo in the 1960s. At the same time, an artificial re-creation of the breed began in the UK, using Oriental shorthair stock (these cats are now known simply as Angoras).

The Turkish Angora is a graceful, slender, silky-coated cat without the fluffy undercoat of the Persian. White is the traditional breed colour, but a much wider range of colours is now available. This cat has a playful, friendly nature.

Turkish Van

The Turkish Van has a white body, usually with a cream or auburn tail and similar areas of coloration above the eyes. The eyes themselves may be either blue or amber, or a combination of the two. This is an active cat which – unusually – enjoys swimming. Its home is on the shores around Lake Van in the east of Turkey.

Maine coon

This is an old American breed, whose name is thought to have come from its racoon-like bushy tail. It has short legs with a squat body and a square head. Originally a tabby, the Maine coon is now bred in a wide range of colours, with the coat becoming much less profuse during the warmer months of the year.

This cat often displays an independent streak, but is also affectionate towards its owners and people in general.

Persian longhair

Norwegian forest cat

Persian longhair

This cat can be recognized by its stocky body type and flat face. The legs are comparatively short, the head is quite rounded with small ears placed well apart, and the fur is long and silky with a thick undercoat. The Persian is placid by nature and makes an excellent companion, but it requires dedicated grooming; its face will also need gentle washing from time to time if the hair becomes stained with food.

Persian longhairs are available in a vast range of colours. Self-coloured varieties (when the cat is just one colour) include white, black, blue, chocolate, lilac, red and cream. Bi-coloured cats are a combination of white with one colour (for example, white and red). There are many patterned longhairs, such as silver tabby, brown tabby and red tabby. Parti-coloured varieties are also available, including tortoiseshell (a combination of red and black) and tortoiseshell and white; as in other cats, these are usually female-only varieties. The chinchilla is particularly attractive, and has a white coat with each hair tipped with black. A stronger degree of black tipping on the hairs produces the grey effect that is described as smoke.

White Persians have varying eye coloration. In some cats both eyes are blue, in others they are orange, and in odd-eyed whites there may be one of each. In common with most other blue-eyed adult cats, a congenital problem means that these white Persians are usually deaf. In the odd-eyed white, deafness is restricted to the ear on the same side of the face as the blue eye.

Norwegian forest cat

The Norwegian forest cat is similar to the Maine coon in appearance. It is an old breed originating from Scandinavia, where its woolly undercoat gives good protection against the cold. Bi-coloured tabbies are common in this breed.

Birman

This is similar in appearance to the colourpoint longhair (see below), but has characteristic white 'gloves' on all four feet and comes in just four colour varieties – seal, chocolate, blue and lilac. It is known as the Sacred Cat of Burma and, according to legend, the first Birman was a temple cat in the ancient south-east Asian kingdom of Khmers. It belonged to a saintly priest whose soul migrated into the cat when he died, whereupon his god gave the cat white feet as a mark of blessing.

Balinese

This is a long-haired version of the Siamese, with a similar lithe body shape; it is bred in all the same colour patterns (see page 97). The coat lacks the thick undercoat of the Persian.

Colourpoint longhair

This is a Persian with the patterning of a Siamese cat (see page 97); in the USA it is better known as a Himalayan. The members of this breed are usually friendly cats and make good companions.

NON-PEDIGREE CATS AND PET-TYPE PEDIGREES

Over many generations cats have been bred in a variety of coat lengths and colours, often with little thought given to their parentage. As a result, pure colours – such as blue (actually a dilute form of black) – are very rare in ordinary non-pedigree cats, but are usually broken by tabby markings and often by pure white areas too. Selective breeding has been carried out to eliminate the markings, but even some show animals have hints of undesirable dark tabby stripes.

Such cats may not be suitable for the show ring but they can make excellent companions, and breeders will generally sell these kittens much more cheaply than potential show winners. Tabby markings may fade as a kitten grows older in any case, and they tend to be less pronounced in long-haired cats.

95

Colourpoint longhair

Short-haired cats

British shorthair

The short-haired cat breeds are justifiably very popular as pets, with their care being no more demanding in most cases than that of an ordinary non-pedigree cat. However, regular grooming with a bristle brush will help to remove loose hairs and keep the coat in top condition. Other good reasons for grooming are that the procedure is enjoyed and appreciated by many cats – particularly if they have been accustomed to it from their kittenhood – and it can also be a very good time to cement the bond between cat and owner.

British shorthair

This cat is compact and powerful, with a deep body and a full chest. It has short, strong legs and rounded paws, and a short, thick tail. The head is massive and round, with a firm chin and a straight nose, and the eyes are round and set well apart. The British shorthair is rather similar to the ordinary non-pedigree cat from which it was originally developed in Victorian times, but it has evolved into a stockier, heavier cat. The fur is short, dense and crisp to the touch, and its texture highlights the darker markings in particular. The coat colours are as varied as those of the Persian (see page 95).

The European shorthair is almost identical to the British variety.

American shorthair

The American shorthair tends to have a slightly more slender, athletic form than its British counterpart. Again, there is a dazzling range of colours and patterns. There is also an American wirehair variety, which has a curled coat rather like that of a lamb.

Manx

The Manx cat is popularly known as the cat with no tail, and for exhibition purposes it must have no trace of a tail. This variety is known as a Rumpy Manx. However, some Manx cats do have tails of varying length, and these are known as the 'Rumpy-riser', 'Stumpy' (or 'Stubby') or 'Longy', depending on the tail length. The shape of the Manx – a round head, and a curved back with a rump higher than the shoulders – is characteristic of the breed, and the cat lopes like a rabbit on its long legs. Some kittens of this breed suffer from birth deformities such as spina bifida because of their appearance. Despite this, the Manx is known for its ability to jump, climb trees and hunt just as well as if it had a tail for balance. It is an intelligent cat, and tends to be long-lived.

Devon rex

Rex

There are two well-known breeds of rex, both originating from the south-west of England, which stand out from the other short-haired breeds because of their wavy coats. Neither is especially hardy, as the coats are relatively thin.

Cornish rex: This has a curly coat with a fairly full, plush texture. It is bred to a slightly oriental body type and is a lithe, athletic cat.

Devon rex: This has a shorter coat and appears more hairless. Its head has a decidedly 'pixie-ish' look.

Japanese bobtail

Outside its homeland, this breed is more commonly seen in the USA than in Europe. Its tail is only a few inches long, and it has bushy fur like that of a rabbit.

Scottish fold

The short-haired version of this breed is currently the best-known variety. The Scottish fold is instantly recognizable by its ears, which are folded over at the tips and point forwards. It is a healthy and robust cat, and the unusual structure of the ears does not appear to cause any hearing problems.

Abyssinian

This is an old breed. It often has pointed ear tufts and head stripes, always with large ears and a very alert, lynx-like appearance. The traditional coloration of the Abyssinian – which is known as the 'usual' – is like that of a wild rabbit. Other new colours have also been developed; these include blue and lilac. Although this breed looks in some ways like a wild cat, it is gentle and can be highly affectionate. A long-haired form of the Abyssinian is called the Somali.

Russian blue

Russian blue

The colour described as 'blue' in cats is really a dilute form of black. The Russian blue is a finely built cat with a wedge-shaped head, and a soft, very silky coat with a marvellous silver sheen. It has an even temperament and makes an affectionate and undemanding pet.

Korat

This breed has been kept pure, and looks exactly as it did 600 years ago to judge from ancient manuscripts preserved in its Thai homeland. It has a silver-blue coat and a heart-shaped face, and is a playful cat.

Burmese

The traditional colour of the Burmese is brown, although it is now bred in a range of colours including patterned varieties such as the lilac tortie. In the UK the Burmese closely resembles the Siamese in terms of its type, but in the USA the breed is more like the American shorthair. This cat is full of energy and always likes to be involved in whatever is going on.

Siamese

This cat almost certainly originated in Siam (now Thailand). It is one of the best known of all the pedigree breeds, with its distinctive eyes of clear blue. The main body colour is always paler than the 'points' on the feet, tail, ears and facial area. The most common point colours are seal (brown), blue, chocolate (dark brown), lilac, red, tabby and tortoiseshell.

Many people admire the Siamese cat for its lithe body and svelte movements. Indeed, breeders in the USA like its lankiness and toughness so much that they have deliberately exaggerated these characteristics in their cats. This is a lively, noisy and affectionate breed, demanding more attention than other types of cat and often almost dog-like, happily retrieving objects and going for walks on a lead. Some people find the Siamese personality a little too overwhelming and prefer a more placid breed as a companion, but for many owners they make very rewarding pets.

Oriental shorthair

As well as the cat we know as the Siamese, cat lovers in ancient Siam used to keep cats that had the same body type (known as 'oriental') but without the pointed colour pattern. In the West these cousins of the Siamese were unfashionable in the early years of this century, but they are now more popular once again.

The Oriental shorthair is available in a wide – and still expanding – range of colours. These include pure black, white, brown, blue or red, bi-coloured (white plus one colour), or patterned (with tortoiseshell or tabby markings). There are four established tabby variants: spotted, ticked (when each hair in the coat is marked with two or three dark bands), mackerel (fishbone-like stripes run down the body) and classic (dark stripes with a prominent black blotch on each flank), along with other types such as smoke. The eyes are normally green rather than blue.

The ever-increasing range of varieties in this category has resulted in some confusion over the names used for these cats, and some of the self (pure-coloured) varieties are simply referred to as 'Foreign', especially in the UK. It has been estimated that there are now over 400 possible colour variants, offering great scope for breeders.

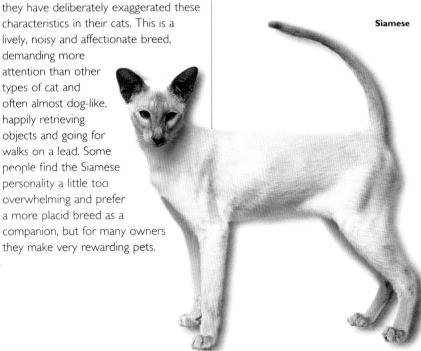

Siamese

Birds

Birds have been kept as pets since the days of Ancient Egypt, some 6000 years ago. The tradition was subsequently maintained by the Greeks, who discovered talking parrots on their overseas conquests and fell under their spell; indeed, the name of the famous Greek commander Alexander the Great is commemorated in the Alexandrine parakeet (*Psittacula eupatria*), which his army brought back to Greece following the conquest of northern India in about 327 BC. Prior to this, the Greeks had kept as pets members of the crow family – such as magpies and jackdaws – both of which can mimic human speech, albeit to a much more limited extent than parrots. They also favoured some other native species – such as goldfinches – both for their colour and for their song.

BIRD-KEEPING IN ROMAN TIMES

Like the Greeks, the Romans appear to have had a keen interest in bird-keeping, with their choice of birds revealing clear social divisions. For instance, while native birds such as magpies were placed outside barbers' shops to amuse customers, the wealthy members of society coveted exotic parrots from Africa, each of which could sell for more than the cost of a slave. These birds were frequently housed in cages made of rare and precious materials such as silver and tortoiseshell. Special tutors were employed to teach the birds to mimic human speech, employing the same techniques used today (see page 108).

Song birds also remained popular. Archaeological research has produced evidence of aviaries dating from this period, although – according to contemporary descriptions – fibrous rather than wire netting was typically used to contain the birds in their flights. Interest in bird-keeping continued after the end of the Roman era, with parrots retaining their status in the royal courts of Europe.

THE MIDDLE AGES AND BEYOND

The overseas voyages of exploration undertaken in the Middle Ages soon brought back parrots – such as cockatoos, which had previously been unknown in Europe – from further afield. Following his successful expedition to the New World in 1493, Christopher Columbus returned with a pair of Amazon parrots, which he presented as a gift to his patron Queen Isabella of Spain.

The indigenous people of the New World had of course already been keeping birds for centuries, and this tradition still continues today with tame parrots often being a common sight in village settlements.

Aviary design flourished in the Renaissance period, and elaborate structures were integrated into the garden landscaping of the great estates. Song birds and ornamental pheasants were both very popular occupants in such surroundings. Overseas influences also became evident in the aviaries of the period, some of which survive today.

The introduction of canaries, first brought to Europe by Portuguese seafarers in the 16th century, was ultimately to lead to the rise of the so-called 'Fancy' in Victorian Britain: the selective breeding of livestock (and plants) for particular features that were considered desirable. Bird shows became popular events, and standards were established for judging purposes. These standards specified the desirable qualities of such birds, which were compared not with one another but against what was perceived as the ideal for the breed concerned.

Whereas canaries enjoyed a strong working-class following, later in the Victorian era the rising middle classes became attracted to the budgerigar, whose powers of mimicry made it a favourite parlour pet. The growth of colour forms which began in the late 19th century continued apace into the next, and the Budgerigar Club (now the Budgerigar Society) was founded in England in 1925 to oversee the development and exhibition of these popular parakeets. From these beginnings in Europe, budgerigars are now kept on a worldwide basis.

BIRD-KEEPING TODAY

The scope for bird-keeping today is very great. Many owners enjoy the company of a single pet bird, but the hobby can be infectious, perhaps leading on to an indoor flight housing a number of birds, or even a garden aviary.

In the past, the breeding of many species was a difficult task, but this is no longer the case. For instance, not only can parrots be persuaded to nest quite readily, but it has also become commonplace for their chicks to be reared successfully by hand, thanks to a better understanding of their nutritional requirements (special diets are now widely available for this purpose). Being accustomed to a domestic environment from hatching, the chicks have no instinctive fear of people and so should develop into excellent companions. They also have a life expectancy that is equivalent to our own in many cases.

Unlike all other pets, birds will actually talk to their owners. Research that has been carried out in this field suggests that at least some parrots have the ability to understand the meaning of learned words, and so really can communicate with us. Another bonus to keeping a pet bird – rather than a cat or a dog, for instance – is that the costs involved are relatively low. You are also likely to have fewer difficulties in arranging care when you go away on holiday, as a friend or a neighbour may well be prepared to look after a bird in your absence.

Choosing and buying birds

First of all, you need to decide on the type of bird (or birds) you would like, and this will depend largely on how you plan to keep it. For instance, if you are hoping to acquire a pet bird to live in your home, a member of the parrot group – which ranges from budgerigars to macaws – will be an obvious choice. However, the larger parrots can be noisy and destructive, which may affect your choice, while the powers of mimicry do vary between species. Another possibility to consider as an indoor pet is a greater hill mynah, although this member of the starling clan is a softbill (see pages 118–19) and so may be messy in the home because of its dietary needs.

KEEPING BIRDS OUTDOORS

If you are looking for occupants for a garden aviary, your choice will be wider. Finches will often live together in relative harmony, so you could keep a mixed collection of several different species. In contrast, most parrots need to be housed either in individual pairs or with others of their own kind. The calls of larger parrots may also be a problem in urban areas, where cockatiels and some parakeets will be a better choice.

Softbills form a diverse group of birds and, while some of these are social by nature, others can be aggressive. They may need heated winter-time accommodation, in common with many finches. Preparing food for these birds is also likely to be more time-consuming.

It is no coincidence that budgerigars and canaries remain so popular today. Both are suitable for an outdoor aviary, or can be kept as household pets. Canaries can even be kept together with other finches, although budgerigars need to be housed in colonies on their own. There is also a strong exhibition following for these two groups, offering further scope for the hobbyist.

WHERE TO BUY BIRDS

Your choice of birds will have an influence on where you buy your stock. If you are seeking exhibition birds, for instance, you will need to go to a breeder rather than to a local pet store, as there is a considerable difference between the average pet budgerigar and its exhibition counterpart.

Similarly, most pet stores do not stock an extensive range of parrots or softbills, and to find the largest range you will need to visit a specialist bird farm (look in bird-keeping magazines for details). These farms are often linked with breeding units, and so may be well-placed to offer hand-reared parrot chicks as well. Bear in mind that the supply of chicks can be seasonal; for example, while African grey parrots tend to be available throughout the year in the Northern hemisphere, Amazon parrot chicks are only available from the late summer onwards.

BIRDS FROM ABROAD

Not all birds on offer will necessarily have been bred in captivity. Some countries in poorer parts of the world export birds to bird-keepers overseas, a practice that is regulated by strict international controls. Many finches are actually serious agricultural pests in their countries of origin, and their sale means that local people receive compensation for the losses inflicted on their crops, without having to revert to more damaging and costly means of control such as the use of poisons or napalm to target the birds' roosting sites.

Imported birds must undergo a period of quarantine after arrival in their country of destination, but this does not mean that they will have become acclimatized to the temperature. Do not place such birds straight into an aviary in winter if the weather is cold, but house them indoors until the spring.

SELECTING A BIRD

Start by looking at all the birds on offer, before asking for any that appeal to you to be caught for a closer examination. A healthy bird should look alert when you approach; if a bird appears dull and has fluffed-up plumage, it is likely to be ill. This may be slightly different with a young hand-reared chick, as its plumage will rarely be as sleek as that of an adult bird. Having been reared with constant human contact, it will probably also be less reactive to you. When handled, however, such a chick should still be alert and responsive.

Missing flight feathers in young budgerigars indicate the feather disease known as French moult, which can be a permanent handicap. Areas of baldness in other parrots could be the result of feather plucking, which may become a habitual vice; or of the serious illness known as psittacine beak-and-feather disease (PBFD), for which there is no cure.

Droppings can also give a good indication of a bird's health: they should be firm, with a creamy-white component (this does not apply with some softbills or nectar-feeding parrots such as lories, as these normally produce liquid droppings).

If a bird is wearing a closed band, it will be coded with the year of hatching. Otherwise, once a bird has moulted into adult plumage, it will be impossible to age it with certainty.

TYPICAL CHARACTERISTICS

Finches
Small, active, often colourful birds. Some – such as the canary – have an attractive song.

Softbills
Very variable in appearance. Some talk; many eat invertebrates.

Parakeets
These often breed well in aviaries, but – with the exception of the budgerigar – are less widely kept as pets than parrots.

Parrots
Long-lived birds; can be excellent mimics and become very tame.

What to look for in a healthy bird

The nostrils should be even in size and must not be blocked.

The bill should be of normal length with no obvious abnormality, such as the upper portion curving into the lower (a problem that is seen in some young budgerigars).

The feathering around the bill and on the head should be clean.

The eyes should be clear, with no discharge or whitish opacity. Dark eyes in a parrot tend to indicate a young bird.

The condition of the plumage may be rough in some cases, but this will be replaced at the next moult. However, check that the bird has a full complement of flight feathers on the wings (especially with a parrot, as these birds are prone to feather ailments) by opening each one in turn.

101

Run your finger down the underside of the bird's body to locate the breastbone here in the mid-line. Distinct hollows on either side will indicate poor condition, which may be the result of chronic illness.

The legs should be relatively smooth. Heavy scaling tends to be a sign of old age, particularly in finches and softbills.

Overgrown claws are a feature of some finches, and these will need to be carefully clipped back (see page 113).

Check that there is no swelling on the bottom of the feet – the result of an infection known as bumblefoot. The toes should all end in claws, although occasionally a claw may be missing (this is not vital, as long as there is no injury).

Check the vent area for soiled feathering, which could indicate a digestive disturbance.

Housing and equipment

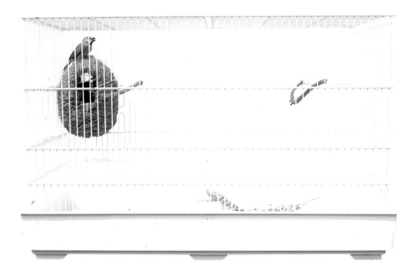

(Above) This is a typical cage for small finches, and is equipped with a nesting basket where the birds may roost. A grey-headed olive-back finch (*Nesocharis capistrata*) is shown here.

(Right) A seed hopper for millet and similar small seeds. The open top allows the hopper to be filled from outside the cage, but always be sure to check the flow of seed at the base as this can become stuck, depriving the bird of its food. Underneath the hopper is a hook-on container suitable for all types of bird food.

If you plan to obtain a pet bird, you will need a suitable cage or flight for your home. Although cages are expensive, they are durable. You must buy a suitably spacious model, but do not be misled by the ornateness of the design. A basic rectangular cage is preferable to a circular one, as this will allow the bird a great deal more space. A parrot kept in a small cramped cage will soon become bored and is likely to start plucking its feathers, as well as becoming obese through lack of exercise. Other behavioural problems – such as persistent screeching and head-weaving – may also develop. A cage with a removable front may be useful when it comes to taming your bird (see page 108).

AN INDOOR FLIGHT OR CAGE

A flight is a large mesh structure on a wooden or metal frame. This will be the best option for housing a large bird, although you may need to re-arrange a room in order to accommodate it. Indoor flights are often mounted on castors, making them relatively easy to move around for cleaning purposes.

Hygiene is obviously an important factor, and, for a small bird such as a canary, a cage with a detachable plastic base is ideal. This will be easy to keep clean, as you can change the floor covering and wash off the base of the cage regularly with minimal disturbance to its

occupant. However, you must take care to ensure that your bird cannot slip out while the units are separated.

Perches

Cages are often supplied with perches made of plastic. Although hygienic, these give parrots in particular little opportunity to use their beaks, and often prove uncomfortable. You should therefore replace these perches with branches of suitable thickness cut from fruit trees (such as apple trees), having made sure that the trees have not recently been sprayed with chemicals. Give the branches a good wash in case they have been soiled by wild birds, and then position them close to the food containers so that your bird is less likely to scatter the contents of the pots by jumping on and off their rims.

Food and water containers

The containers supplied with many cages are inadequate, as they are often too small and positioned where they will become soiled by seed husks and droppings. Move your bird's food containers so that they are above a perch (where the bird can reach up to the containers but not stand on them), and use a separate drinking container firmly attached to the outside of the cage. Bear in mind that parrots are very destructive birds and extremely adept at dislodging ordinary hook-on containers, so choose stainless-steel coop cups which fit tightly into wire hangers and can be hooked on to the sides of the cage where they will not be dislodged. For other birds, beware of tubular feeders, as the seed flow can sometimes become blocked and cut off the food supply.

A cuttlefish-bone clip

Cuttlefish bone is an important source of minerals, and you will need a clip to hold it in place on the cage. A design that holds the cuttlefish in place from the exterior of the cage is less likely to be destroyed by a parrot.

Toys

A wide variety of toys is now available for pet birds. These can provide hours of interest for parrots in particular, but do not clutter the cage with them. You must also choose any toys carefully and ensure that they are

Do not give a ladder to a young budgie, as it could become stuck between the rungs.

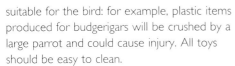

suitable for the bird: for example, plastic items produced for budgerigars will be crushed by a large parrot and could cause injury. All toys should be easy to clean.

Birds other than budgerigars and parrots do not generally appreciate toys, although a mynah or canary may be interested in a mirror. Most budgies will enjoy a mirror, especially if they are kept on their own. However, if your bird starts to become over-devoted to this toy, feeding its reflection repeatedly, you must remove the mirror for a period or the bird could starve itself. Do not give ladders to a young budgerigar as, being small in size, the bird could easily become trapped in the rungs. A table-tennis ball on the floor of the cage is often enjoyed by budgies of all ages, and is easy to wipe clean when soiled.

Various types of chews are available, and make a good choice for a larger parrot as they will appeal to its destructive nature. A mirror placed out of reach beyond the cage can also be a source of fascination. A good range of 'exercise gyms' – comprising a climbing frame, swings and similar activity toys – will help to occupy a parrot when it is out of its cage.

A BOX CAGE

Most cages sold for use in the home have a wire-mesh design, but breeders prefer to use box-type cages. These are a good idea for housing finches indoors, as they provide greater security for these rather nervous birds. You can buy a cage of this type complete, or simply buy a cage front of suitable size and then construct the cage yourself. The fronts are manufactured in budgerigar, canary and finch designs, and it is important that you select the correct one for your purposes: the finch design, for instance, has a narrower bar spacing. You could use hardwood to make a box cage for finches, but plywood is certainly a better option for budgerigars as they can destroy the softer material with their powerful beaks.

If you are making the cage yourself, allow sufficient space under the front to fit a removable sliding tray here for cleaning, and remember to incorporate this extra height into the surrounding measurements for the side and back of the box. Perches extending across the cage can be held in place with panel pins driven in from the back and supported on the wire at the front.

AN AVIARY

You could build an outdoor aviary from scratch, although it will probably be as cheap to buy the components in sections and to assemble them on site. A typical aviary consists of two parts: the flight (made of wire mesh) and the shelter, where the birds will be fed and will hopefully roost at night.

It is also a good idea to incorporate a safety porch into the design of your aviary, so that you can enter with no risk of your birds escaping. The outer door of a safety porch should open outwards for easy entry and, once this is firmly closed, you can go into the aviary itself (this second door should open inwards). If possible, position the safety porch behind the shelter, out of sight.

The flight

The hole size of the wire mesh for the flight should be no more than 2.5 x 1.25 cm (1 x ½ in), as dimensions any larger than these would give easy entry to rodents such as mice, which will threaten the birds' health. The other important aspect is the gauge (thickness) of the wire. For finches and canaries 19-gauge will be adequate, whereas large parrots may require a flight made of thicker 14- or 12-gauge mesh.

You must also keep large parrots in an all-metal aviary, while for other birds a wooden framework of 3.75–5 cm (1½–2 in) timber will be suitable. Treat the wood with a non-toxic preservative and allow it to dry before putting birds in the aviary.

The shelter

This part of the aviary should consist of a shed or similar structure attached to the flight, covered with roofing felt. The shelter must be well lit to attract the birds inside, and should have an entry/exit platform. Some shelters also have a doorway leading into the flight. (*Continued overleaf.*)

This typical covered flight forms part of an outdoor aviary, which is high enough to allow a person to walk around in easily. Concrete is the ideal flooring for an aviary, being simple to clean and disinfect; it should slope so that water runs away through a drainage hole.

103

HEATING

Some birds – such as the smaller finches and some softbills (see page 119) – will need extra warmth during the cold winter months. You will be able to provide this easily in a birdroom environment (see overleaf) with a thermostatically controlled tubular heater. However, be sure to position the heater where the birds cannot get to it, especially if you have parrots, as they may well attempt to gnaw the cable.

A sick bird will also require extra heat, and you can supply this by means of a dull-emitter infra-red lamp (see page 112).

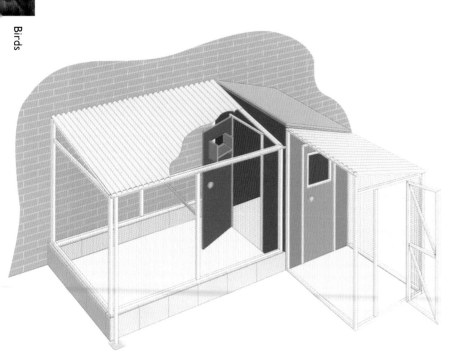

A typical aviary with a safety porch attached to the shelter. A solid back wall will give your birds greater protection from the elements. If a wall is not available, a wooden (rather than a wire-mesh) back may be suitable for the less destructive species such as finches. Note the plastic covering on the flights, and the secure foundations on which the flight panels are assembled.

Siting and building the structure

The site that you choose for your aviary should be relatively level, and out of the path of prevailing winds. In addition, try not to position it anywhere too conspicuous, to avoid attracting potential thieves or vandals.

Mount the frames on a secure course of blockwork, set below the ground and extending approximately 30 cm (12 in) above it. The aviary should be sufficiently high to allow you to walk about in it easily. If you are building the framework yourself, construct it around the width of the mesh: this is normally 91 cm (3 ft). Frame fixers will anchor the aviary securely to its base, and bolts will hold the panels together. Keep these well oiled so that you can easily move the aviary at a later date if necessary.

Plastic sheeting, extending about 91 cm (3 ft) from the shelter over the roof and sides of the flight will provide protection from the elements, while guttering on the roof area will ensure that the flight does not become flooded in the event of heavy rain. You could use a range of floor coverings, but concrete is the best option as it is easy to clean and disinfect. Slope the concrete so that water runs off from the flight through a drainage hole.

A BIRDROOM

A birdroom is an area containing flights and/or cages, used to house birds under cover. Many breeders and owners prefer to use indoor birdrooms, which reduce the noise levels of an outdoor aviary and can accommodate breeding cages in easily supervised surroundings. Other features might include a food-preparation area and training cages for exhibition birds.

A birdroom is also useful for overwintering more delicate species, as you can provide heating and artificial lighting here for them. Alternatively, you could avoid the need for separate winter quarters by incorporating the shelter part of an aviary in the birdroom, and then simply close off your birds' access to the outdoor flight in cold weather.

Feeding

Most of the birds covered in this book can be fed on a diet consisting partly of seed. However, they will also need other items – such as greenstuff – if they are to remain in good health, as seed is deficient in a number of very important dietary ingredients such as vitamin A and calcium. When you first acquire your bird or birds, you must keep to the diet to which they are accustomed at first, and then only make changes gradually, in order to avoid causing digestive problems (see also page 112).

SEED MIXES

The seeds used for bird food fall broadly into two categories. There are the cereals – millets, plain canary seed and groats (de-hulled oats) – which are relatively high in carbohydrate and low in fat; and the so-called oil seeds – hemp, sunflower, peanuts, pine nuts and perilla (the last is a valuable tonic seed, used in particular during the moult) – which have a much greater oil (fat) content in comparison with the carbohydrate.

Not surprisingly, therefore, many seed mixes contain both types of seed. Cockatiels and parakeets – including conures – will eat cereals readily, although larger parrots will prefer an oil-based seed diet. The biggest species – such as macaws – will also readily eat nuts such as walnuts and hazelnuts, cracking the casings easily in their powerful bills.

Seed mixes for specific birds are available, and some of these are supplemented with vitamins and minerals. The basis of many seed mixes for finches and budgerigars is a combination of various types of millet (recognizable as a round seed, varying from pale yellow to red) and plain canary seed (oval with pointed tips); millet sprays are also often provided. For canaries there is not only plain canary seed but also red rape (a dark-reddish seed). Other ingredients in a canary-seed mix may include hemp (a dark, fairly large, circular seed) and niger (thin and black in colour).

Breeders often provide their birds with additional seeds at particular times of the year: for example, blue maw seed (which is obtained from poppies) is valued as a weaning food for young canaries, encouraging them to eat hard seed on their own.

Complete food for parrots

Millet

Groats

Softfood used as a rearing food

Millet spray

Plain canary seed

Unsalted peanuts

Cuttlefish bone

Buying and storing seed

Only obtain seed from a reputable source, as poor-quality seed will be dangerous to your birds' health, especially if it is contaminated with rodent droppings. Check that it is free from harvesting debris and dust by running a sample through your fingers, and sniff at the seed – a sweet, sickly smell is very likely to indicate the presence of harmful fodder mites.

Always store your seed in a cool, dry place, preferably in metal containers so that rodents cannot gain access to it in aviary surroundings. Some breeders have a designated birdroom incorporating seed-storage facilities (see opposite, below). You will be able to keep seed for several months without its nutritional value deteriorating significantly, but rotate your supplies rather than simply pouring new seed on top of the older supply.

SOAKED SEED

Soaking seed stimulates the germination process, raising the vitamin B and protein levels. Breeders often use soaked seed for birds during the breeding period, or for those which are unwell and may be unwilling to crack dry seed for themselves; it also makes a useful occasional addition to the diet of any bird.

If you use soaked seed, only prepare a limited quantity – no more than will be consumed in a day – or it is likely to turn mouldy and will become a hazard to your birds' health. Rinse the seed in a sieve under cold running water, tip it into a bowl and cover with hot water. Leave it to stand overnight, then rinse again thoroughly before giving it to the birds in separate containers from their regular supply of seed (birds will generally eat soaked seed readily in preference to their usual ration).

GRIT AND CUTTLEFISH BONE

As well as seed, grit and cuttlefish bone are usually provided. Grit assists the digestive process by passing into the gizzard and helping to grind up the seed kernels, as well as preventing the kernels from sticking together. Many of the larger parrots do not appear to consume large quantities of grit, but you should still make it available for them. When cuttlefish bone is offered, birds will nibble away its soft side. This helps to keep their beaks in trim and provides a source of extra calcium, which is especially important during the breeding period for the formation of healthy eggshells.

GREENSTUFF AND FRUIT

A variety of greenstuff and fruit should feature in the diets of seed-eating species. Always wash these items thoroughly, and be very careful if gathering them outside your garden – avoid sites such as roadside verges where chemical sprays could have been used. Chickweed, dandelion and spinach are popular with many birds, and you can also offer sweet apple, carrot, berries in season and even pomegranates (the latter are a particular favourite of parrots).

FEEDING SOFTBILLS

By definition, softbills are birds which do not feed on seed as a major part of their diet. Many of these species eat fruit, along with various insects such as mealworms or crickets. Special softbill food is available, and you should sprinkle this over fruit (diced to a suitable size) to provide a well-balanced range of nutrients for your birds. You may also be able to buy softbill pellets, which are often preferred by the birds because they are similar in size to berries.

Some softbills are also nectivorous (in other words, they need nectar in their diet). You will be able to buy nectar from bird farms and from larger pet stores, and this simply needs mixing with water at the appropriate dilution (follow the instructions on the packaging). Always keep the containers for nectar scrupulously clean or they may become a source of infection to your birds; provide fresh nectar at least once and ideally twice daily.

COLOUR FEEDING

Colour feeding is an artificial way of improving the coloration of certain birds – such as the Norwich fancy canary (see pages 116 and 117) – for showing, by adding a colouring agent to the drinking water or to the birds' food. The colouring is absorbed into the body and passes from the bloodstream to the site of feather development. This fact was discovered by a canary breeder at the end of the 19th century, who gave some cayenne pepper to an unwell bird and found to his surprise that the plumage in its new feathers improved considerably. Other foods such as carrots also have this effect, but most breeders use synthetic colouring agents. Colour feeding should be started before moulting, so that there is an even uptake of the colouring agent into the new feathers. If you wish to colour feed exhibition birds, ask a breeder for further advice.

General care

Bring a new bird home in a box rather than in a cage, as it will find this less stressful and should settle rather than flapping about and possibly becoming injured under the wings. Pet stores and bird farms will be able to supply suitable carriers, but if you are buying from a breeder you may need to take one with you. Check that the box is stout, and punch some small ventilation holes around the top, close to the lid. Line the base with old newspaper, and take tape and scissors with you so that you can seal the top securely once the bird has been placed inside.

Holding a budgerigar in this way, with its head resting between the first and second fingers of your hand, will prevent you from being bitten.

106

A finch can be restrained more easily as it will not bite, but these birds are very fast in flight and so can be harder to catch.

PREPARATIONS AT HOME

You will need to make some preparations in advance at home for your pet's arrival. Even if you have bought a new cage, it is a good idea to wash and disinfect it with a safe product (your pet store will advise you on what to use) as it could have become dusty before you bought it. Wash and dry the food and water containers, and check that the perches are secure and positioned close to the food so that the bird is less likely to scatter it by jumping on and off the rims of the pots (see also page 102).

When you get home with your bird, leave it in its carrier while you fill up the food and water containers. If you have a young budgerigar, you may also want to sprinkle a little seed around the seed container if this is hooded, as a young bird can have difficulty in locating food when first confronted with this type of feeder.

PUTTING A BIRD IN ITS CAGE

You will almost certainly need to handle your bird in order to put it into its cage. Bear in mind that even a tame parrot may bite if it is frightened, so wear a pair of sturdy gloves to avoid a nasty nip.

Gently reach down into the bottom of the box and locate the bird with your hand, then place your hand over its shoulder area so that it cannot flap its wings (once these are held closed, the bird will be far less likely to struggle). Next, try to slide your first and second fingers on either side of the neck, but be very careful not to apply any pressure or you will make it difficult

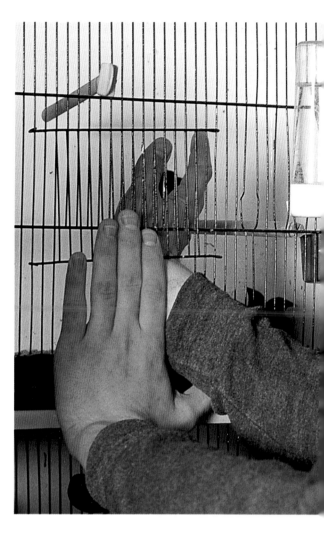

for the bird to breathe. Gently lift the bird out of the box, and transfer it directly to the cage. At this stage even a tame bird is likely to be a little nervous, so leave your pet alone to settle down quietly on its own.

PUTTING BIRDS INTO AN AVIARY

If you have bought aviary stock, it may be a good idea to keep the birds confined to the shelter section of the aviary (see page 103) for a day so that they can orientate themselves here and eat properly. Otherwise they may fly straight out into the flight and be reluctant to go back into the shelter for food.

If you are adding new birds to an existing collection, you should house them in separate quarters for two or three weeks, in order to ensure as far as possible that they are healthy. During this period, you should treat the new birds with a spray to kill external parasites (see page 113), and you may also need to de-worm them. Your vet will be able to advise you in detail about what to do.

(Above) Feather-plucking is a problem that is most commonly encountered in parrots. This can be linked with an underlying illness, or it may be the result of boredom or a poor diet. Provide some diversion in the form of toys, and spray the bird's feathers with tepid water to allay any irritation.

(Left) Always make sure that a bird cannot slip out of its cage when you are trying to catch it. Block off the gap at the open door, as shown here, until you are holding on to the bird securely.

CATCHING A BIRD

You may find it easier to catch birds in a flight with the help of a special net; this must be well-padded around the rim to reduce the risk of causing any injury. Only catch birds individually. Close off the entry point to the shelter, and lower the perches so that they are out of the way. This will also force the birds to rest either on the ground or to hang on to the aviary mesh, where you will be able to catch them more easily. Use your spare hand to guide each bird towards the net if necessary.

Once a bird is in the net, place your hand over the top to prevent it from flying out again, and then reach inside to restrain it. Bear in mind that the bird will anchor on to the net using its claws, so do not try to lift it straight out. Instead, be ready to prize its claws from the fabric very carefully, to avoid harming it.

RODENT WORRIES

Always feed your birds in the shelter section of the aviary, as this will keep their food dry and should also help to ensure that rodents are not attracted to it. Be alert to possible signs of these pests, which are most likely to reveal themselves by dark droppings left in the vicinity of the food.

Neither poisons nor break-back traps can be used safely in an area where birds are kept, but 'live' traps can be very effective for catching rodents; some types will even catch a number of them at a single setting. You must take immediate action if you suspect that rodents are about, because they will multiply rapidly when they are able to gain access to a constant supply of food, as is likely to be the case in aviary surroundings.

SPRAYING BIRDS

One of the most important ways of keeping a bird in good plumage is to provide it with access to water, but few birds will bathe in a cage, as they would do in an outdoor aviary, because their water containers will not be large enough. Many softbills – such as this sugarbird – will benefit from being sprayed at least twice a week, or daily if possible, with warm water (remove the food pots first, so that their contents do not become wet). A plant mister is ideal for this, and you should direct the jet so that the water falls down in a fine mist. Your bird will soon look forward to its regular shower.

Birds as pets

Taming is only really possible with members of the parrot group. The mynahs may be amenable to handling, although they are very messy birds and so are generally kept just for talking. The taming process will be quickest with a hand-raised bird, although a young parent-reared bird will also settle fairly quickly in the home. An older bird will be much harder to tame successfully, and almost certainly will never become as friendly or talk as much as a parrot acquired as a youngster.

THE TAMING PROCESS

The first step with taming is to encourage the bird out of its cage on to your hand. Offer your finger as a perch – placing it alongside the perch on which the parrot is resting – and move your finger gently up under the parrot's toes so that it steps on to your hand. Once you have built up a rapport, gently draw the parrot out while it is on your hand (this will be easier if the cage has a removable front).

Never make sudden movements when you are near the bird, as you may well frighten it. Nor should you ever seek to punish it by tapping it on the beak if it fails to respond as required: this will simply hamper the taming process, and may well cause the parrot to dislike you.

You are likely to find that your bird is initially reluctant to return to its cage. In this case, draw the curtains in the room and turn off the light, having placed a stool at a convenient place to reach the parrot. Plunged into sudden darkness, the bird will not fly away, so you will be able to catch it easily; otherwise, you could well be faced with a long and stressful period of pursuing it around the room.

TEACHING YOUR BIRD TO TALK

Parrots do differ in their powers of mimicry, the most talented in this respect being the African grey parrot (*Psittacus erithacus*), which can build up a vocabulary of as many as 800 words. Some budgerigars can also become exceptional mimics. One of the most famous of these, a bird called Sparkie Williams, even managed to learn eight entire nursery rhymes, taught one line at a time. Other parrots – such as cockatoos and Amazon parrots – generally have a much more limited vocabulary, often of 50 words or less.

The hill mynah is an exceptional mimic of noises – such as ringing telephones – and speaks with amazing clarity. It also has the distinction of having mastered one of the longest words in the English language: antidisestablishmentarian. The main drawback of the mynah as a pet is its relatively short lifespan. This bird may only live for 12 years, which – although

108

An African grey parrot on a swing. Many toys are commercially available for these bigger birds, but always supervise your pet when it is free in a room as it could become bored and gnaw your furniture instead of its perch.

A budgerigar play station should keep your bird occupied for some time; this one is designed to fit on the top of the cage.

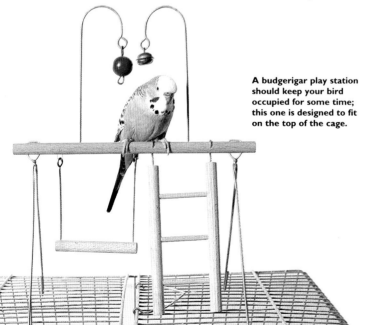

Potential hazards for a bird in the home

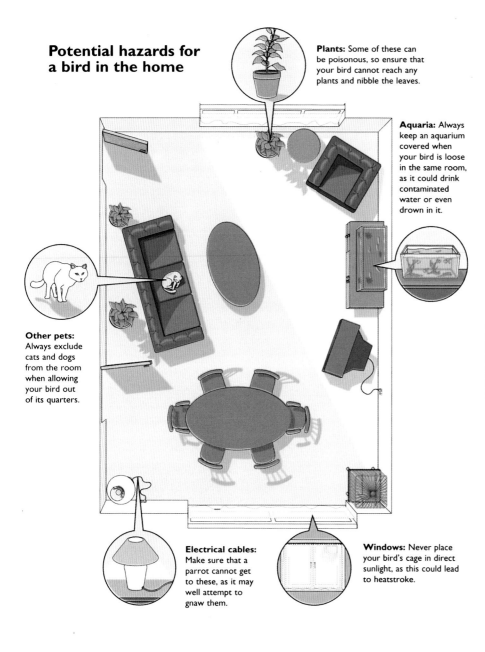

Plants: Some of these can be poisonous, so ensure that your bird cannot reach any plants and nibble the leaves.

Aquaria: Always keep an aquarium covered when your bird is loose in the same room, as it could drink contaminated water or even drown in it.

Other pets: Always exclude cats and dogs from the room when allowing your bird out of its quarters.

Electrical cables: Make sure that a parrot cannot get to these, as it may well attempt to gnaw them.

Windows: Never place your bird's cage in direct sunlight, as this could lead to heatstroke.

AVOIDING ACCIDENTS

As shown on the left, you must always make a number of safety checks before letting a bird out of its cage, and remove or cover potential hazards such as an open-topped aquarium or any plants which could be poisonous (such as ivies). Make sure that an open fire is well screened, close all doors and windows, and exclude dogs or cats. Remember that even a tame bird will fly off if frightened, so put ornaments out of harm's way.

longer than the majority of budgerigars – does not compare with the longevity of most larger parrots. Young hill mynahs may be recognized by the relative absence of fleshy lobes on the back of the head. They may also still beg for food, and so are often described as 'gapers'.

Parrots usually find it easier to learn from women or children because of the pitch of their voices. When teaching your bird, you should avoid distracting sounds such as those of the television or radio. Start by repeating a simple phrase – such as 'Good morning' – when you first go into the bird's room and remove the cover from its quarters (it is important to keep the cage covered every night in order to give your bird an adequate period of darkness, even if you stay up late

yourself). Before very long, the parrot should be responding to you in a similar way.

Once it has mastered a few simple phrases the parrot may learn further words spoken by other members of the household, or may pick these up on its own. It may also mimic frequently heard sounds, such as a creaking door or a barking dog. It is advisable not to keep your parrot in the same room as the telephone, because some parrots can mimic the tone so faithfully that utter confusion results! On the subject of telephones, the most useful phrase to teach any bird is your own telephone number and address. If your pet ever escapes or is stolen, anyone who finds it will then be able to get in touch with you easily to return it.

Breeding

Breeding birds is not generally difficult and can become a very interesting pastime, but first of all you will need to establish that you have a true pair of birds. While this is easy to ascertain in some cases because of a distinctive difference in appearance between cock and hen, recognizing pairs – particularly in the case of many parrots – can be difficult as there is no means of visually distinguishing the sexes.

SEXING

Two techniques are now used for reliably establishing a bird's sex. The first of these – surgical (endoscopic) sexing – has been used for many years, but is not suitable for young birds; the use of an anaesthetic also carries a slight risk. These drawbacks have made DNA sexing the preferred option. Here, a blood sample is taken and then normally sent off to a laboratory by courier; laboratories offering this service advertise in bird-keeping magazines, or your vet may be able to carry out the procedure for you.

Surgical sexing

Here, the bird is anaesthetized by a vet (normally using a gaseous anaesthetic, from which the bird will recover rapidly once the procedure has been completed). A small incision is made in its left flank and an endoscope (a viewing tube) is inserted. This enables the vet to see the reproductive organs and therefore to sex the bird.

DNA sexing

This requires just a small blood sample, and, as the blood can be taken from a feather, there may be no need to remove the bird from its aviary (do ensure that samples are labelled accurately if several birds are tested). The blood sample is placed in a special transport tube and dispatched to a laboratory for analysis.

CONDITIONING

This is as important a part of breeding as having a true pair of birds. Some birds – such as canaries – have a breeding period that is confined to the spring and summer, while others will breed throughout the year. However, allowing birds to nest during bad weather is likely to be less successful, and will also entail extra expenditure on heating and lighting.

Birds need time to settle in their quarters before starting to breed: in the case of the larger parrots, this could even take several years. The pair bond between the larger parrots is strong, and they may not accept new partners readily; this is why breeders are often prepared to pay a premium price for a proven pair of parrots which are known to be compatible.

NESTING SITES

Your choice of nesting sites will be important for successful breeding. For instance, while canaries build cup-shaped nests in suitable nest pans, budgerigars and other parrots require nest boxes. Budgerigar nest boxes should be lined with wooden concaves; other parrots may gnaw at soft-wood battening to create a nest lining themselves, or you could provide coarse woodshavings in the nest box for this purpose. Lovebirds and hanging parrots build nests of twigs, as does the monk or quaker parakeet (*Myiopsitta monachus*).

HAND-REARING A CHICK

If a chick is unable to feed itself, you will need to rear it by hand. After hatching, the chick's yolk sac will continue to sustain it for about four hours; the first feed should then be given. A simple dropper, or a teaspoon with the edges bent inwards to act as a funnel (as shown here with this young lorikeet chick), will make an ideal feeding tool. Feed a very tiny chick every two hours around the clock; every four hours will be sufficient for a larger individual. As the chick grows, increase the intervals between feeds.

The best way of monitoring a chick's progress is to weigh it daily before the first feed (use scales graduated in 0.1 g units). By keeping a record, you will soon detect any problems. For further advice on hand-rearing chicks, contact your vet.

(Left) A typical double breeding cage housing canaries. This has a removable central partition, so it can be used as a stock cage for the young birds after the breeding season and before they are moved to the aviary.

An injection of a calcium compound is usually effective if given rapidly; otherwise your vet will probably need to remove the egg surgically.

FEEDING AND GENERAL CARE

The first sign of a successful hatching may be the appearance of eggshells in the flight, or the sound of young chicks being fed. At this stage, you should increase the amount of rearing food being given. You will be able to obtain a range of suitable egg foods from pet stores, which are usually ready to feed straight from the packet. Provide fresh supplies morning and evening. Some birds may require other foods at this stage (for example, waxbills and softbills will need invertebrates in large quantities) to ensure that their chicks are reared successfully. If you need further information on feeding, ask the advice of your vet or an experienced breeder.

Do not interfere too much with your birds during the rearing period, although some species – such as budgerigars – are likely to be more tolerant than others of having their chicks handled. In this case, you may want to clean out the nest lining and replace it with a fresh one. Check for any accumulation of dirt on the young budgerigars' toes (you will need to soak this off carefully with warm water) or inside the beak (gently prize this out using a blunt cocktail stick or the bare end of a matchstick).

REMOVING THE CHICKS

Once the chicks are ready for fledging, their parents will continue to feed them for a variable period. After this you should remove the young birds to separate quarters, as the adults may wish to nest again, and will resent their presence.

A newly hatched budgerigar chick. If you plan to breed your budgerigars, you will need to provide them with a nest box for egg-laying.

Budgerigar eggs hatch on alternate days, so there can be a considerable variance in the size of the chicks. Despite this, they will usually all be reared successfully.

Finches may use nest boxes or pans, or may even build their own nests if housed in a planted flight, as will softbills. You will generally need to provide suitable nesting material (available from a pet store) for these two groups of birds.

Exhibition canaries, budgerigars, and Bengalese and zebra finches are usually housed in breeding cages. This enables breeders to pair birds as they wish so that, with luck, young of a particular colour or an improved show quality will result. The pair bond between these birds is weak.

BREEDING ACTIVITY

Signs of breeding activity will depend largely on the species concerned. For instance, finches will often carry nesting material in their bills, while cock birds will start to sing frequently and may also show signs of aggression to potential rivals. Most parrots will become noisier as the time for egg-laying approaches, with hens spending longer in their nest boxes. They will also consume cuttlefish bone more avidly at this stage, while immediately prior to egg-laying the hens' droppings often become significantly larger.

In some cases incubation duties will be shared; in others the hen sits alone. Keep a note of when egg-laying is likely to have occurred, at the stage when the hen disappeared into the nest. Avoid disturbing sitting birds unless absolutely necessary, but keep an eye on how much food they eat as this is a good indicator of anything being amiss.

The problem that you are most likely to come across is egg-binding, when an egg remains trapped in the hen's body. In this case, she will emerge from the nest box and appear unsteady on her feet, soon losing her ability to perch. This condition requires urgent veterinary attention.

Health care

Careful observation is an important part of looking after any bird. You will soon discover how much food your pet normally eats in a day (you should always supply food – never ration it), as well as the usual colour and consistency of its droppings and its sleeping habits. If a bird is unwell it will usually eat less and sleep more, and its droppings may be an unusual colour or have a very watery consistency. The bird will also appear listless and disinterested in what is going on around it.

IF YOUR BIRD IS ILL

If you believe that your bird is ill, you must act quickly. Many pet birds die simply because their owners fail to notice in time that they are unwell, or to act quickly enough once they do so. The first step is to provide additional heat, because ordinary room temperature will be inadequate for a sick bird. The most beneficial form of heat is a dull-emitter infra-red lamp, which produces heat rather than light. If this type of lamp is not available, increase the temperature by other means to approximately 29°C (85°F), and also cover the bird's cage with a towel. Consult a vet immediately – ideally, one who is experienced in dealing with avian patients.

Most birds are actually very healthy, and rarely fall ill once they are well established in their quarters. Young birds, and especially newly acquired individuals, will be at the greatest risk of illness. Keeping to the diet to which they have been accustomed initially, and then only making changes gradually, is a sensible precautionary measure. Giving a probiotic product (this promotes beneficial bacteria in the gut, and will be available from your vet or from a pet store) can also help to prevent digestive upsets from occurring during the settling-in period.

Unfortunately, the symptoms of many avian illnesses tend to be rather similar, but modern drugs will help to ensure recovery in many cases. There are even special foods now available to maintain the condition of a sick bird which is no longer eating, thus giving time for treatment to be successful. In the past such birds would almost invariably have died – essentially because of their loss of appetite.

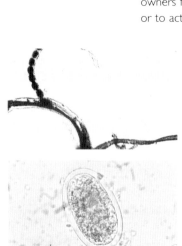

A female roundworm seen under a microscope (top), with one of its eggs in magnified detail (above). These parasites are a particular problem in Australian parakeets, and young birds may be infested in the nest from worms present in the adult birds' droppings.

AVIAN PARASITES

Breeders in particular must watch for parasites in their stock. Not surprisingly, parasites spread most readily in species kept in groups, such as budgerigars; they are less likely to be a problem for pet birds housed on their own.

Red mites (*Dermanyssus gallinae*)

These mites are one of the most significant avian parasites. They are barely visible to the human eye and hide away during the day, emerging at night. They obtain their red coloration from feeding on birds' blood. Even a mild infestation can cause severe irritation, while a large number of the mites are likely to cause anaemia (lack of red blood cells) and even death in young chicks.

Red mites are more likely to be a problem when many birds are kept together. Treatment involves spraying adult birds with a special preparation, and washing their accommodation – particularly nest boxes and breeding cages – to prevent any accumulation of the mites (most owners spray new birds before putting them in with others, and strip down and wash the aviary at the end of the year). If this is not done, the mites can survive without feeding from one breeding season to the next, and will then multiply rapidly when the birds are re-introduced.

Lice

Lice can sometimes be a problem, and may give a ragged, chewed appearance to the edge of the feathers. The same spray used for red mites will kill these pests, which will spend their entire lives on the birds rather than in the environment.

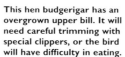
This hen budgerigar has an overgrown upper bill. It will need careful trimming with special clippers, or the bird will have difficulty in eating.

roundworms and similar parasites. In aviary surroundings, you must also clean the floor thoroughly and disinfect it to prevent the birds from re-infecting themselves.

CLIPPING CLAWS AND BEAKS

Claws can sometimes grow too long, which will be dangerous as a bird could become caught up in its quarters. You must carry out claw clipping in good light so that you can locate the blood supply first. Using sharp clippers (these must be specially designed for the purpose), carefully snip off the end of each claw beyond the point at which the red streak disappears, so that you do not cause bleeding.

A bird's beak is less likely to require cutting, but may become overgrown (this especially likely in pet budgerigars) and will then need careful trimming. If you do not wish to do this yourself, ask your vet to do it for you.

Clipping a bird's claws is fairly straightforward, but you must first locate the blood supply, or 'quick' (visible as a pink streak).

Using special clippers, carefully trim off the overgrown part of the claw beyond the 'quick'.

Scaly face

This is a problem associated especially with budgerigars. However, the mites responsible for the condition can also affect other birds – such as zebra finches – and may be found on the legs and feet as well as on the beak, around the eyes and on the cere (the waxy swelling around the base of the upper bill). The earliest sign will be minute snail-like tracks across the upper bill, which will give rise to distinctive coral-like growths. If the condition is left untreated, the growths will result in permanent malformation.

Proprietary treatments will resolve scaly face, but they must be applied every day. Alternatively, a drug called ivermectin has proved very effective at overcoming the parasites in a single treatment. The drug will also kill air-sac mites, which live within the airways and cause breathing distress, especially in canaries and in some other finches.

Other parasites

Some birds are more prone to certain parasites: for instance, cockatiels and Australian parakeets often suffer from intestinal roundworms because they feed on the ground and so pick up the parasitic worm eggs. You should de-worm all new birds before putting them into an aviary, as it is much easier to exclude the parasites rather than having to deal with them *in situ*. You can add this medication to the drinking water, but giving it directly to the individual birds is likely to be more effective. Your vet will advise you on the best product to use and how to administer it, and will also be able to screen your birds' droppings if necessary for any evidence of

COMMON AVIAN AILMENTS

Ailment	Symptoms	Treatment
Egg-binding	*Distressed hen, difficulty in laying.*	Keep bird warm, at 32°C (90°F); contact vet for administration of calcium-compound injection.
Enteritis	*Greenish droppings, rapid weight loss, dejected appearance, refusal to eat.*	Keep bird warm, at up to 32°C (90°F). Give course of antibiotics from vet. Wash soiled vent feathers with veterinary-antiseptic solution.
Feather-plucking	*Bird nibbles its own feathers.*	Provide diversion (toys); spray feathers with tepid water to allay any irritation.
Infection	*Loose droppings, laboured breathing.*	Treat as for enteritis.
Moulting	*Ragged plumage, excessive loose feathers in cage.*	Place cage in airy position with even temperature; spray bird with tepid water to tighten feathers.
Scaly face	*Greyish, scurfy encrustation on beak, cere, eyes, legs and feet; common in budgerigars.*	Keep bird isolated; apply drops, cream or ointment as directed on package instructions, or treat with ivermectin from vet.
Stroke or fits	*Violent trembling movements, spread wings.*	No treatment; leave bird to recover quietly and seek veterinary advice.

Finches

Finches are often colourful birds and will nest readily – even in the confines of a cage kept inside in the home – but they are generally not tameable, nor do they rival domesticated canaries as songsters. These small birds will not cause pain if they bite, but they can still be difficult to handle, especially for elderly or infirm owners living on their own. Most species are very quick on the wing, and if a pair of the birds were to escape from their cage in a room, it could be difficult to catch them again without the assistance of a long-handled net. In temperate areas, the smaller finches will need heating and lighting during the winter months.

Chestnut-and-white Bengalese finches

Bengalese finch (*Lonchura domestica*)

⬤ 11 cm (4½ in) ⬤ 6 eggs ⬤ 15 days
⬤ 24 days ⬤ 34 days

This species is better known in the USA as the 'society finch'. It does not occur in the wild, and is thought to have been created in China by the hybridization of *Lonchura* species, before being taken to Japan in the 1700s.

A range of colours has now been developed, together with a crested mutation (as in the zebra finch). The chocolate self (solid-coloured) Bengalese has a deep brown head and back, with paler underparts. Chocolate-and-white pieds are often seen, too, with their brown areas broken by white markings. The fawn self Bengalese is lighter than the chocolate, with a pinkish hue to the bill and legs. There is also a fawn-and-white form and a pure-white Bengalese.

Breeding requirements are similar to those of the zebra finch. Pairs can be prolific and breed readily indoors, but sexing can be problematic because the only means of distinguishing the cock and hen is by the cock's song.

Zebra finches: cock (left) and hen (right)

Zebra finch (*Poephila guttata*)

⬤ 11 cm (4½ in) ⬤ 6 eggs ⬤ 12 days
⬤ 21 days ⬤ 31 days

This is an excellent choice if you wish to breed finches either in your home or in aviary surroundings. Measuring about 11 cm (4½ in) in length, these birds were first brought to Europe from Australia in the 1840s. The name comes from black-and-white stripes on the cock bird's flanks; the hen is generally duller, with a paler beak. Young birds resemble hens on fledging, but are distinguished by their black bills.

A wide range of colour forms of the zebra finch is now established and exhibited on a regular basis; there is also a crested mutation. There are several white forms, including pure white and albino (the latter has red eyes). On the chestnut-flanked white, markings are retained so that sexing does not depend on bill coloration. Pied finches – which have variable areas of white and dark markings – are common, as are fawns. There are also silvers and creams; newer colours include black-breasted and orange-breasted forms.

A nesting box or basket, with nesting material provided, will be suitable for breeding these birds. Incubation lasts about 12 days, with perhaps six chicks fledging three weeks later.

Mannikins

⬤ 10–12.5 cm (4–5 in) ⬤ 4–6 eggs
⬤ 13 days ⬤ 21–27 days ⬤ 31–37 days

Also known as munias and nuns, these birds include the ancestral forms of the Bengalese finch. However, they tend to be less free-breeding (certainly in cages) and are best kept in small flocks. Shades of brown, white and black tend to predominate in the coloration.

Sexing is generally established on the basis of the cock bird's song. Egg food is often eaten when there are chicks in the nest, but livefood is rarely required.

Blue-capped waxbills

Waxbills

⬤ 10–12.5 cm (4–5 in) ⬤ 3–5 eggs
⬤ 12 days ⬤ 16–21 days ⬤ 30–35 days

This group originates mainly from Africa. The birds are often very colourful, and average about 10 cm (4 in) in length. They may need heating and lighting during the winter months in temperate areas, or they can be over-wintered in an indoor flight or bird room (see page 102). Generally social birds, waxbills can be kept in mixed groups. Sexing them can be difficult, so having at least four birds of one species is recommended to try to ensure a true pair. Waxbills are most likely to breed successfully in a planted aviary, where the roof must be well covered to prevent the nests from being flooded in a summer downpour. Although they will eat mainly seed for much of the year they become highly insectivorous during the breeding period, and small livefood – such as hatchling crickets and whiteworm – will be essential if chicks are to be reared successfully.

Singing finches

⬤ 11 cm (4½ in) ⬤ 4 eggs ⬤ 14 days
⬤ 14 days ⬤ 25 days

These African finches are closely related to canaries (see pages 116–17), and they need similar management and care. Their song is less well developed than that of canaries, but they may have a longer lifespan – some individuals have lived for over 20 years.

Weavers and whydahs

⬤ 12.5–15 cm (5–6 in), excluding the long tail plumes of whydahs ⬤ 2–4 eggs
⬤ 14–16 days ⬤ 12–14 days ⬤ 30 days

The cock birds of this interesting group often undergo a spectacular change in appearance at the onset of the breeding period. Some whydahs are parasitic, laying their eggs in the nests of specific waxbills rather than rearing their own offspring; in contrast, the weavers, as their name suggests, delight in making their own nests.

Breeding from weavers and whydahs that are kept in cages is very unlikely to be successful, so these birds should be housed in flights; they are also polygamous, so several hens should be put in with each cock bird.

Once they have had time to become acclimatized to their environment, both the weavers and the whydahs can be relatively hardy birds.

Australian finches

A number of other Australian species are well established in aviculture, in addition to the zebra finch. The stunning Gouldian finch (*Chloebia gouldiae*) is one of the most widely kept species, and occurs in three different head colours: black, red and yellow (the latter is actually a shade of orange). Various mutations – such as a white-breasted form – have also been developed. The cock bird is easily recognizable by having a red tip to its bill when it is in breeding condition; it also tends to have more brightly coloured feathering than the hen. Australian finches need to be kept warm and so are ideal occupants for an indoor flight (see page 102).

WEANING TIMES
Note that the weaning times given here and on the following pages are approximate, and that you may need to move the young birds earlier than this if either of their parents appears aggressive towards them.

However, you should try to avoid weaning too soon, as it will be better if the young remain in the aviary undisturbed until you are quite certain that they are feeding independently.

115

Orange weavers: hen (left) and cock (right)

Canaries

Canaries are broadly divided into the following three categories: those bred for their 'type' or appearance (these are popular show birds, although they can also be kept as pets); the coloured canaries, whose coloration is of the greatest significance in exhibition circles; and the small number of breeds – of which the roller is the best known – which have been developed specifically for the quality of their singing. Canaries should not be used for breeding purposes until they are 12 months old.

Gloster fancy (Corona)

Gloster fancy (Consort)

Border fancy

This is one of the best-known 'type' canaries. It arose in the Border region between England and Scotland, and, in common with many type breeds, is named after its area of origin. This bird presents a great challenge to the exhibitor, for not only is it the most popular variety of canary, producing fierce competition; but considerable skill is also needed to combine the many features that make up a well-balanced specimen. Show judges will look for a small, round, neat head, a distinct neck, a nice rise to the back and a well-rounded chest. The wings should be held close to the body, and the tail tightly folded. Feather quality and depth of natural colour are also very important.

Fife fancy

The Fife was developed in the 1970s by fanciers who felt that the Border fancy was becoming too big and no longer lived up to its old name of the 'Wee gem'. It is simply a smaller version of the Border and, apart from its size, should resemble that breed in every detail.

Norwich fancy

The Norwich is more sedate in its movements than the Border and Fife varieties, as befits a bird of its rotund proportions. The required qualities are a broad head with a short neck merging imperceptibly into a stout and nicely rounded body, and a short tail. Although its 'bullfinch' shape gives the impression of size, this bird should not exceed 16.5 cm (6½ in) in length. It is customary to colour-feed Norwich fancy canaries for exhibition purposes; this will impart an orange tint to yellow plumage. A suitable colouring agent – which can be added to drinking water or mixed into soft food – will be required just prior to and during the moult for this purpose (see also page 105).

Yorkshire fancy

'Guardsman' and 'Gentleman of the Fancy' are names that are often given to the Yorkshire, and they allude to its upright stance and swaggering manner. At one time it was a tall, slim bird – a good specimen was said to be able to pass through a wedding ring. However, in recent years individuals with broad, round heads and wide shoulders have been more favoured and, although the qualities of stance, smooth feather and nervous energy have been maintained, a much bolder form has been the result. The Yorkshire can be up to 20 cm (8 in) in length and, like the Norwich, is colour fed for exhibition purposes.

Gloster fancy

This is now the best known of the crested breeds. Its neat daisy crest must not obscure the eyes, and type is also important – the aim being to breed a dainty, lively small bird that still manages to convey an impression of solidity and 'cobbiness' in its shape.

Crested Glosters are known as 'Coronas', and their plainhead mates as 'Consorts'. The Gloster has been used in the recent development of the Stafford fancy, which is now becoming increasingly popular.

Yorkshire fancy

Norwich fancy

Red factor

Roller

This canary is bred exclusively for its song, which is so superior in sweetness and tone to that of any other breed that it really needs to be heard to be appreciated. The song comprises a number of 'passages', or 'tours', with specific names such as 'glucke', 'bass', 'water roll', 'flutes' and 'bell roll'. A trained roller will utter the different song passages when required, passing effortlessly and without pause from one tour to another. The song can range across three octaves.

The origins of this breed lie in the Harz mountains, where these canaries were taught to mimic the sounds of the mountain streams. Today, top-quality 'schoolmaster' birds or audio-cassette tapes are used for teaching purposes.

Red factor

This bird is descended from fertile hybrids bred from crosses between yellow canaries and a South American finch called the black-hooded red siskin (*Carduelis cucullatus*). The aim of this was simply to produce a true-breeding red canary which owed its coloration to its genetic make-up rather than to specialized feeding. Some progress was made, but it was not until a superior

proprietary colouring agent became available in the 1960s that deep red-orange and apricot canaries appeared on the show bench in large numbers. Increased interest has given rise to other mutations, and this is now a wide field for experimental breeding.

Lizard

This is the oldest surviving breed of canary, whose origins date back to the early 1800s. It has black wings and a black tail, and – apart from a crown of light feathers on its head, which is called the 'cap' – is a dark bird. Rows of spangles are displayed on its back, which are thought to resemble the scales of a lizard in appearance – hence the breed's name. Not all lizard canaries actually have a distinct cap, and in some individuals the cap is divided by a darker area; these birds are described as 'broken caps'.

The lizard is colour fed for exhibition purposes, and is the only variety judged on the pattern of its plumage.

Crested canaries

All crested canaries display the same form of circular crest, which radiates from a distinct centre on the top

of the head. It is not genetically viable to breed crested canaries together; the recognized mating is crest × plainhead (non-crested). This gives a 50/50 expectation of both types, as is the case with crested mutations in other birds such as the Bengalese finch and budgerigars (see pages 120–1).

Breeding data

🥚 4 eggs 🥚 13 days
🥚 14 days 🥚 21 days

Roller

Softbills

There is tremendous diversity in this group of birds, which ranges from small nectar-feeding species such as hummingbirds and sunbirds up to large toucans and touracos. The feature that they have in common is that none of these birds feeds mainly on seed. Some require experienced owners if they are to thrive – this tends to apply to the more insectivorous species, although the increased availability of balanced diets and commercially cultured supplies of livefood (such as different-sized crickets – see also page 105) has made it much easier to keep and breed these birds successfully.

Black-headed starling

Starlings

2–5 eggs **⏱** 16 days **◑** 20 days **➷** 50 days

For the pet-seeker, only the greater hill mynah (*Gracula religiosa*) will prove to be a talented mimic, although other starlings – such as the attractive purple, glossy starling (*Lamprotornis purpureus*) – are relatively easy to maintain in aviary surroundings. A pair (recognizable by surgical sexing – see page 110) may well attempt to breed in a cockatiel-type nest box lined

with a variety of small twigs and similar materials gathered around the aviary. Pairs should be housed on their own for the greatest likelihood of breeding success, as they can become aggressive. Starlings require a varied diet of fruit, softbill food or pellets, and livefood.

Bulbuls

2–4 eggs **⏱** 13 days **◑** 13 days **➷** 30 days

A number of softbills have an attractive song, and the bulbuls fit into this category. While most are not especially colourful, these birds are

Greater hill mynah

easy to keep and can be housed in the company of certain finches and other non-aggressive softbills of similar size.

Bulbuls cannot be sexed visually. There is a good chance of these birds breeding successfully in a planted aviary, where the hen will lay her eggs in a cup-shaped nest made of moss, twigs and similar material. You will need to supply a typically mixed softbill diet with an increased proportion of small livefood during the nesting period, particularly once the chicks have hatched.

Pekin robin

4 eggs **⏱** 14 days **◑** 14 days **➷** 30 days

This is a widely kept species of softbill. Its name is rather misleading, as it is not a robin in spite of its shape; nor does it originate from the vicinity of Peking (now Beijing) but is found instead further south in Asia. These birds are omnivorous in their feeding habits, taking both a softbill diet and small seeds such as millet when they are kept in a mixed collection. Unfortunately, they may steal the eggs of other birds in such surroundings, although they are not aggressive by nature. As with bulbuls, it is generally not possible to distinguish the sexes easily; any slight differences in coloration between a male and female may be the result of regional variations in the birds' origins, rather than reflecting sexual differences.

Laughing thrushes

3–4 eggs **⏱** 12 days **◑** 12 days **➷** 30 days

These birds make up a group of larger softbills that need to be housed on their own, as they are often fairly aggressive by nature. A number of species – such as the hoami (*Garrulax leucolophus*) – are highly prized for their song. Originating from northern parts of Asia, laughing thrushes are generally hardy once they are acclimatized to an environment, and can be housed outdoors through the winter without additional heat, provided that they have

Chestnut-flanked white-eyes

Bay-headed tanager

access to a suitable snug shelter. Placing some dense bushes in the flight will encourage nesting. Visual sexing is again generally impossible.

As with many birds, the most difficult stage is the post-hatching period, as laughing thrushes have a reputation for cannibalizing their offspring soon after they hatch. This may be related to the ease with which they can obtain their food in aviary surroundings, resulting in boredom. Dispensing livefood on the floor of the aviary to encourage the birds to hunt for it here will reduce the likelihood of the chicks being eaten by their parents. You must also restrain your curiosity: do not disturb the birds more than is strictly necessary at this stage and avoid poking around in the nest, as this could result in chicks being abandoned by the parents.

Tanagers

🐣 2 eggs 🕐 12–14 days 🥚 12-19 days 🐦 26–33 days

These often colourful softbills originate from the New World, with most species found in Central and South America. Fruit and berries should feature prominently in their diet, along with a low-iron softfood and some livefood. The birds vary in size from about 10 cm

(4 in) to 23 cm (9 in) and, while the larger species such as mountain tanagers are relatively hardy, the more commonly kept *Tangara* species will need winter warmth when kept in a temperate climate. Sexing tanagers by visual means is generally impossible.

Barbets

🐣 3–5 eggs 🕐 14 days 🥚 23–33 days 🐦 37–50 days

Stockily built and with their broad bills, barbets are rather like miniature toucans in appearance. Some are more insectivorous than others. These birds are hole-nesters, and are often willing to adopt a nest box or a stout hollow log for roosting and nesting purposes. They may attack the woodwork in their aviary, or may even tunnel into the floor if this is not solid. As a general rule, barbets are not especially hardy birds.

Compatibility for breeding can be a problem, with even true pairs not agreeing at all times. The cock bird is most likely to become aggressive at the start of the breeding period if the hen does not respond immediately to his advances. Be prepared to separate the pair if necessary, taking the male away and then re-introducing him to the female at a later stage.

White-eyes (*Zosterops*)

🐣 2–4 eggs 🕐 12 days 🥚 12 days 🐦 27 days

These are the most easily managed of the nectivorous softbills. Several species of white-eyes are often available, including the chestnut-flanked zosterops (*Z. erythropleura*), which is so called because of the chestnut plumage on the sides of its body. All species have a distinctive area of white feathering encircling the eyes.

As well as finely chopped fruit and some softbill food, these birds require nectar and some livefood. Always provide the nectar in a suitable tube – never in an open dish – or the birds may be tempted to immerse themselves in the sticky solution. Like many softbills they will bathe readily, and you should provide an open pot of water in their quarters for this purpose.

The sexes are identical in appearance, but the male zosterops will sing during the nesting period. The hen will lay her eggs in a nest made of fine fibres and moss.

Zosterops can be housed in groups together with other small birds such as finches, and, like them, will need to be given extra warmth during the winter months (see page 103).

119

Budgerigars

The budgerigar was originally introduced to the UK by the explorer and artist John Gould, who returned with a pair from Australia in 1840. These birds passed into the care of his brother-in-law, Charles Coxen, who bred them for the first time in Europe.

The budgerigar's name is derived from the Aboriginal word 'betcherrygah', meaning 'good food', while the scientific description, *Melopsittacus undulatus*, was constructed from the Greek words 'melos' and 'psittakos' ('song parrot') and the Latin *undulatus* ('wavy-lined') – the latter describing the pattern of feathering on the birds' backs. A budgerigar's colour will have no effect on its talking ability.

Recessive pied cock

Albino cock

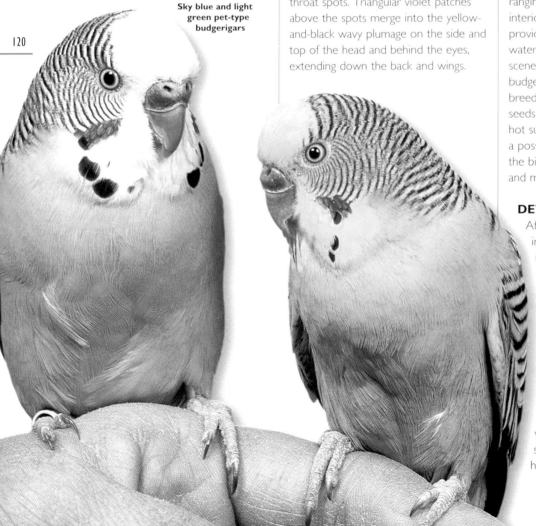

Sky blue and light green pet-type budgerigars

NATIVE BUDGERIGARS
The native form of the budgerigar is light green with a yellow face and black throat spots. Triangular violet patches above the spots merge into the yellow-and-black wavy plumage on the side and top of the head and behind the eyes, extending down the back and wings.

The tail feathers are dark blue, and the bird's total length is about 18 cm (7¼ in).

Budgerigars in the wild are nomadic, ranging over much of Australia's dry interior in search of the rains which provide them with both food and water. These rains transform the arid scenery into flourishing grassland. The budgerigars then move in to feed and breed, rearing their young on the grass seeds which ripen quickly under the hot sun. As soon as they are faced with a possible shortage of food or water, the birds move off to another district and may not return for several years.

DEVELOPMENT OF COLOURS
After the budgerigar's appearance in Europe, reported sightings of mutations in the wild flocks of Australia were soon circulating. Yellow individuals were observed, and the skin of a wild, dark green budgerigar confirmed that the reports were indeed accurate. The first mutation to be bred in captivity was the yellow, which appeared in Belgium in 1872. Yellow budgerigars can be distinguished from the lutino variety – which became known seven years later – as the latter has red, rather than black, eyes.

Light green cock (exhibition type)

Lutinos are deep yellow in colour and lack throat spots; a white patch on the cheeks also replaces the mauve colour found on the true yellow budgerigar. Albinos – which are pure white with red eyes – became known in the 1930s. Both these varieties are more difficult to sex than normals, especially if the birds are immature. However, the majority of cock budgerigars have a blue cere above the beak, while hens have a brown cere which darkens when they are in breeding condition. In the case of chicks, young cocks have a more purplish cere than the hens, with this slightly darker coloration being most pronounced around the nostrils.

No-one living in the 1870s when the budgerigar mutations first appeared could have foreseen today's profusion of colours. Changes in the colour of the normal green budgerigar led to dark greens being bred in France in 1915. These were followed by olive greens – an important breakthrough, as it proved that budgerigars could be bred in light, medium and dark forms.

Blue budgerigars were first bred in Belgium towards the end of the 19th century. The initial strain appears to have been weak, and only in 1910 were sky blue budgerigars first seen in the UK. These were the blue-series equivalent

of the light green. As with the greens, darker forms were subsequently bred, beginning with the cobalt variety in 1920 and leading on to mauves shortly afterwards. Violet budgerigars appeared in 1936, and were immediately very popular.

Any of the three shades of green and blue can be present in a pied budgerigar, in conjunction with yellow and white respectively – so, for example, a pied cobalt may be bred. Two genetically distinct forms of the pied budgerigar – the Australian dominant pied and the Danish pied – are recognized, each being named after its country of origin. The Australian dominant pied was bred in Sydney in about 1935, and is easily distinguished from its Danish recessive counterpart by its larger size and – in the case of adult birds – by white irises around its black eyes. The Danish pied has eyes resembling those of a young bird (the white irises which develop in most budgerigar varieties at about 12 weeks do not appear), and when viewed in a good light they look more reddish in colour. As with adult cock lutinos and albinos, the cere is reddish-mauve, not blue.

Other changes to the markings have occurred, giving rise to opalines, where the barring on the head is significantly reduced. Then there are greywings, whitewings and yellow-wings, as well as yellow-faced forms of the grey and blue budgerigar. One of the most recent mutations, which is called the spangle, has light markings in the centre of its darker feathers, and this characteristic can be combined with any colour. In fact, there are many thousands of different combinations now available. One colour that is theoretically possible but has yet to emerge is a black form.

DEVELOPMENT OF FEATHERING

Alterations to the feathering have also occurred over the years, with crested budgerigars being developed in the USA in the late 1930s, as well as in Australia and France. Three distinct types are

Lutino hen: the cere is still pale, rather than dark brown which would indicate that the bird is in breeding condition.

recognized: the tufted form, which has an upright crest extending above the cere; the full circular-crested budgerigar, whose crest is similar to that of the Gloster corona canary (see page 116); and a third variety which has a semi-circular crest extending forward on the bird's head. As is the case with other crested mutations, such budgerigars need to be paired to normals, and not to one another.

BREEDING

Budgerigars do not require any nesting material, and they will lay quite happily on the wooden concave of a nest box attached to a breeding cage (see also pages 110–11).

When they are kept together in groups, these birds are normally reliable breeders either in cages or aviaries. However, if one pair of budgerigars is kept out of sight and sound of others they will often fail to nest – presumably because the birds lack the stimulus of their companions – and this is a major reason for breeding disappointments in the home.

As with canaries, budgerigars should not be used for breeding purposes until they are 12 months old.

Breeding data

4–6 eggs   18 days   5 weeks
6 weeks

Cockatiels and parakeets

Cockatiels are suitable both as pets and as aviary occupants, but parakeets are kept mainly in aviaries. Their attractive coloration, lively personality, ease of care and readiness to breed have made them firm avicultural favourites. In recent years a number of colour mutations have been developed, adding to the interest among bird enthusiasts in this group of birds.

Cockatiel (*Nymphicus hollandicus*)

⬤ 30 cm (12 in)   ⬤ 6 eggs   ⬤ 18 days
⬤ 28 days   ⬤ 42 days

A native of Australia, the cockatiel has been known in Europe since the 1840s. Quiet and gentle by nature, cockatiels can be housed in colonies or in the company of other non aggressive birds such as finches and some softbills. They are fairly hardy, and are easy to care for.

Cockatiels also make excellent pets in the home, but it is best to start out with a youngster of about 10 weeks old. Both sexes settle well, but a cock may turn out to be the better mimic.

Grey cockatiel cock

Cockatiels can be allowed to breed from the age of 12 months. Unusually among parrots, both sexes share the task of incubation, with the cock bird sitting on the eggs during the day.

Colour forms of the cockatiel are now well established. These include a stunning, pale lemon-yellow lutino form; pied cockatiels, with highly variable areas of dark and light plumage; and the cinnamon, whose grey plumage has a warm brownish hue. Among the recent additions to the colours is a pure snow-white albino. There is also a white-faced variant, which lacks the yellow facial coloration and the orange cheek patches; and an unusual pearl variety, with pale iridescent markings that are most in evidence over the wings.

Australian grass parakeets
(*Neophema* species)

⬤ 20 cm (8 in)   ⬤ 6 eggs
⬤ 19 days   ⬤ 28 days
⬤ 49 days

Justifiably popular as aviary occupants but rather too nervous to settle well as pets in the home, this group of parakeets is ideal for back-garden aviaries in urban surroundings because their calls are not disturbing, nor do they require particularly spacious flights. Another advantage is that they can usually be sexed visually. These birds tend to be most active at dusk.

Among the most popular of the grass parakeets are the turquoisine (*N. pulchella*), a variety whose cock bird has red wing patches; and the splendid (*N. splendida*), also known as the scarlet-chested because of the

Mealy rosella

prominent area of red feathering on the cock's breast. A species with highly distinctive coloration is Bourke's grass parakeet (*N. bourkii*), with its pale pinkish underparts – a feature that has been developed in the rosa mutation.

Rosellas (*Platycercus* species)

⬤ 25–36 cm (10–14 in)   ⬤ 5–7 eggs
⬤ 21 days   ⬤ 35 days   ⬤ 50 days

These parakeets, which occur only in Australia, are sometimes known as broadtails because their long tail feathers do not taper towards the tips. They can also be recognized by the scalloped markings over their backs and wings. Caring for these birds is straightforward, although, as with other Australian species, their habit of foraging for food on the ground leaves them vulnerable to parasitic roundworms; you should therefore de-worm all new birds before introducing them to their permanent aviary quarters (see also pages 112–13).

Two of the most popular rosellas are the golden-mantled, or eastern (*P. eximius*), with its red head and underparts; and the stunning crimson rosella, also called Pennant's parakeet (*P. elegans*). Visual sexing of these birds can be difficult, although the cocks are generally more brightly coloured. The western rosella, or Stanley's parakeet (*P. icterotis*), is the smallest member of this group of eight species.

Other Australian parakeets

Some other parakeets from Australia that may be available include members of the *Psephotus* and *Polytelis* species.

Psephotus species

🔵 27 cm (11 in)   ⊕ 4–6 eggs   🕐 19 days
🌑 42 days   ◐ 63 days

Together with some other *Psephotus* species, such as the many-coloured (*P. varius*), the red-rumped parakeet (*P. haematonotus*) is fairly commonly seen in aviculture. A pair of these birds will breed freely, but you must remove the young from the aviary as soon as possible; this is because they may be attacked by the cock bird, which is likely to be wishing to nest again.

Polytelis species

🔵 40–45 cm (16–18 in)   ⊕ 4–5 eggs
🕐 19 days   🌑 42 days   ◐ 63 days

The Princess of Wales's parakeet (*Polytelis alexandrae*) is ranked as one of the most beautiful of all Australian species because of its beautiful pastel coloration. The hen has a greyish head. Another member of this group, also well represented in aviculture, is the slim and elegant barraband parakeet (*P. swainsonii*); the cock bird is easily distinguishable by its yellow face.

Conures

🔵 25–46 cm (10–18 in)   ⊕ 3–8 eggs
🕐 26 days   🌑 49–56 days   ◐ 60–86 days

The unusual name of these parakeets comes from *Conurus*, an old scientific description. They are found in Central and South America. Members of the *Aratinga* genus include the beautiful sun conure (*A. solistalis*), which is now widely bred. Hand-reared chicks can make excellent pets (at this stage they are duller in coloration than the adult birds). Most other *Aratinga* conures are predominantly green, sometimes with red markings. They can be destructive and fairly noisy birds.

The scaly-breasted conures form a significantly quieter group, which includes the widely bred maroon-bellied conure (*Pyrrhura frontalis*). The markings

on the chest give this bird its name; the rest of the plumage is predominantly green. Like other conures, it cannot be sexed visually. However, a true pair will breed readily, and their calls are unlikely to cause offence in urban surroundings. In contrast, the large, noisy Patagonian conure (*Cyanoliseus patagonus*) should be avoided in a town.

Brotogeris parakeets

🔵 18–23 cm (7–9 in)   ⊕ 4 eggs
🕐 26 days   🌑 49 days   ◐ 66 days

These species all have a decidedly dumpy shape, with relatively short tail feathers. Predominantly green in coloration, the group includes the tovi parakeet (*B. jugularis*) and the canary-winged parakeet (*B. versicolorus*), which is recognizable by its bright yellow wing markings. Young birds can develop into excellent companions but may become jealous of other pets, such as dogs, and will express their feelings by screeching loudly; they can also be very destructive. A pair of these birds may prove more reluctant to nest than other parakeets, but it may help to place their nest box (which will be used regularly for roosting) in a shaded part of the aviary.

Psittaculid parakeets

🔵 33–58 cm (13–23 in)   ⊕ 3–5 eggs
🕐 21 days   🌑 35 days   ◐ 65 days

Members of this genus have been kept in captivity for thousands of years. The ring-necked parakeet (*P. krameri*) was known and highly prized by the Romans, who housed these birds in cages decorated with precious materials such as tortoiseshell. Later, Indian princes cherished the rare blue and lutino mutations, which are common in aviculture today. Other colours – including greys and an albino form of the ring-neck parakeet – have also been bred. As with the Alexandrine parakeet (*P. eupatria*), it takes about three years for a cock bird to acquire its distinctive collar.

The plum-headed parakeet (*P. cyanocephala*) is another old

Alexandrines: hen (left) and cock (right)

favourite. The sexes are distinguished by the head colouring, although all young birds have grey plumage here and so tend to resemble adult hens. The calls of the plum-head are more musical than those of its larger relatives. These parakeets are best kept in an aviary.

Sun conure

Parrots and cockatoos

African grey parrot

Many members of this group are popular pets, with hand-reared chicks often developing into talented mimics. However, it is important to realize that the larger species can be as demanding as young children in terms of the care they require, especially when kept on their own. If a pet parrot becomes bored it will turn noisy and destructive, and may also start to pluck its feathers – behaviour which rapidly becomes habitual. A smaller species – such as the Senegal parrot – may therefore be a better choice if you are inexperienced, as it will be easier to manage. Its calls are also unlikely to cause complaints from neighbours, in contrast to those of a large parrot.

African grey parrot
(*Psittacus erithacus*)

⬤ 35 cm (14 in)　#️⃣ 3–4 eggs　🕐 28 days
🥚 90 days　🔷 120 days

The African grey parrot is probably the most talented of all avian mimics, although the birds can be shy in front of strangers. The distinctive coloration is predominantly grey with a red tail. A smaller, duller subspecies, called the Timneh grey parrot (*P.e. timneh*), is easily identified by its maroon tail feathers. Once acclimatized to aviary surroundings, grey parrots are fairly hardy birds.

You should only choose a mature grey parrot for breeding, not as a pet, because its temperament will become unpredictable and it is likely to be very destructive (a young bird is recognizable by its dark irises, whereas these are pale yellow in an adult). Grey parrots cannot be sexed reliably by visual means. Compatibility is an important factor to achieve breeding success but, once established, the pair bond will be strong. Breeding is usually confined to the warmer months of the year, although a pair kept indoors may nest at any stage.

Amazon parrots (*Amazona* species)

⬤ 25–38 cm (10–15 in)　#️⃣ 3–4 eggs
🕐 26 days　🥚 56 days　🔷 86 days

Amazon parrots are sometimes referred to as green parrots, because this is the dominant colour in the plumage of many species. They are found from the southern border of the USA southwards to Argentina, with the rarest of the 26 species occurring on individual islands in the Caribbean.

The blue-fronted Amazon (*A. aestiva*) has been a popular pet for many years. Hand-reared chicks can be identified by their dark eyes, as can other young Amazons. They have an area of blue plumage which is variable in extent above the nostrils, and a bright red area on the wings. The orange-winged Amazon (*A. amazonica*) is similar but smaller. It has a horn-coloured rather than a black bill, and characteristic orange rather than red wing markings.

The yellow-fronted Amazon (*A. ochrocephala*) shows the greatest variation in appearance. In some cases the yellow is restricted to a small area above the bill, while on other birds it covers the entire head. Other species which may be available include the white-fronted (*A. albifrons*) – one of the smallest members of the group – and the much larger and noisy mealy Amazon (*A. farinosa*).

Unfortunately, most Amazons are prone to screeching – particularly early in the morning and at dusk – which can become tiresome for anyone living at close range. However, covering the parrot's quarters at these times may help to curb the behaviour. Amazons are reasonably talented mimics, but less so than the African grey parrot.

Pionus parrots

⬤ 27.5–30 cm (11–12 in)　#️⃣ 3–5 eggs
🕐 26 days　🥚 56 days　🔷 86 days

These birds are likely to prove better pets than Amazon parrots, as they are quieter and have more trustworthy temperaments as they mature; they are also less destructive. The species that you are most likely to find for sale are the blue-headed (*P. menstruus*) and Maximilian's (*P. maximiliani*). Both are mainly dark green, with chicks that are less colourful than the adults. As in the case of the Amazon parrots, these birds cannot be sexed visually.

Macaws

⬤ 30–91 cm (12–36 in)　#️⃣ 2–3 eggs
🕐 25–28 days　🥚 60–90 days
🔷 90–120 days

This group includes the largest members of the parrot family. Accommodating these in the home is difficult, although they can become very affectionate companions. Like grey parrots, young macaws can be identified by the dark irises in their eyes.

The so-called dwarf macaw species are mainly green in colour, although some birds – such as the yellow-collared macaw (*Ara auricollis*) – have distinctive markings. Despite their size, dwarf macaws can still have loud calls. The smallest member of the group is the Hahn's macaw (*A. nobilis*), which displays the bare facial patches that are characteristic of these parrots.

Cockatoos

⬤ 30–46 cm (12–18 in)　#️⃣ 2–4 eggs
🕐 28 days　🥚 60–84 days　🔷 90–115 days

Cockatoos are easily recognizable by their crest of feathers, which they will raise when alarmed or excited. Although hand-reared cockatoo chicks are very appealing, they are highly strung and rank among the most demanding of

Senegal parrot

Blue-headed pionus

Lesser sulphur-crested cockatoo

all parrots kept in the home. They are potentially very destructive birds – especially when they mature at about four years of age – and do not make especially good mimics.

The majority of captive species have predominantly white feathering. It is usually possible to sex adult cockatoos by their eye coloration, because the cocks have black irises while those of the hens generally appear reddish-brown when viewed in good light.

Parrotlets

- ◐ 12.5–15 cm (5–6 in) ⊕ 4–6 eggs
- ◐ 18 days ◐ 42 days ◐ 56 days

A number of the smaller-sized parrots, including the parrotlets (*Forpus* species), are more frequently kept in aviary surroundings than as household pets. However, if you are lucky enough to obtain a hand-reared youngster it should develop into a marvellous companion, although its talking abilities will be very limited.

Lovebirds

- ◐ 15 cm (6 in) ⊕ 5 eggs ◐ 23 days
- ◐ 42 days ◐ 60 days

Lovebirds are very popular among bird-keepers, and this is especially true of the peach-faced lovebird (*Agapornis roseicollis*), which has been bred in a wide spectrum of colours ranging from yellow through to greenish-blue. The creamino, which has a pale yellow

plumage, is one of the most distinctive colour varieties of lovebird.

These small parrots cannot be sexed by visual means. They can tend to be rather vicious towards one another, and for this reason they are generally kept as individual pairs in aviary surroundings. Young lovebirds kept as pets will learn a few words.

Senegal parrot
(*Poicephalus senegalus*)

- ◐ 23 cm (9 in) ⊕ 4 eggs
- ◐ 26 days ◐ 63 days
- ◐ 90 days

This parrot is slightly larger than the lovebird. It will be shy as an adult, but dark-eyed youngsters can develop into delightful pets. The Senegal's bright, orangish-yellow abdomen is offset by its grey head and green wings. It is not a noisy bird, as its calls consist mainly of a series of whistles.

Lories and lorikeets

- ◐ 18–38 cm (7–15 in) ⊕ 2 eggs
- ◐ 22–26 days ◐ 63–72 days
- ◐ 90–100 days

These rank among the most colourful of the parrots, often being vivid shades of red, blue and yellow. The sexes are similar in appearance, making visual sexing difficult, but a pair of lories or lorikeets will usually breed readily.

A young bird may make a lively companion, although its diet – which needs to be based on nectar and fruit rather than on seed – means that it is likely to be messy if kept in the home. Nectar preparations for lories and lorikeets are available in powder form, ready to mix with water. You should provide a fresh solution for the birds at least once and preferably twice daily.

125

Green-winged macaw

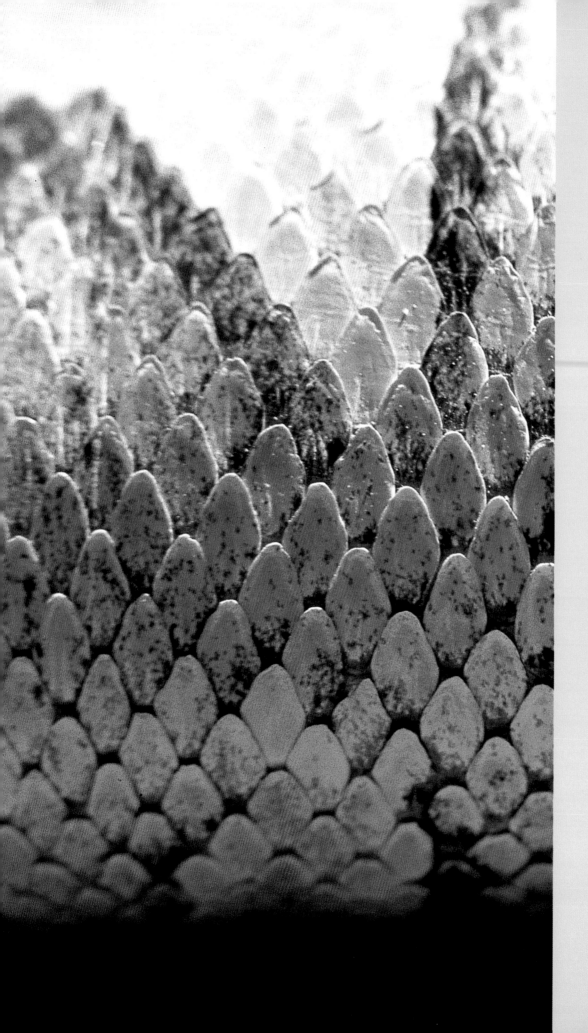

Reptiles and Amphibians

Reptiles and amphibians are collectively known as herptiles. Interest in keeping and breeding this group of creatures in the home has grown significantly in recent years, which is likely to be partly the result of changing lifestyles: as households have become smaller and more people live in urbanized areas, so the choice of suitable pets has become more limited. For instance, the demands of caring for a dog and the fact that it will not be ideally suited to town life mean that someone living alone may not feel able to keep this type of pet; while a cat, although more independent, will be at risk of road-traffic accidents, especially in urban areas. Even a pet bird demands a good deal of attention; and small mammals, although they are generally less time-consuming to care for, have the drawback for many owners of having only a short lifespan.

5

WHY KEEP REPTILES AND AMPHIBIANS?

In a world which tends towards ever-greater uniformity, the bizarre and exotic appearance of some of the creatures in this group holds an appeal for many people, and choosing them as pets has a number of advantages. Some species can become remarkably tame, and their care is quite straightforward. Indeed, in some cases – such as with snakes and toads – it may be inadvisable to feed the adult animals on a daily basis because of the long-term risk of obesity, so arranging care for them when you go on holiday should not present too many problems.

Some reptiles – such as tortoises – may even have a life expectancy exceeding our own and, provided that their environmental needs are properly met, they are unlikely to fall ill. They require no routine vaccinations, and the general cost of their care is normally much lower than that of other pets such as dogs or cats. It is also possible to breed many herptiles successfully, adding to the interest of keeping these creatures in the home.

The housing that is required for a reptile or amphibian – which is known as a vivarium – can become a focal point in a room, especially since the requirement for natural lighting to keep the occupant healthy means that plant life within the vivarium will often thrive, adding another dimension to the attraction of keeping reptiles and amphibians. However, you will need to choose your pets carefully, as not all reptiles and

amphibians require a tropical planted setting for their living quarters – a number of popular species originate from more temperate parts of the world or from desert environments, while others may readily destroy any tropical vegetation that is provided in the vivarium.

CHOOSING SUITABLE SPECIES

You will need to have a good understanding of the environmental needs of any reptile or amphibian to be able to care for it properly. For instance, the Mediterranean spur-thighed tortoise (*Testudo graeca*) can be allowed outside in temperate areas when the weather is warm and sunny, but a tropical species – such as the leopard tortoise (*Geochelone pardalis*) – will be very susceptible to chilling and so should be housed indoors. Tortoises in general form a group of creatures which can become very tame and enjoy interacting with their owners. They do seem to be able to distinguish between different people and, like other long-lived creatures, they also appear to have a memory.

In terms of appearance, lizards are the reptiles which display the greatest diversity of all. There are species which resemble modern-day mini-dinosaurs, and some are strikingly coloured. A number of lizards can become very tame – notably the green iguana (*Iguana iguana*). If you acquire one of these as a hatchling, you will even be able to exercise it out of doors on hot days using a special lead and harness.

People are either fascinated by snakes, or dislike them intensely. This field of reptile-keeping has grown greatly over recent years thanks to successful captive breeding. Many colour variants have emerged in the more free-breeding species in particular, adding to the appeal of these reptiles.

Some amphibians are also now being bred consistently, and a single spawning can result in a large number of offspring. Proximity to water remains a dominant factor in the lives of amphibians, as their skin is unable to resist desiccation effectively without it. Their reproductive biology is also tied to an aquatic environment, although only a relatively few species live entirely in water. Tree frogs, for example, will spend much of their time climbing around a vivarium, which should be designed accordingly.

Some amphibians – especially toads – can in time become surprisingly tame and will feed from your hand. Despite popular mythology, touching the wart-like swellings found on the bodies of some species will not cause you to develop warts. However, the more brightly coloured frogs – notably the 'poison-arrow' variety – are more dangerous, with their coloration serving as a warning of their toxic skin secretions. As a precaution, you should only handle these creatures while wearing disposable gloves. This also applies to some members of the other amphibian grouping – newts and salamanders – although, as it is not normally necessary to handle amphibians, this is unlikely to create any problems or to spoil your enjoyment of keeping them.

Choosing and buying reptiles and amphibians

Amphibians are all fairly small – without water to support their weight, they would find it difficult to breathe on land – but reptiles can vary significantly in size. Before deciding on a particular species, you must therefore be aware of how big it could grow. For example, while an adult gecko generally measures less than 30 cm (12 in), a cute-looking green iguana hatchling of this size is likely to grow to over 1.2 m (4 ft) within two or three years. Providing adequate housing may then be problematic, as well as costly.

FARMED SPECIES

Green iguanas are one of the increasing number of reptile and amphibian species now being farmed or ranched in their countries of origin. Local people encourage the lizards to breed, then hatch the eggs in an area free from predators. Some of the resulting hatchlings may be returned to the wild, while others are sold for food or as pets. This system helps to protect both the habitat and the species themselves.

Rules governing international trade in these creatures are laid down under the Convention on International Trade in Endangered Species (CITES), which imposes strict conservation and welfare controls regarding live animals. Quotas based on field studies are also frequently used to prevent any risk of a species becoming threatened due to trade. At a local level, you should never collect herptiles unless you are certain that it is legal to do so.

STARTING OUT

If you are new to keeping herptiles it is better to choose those bred in captivity. Although these are likely to be slightly more expensive than imported stock, they should be much easier to manage and you will also have the advantage of knowing their age. There will be no need to adjust them to unfamiliar foodstuffs, nor should you have to worry greatly about parasites, which can be a major problem with imported animals. A heavy burden of parasites will cause a lack of appetite and a corresponding loss of condition, leaving the herptile more vulnerable to illness.

FEEDING HABITS

Before buying a reptile or amphibian, you will need to learn something about these creatures' different feeding requirements. For instance, many people would like to keep snakes – which are fascinating reptiles – but dislike the idea of feeding them on dead mice or rats (although it is now possible to buy special sausages for snakes, so this need no longer be a drawback).

Commercially prepared diets have also greatly simplified the care of terrapins, but amphibians generally need to be fed on invertebrates such as crickets (these are available from specialist suppliers – look in pet magazines for details). Some lizards – like tortoises – are mainly vegetarian in their feeding habits, but others are also insectivorous.

Unpleasant odours can be a problem with this group of pets, simply because of the foods that they eat. You may therefore need to give their quarters a quick clean every day, and a more thorough clean at least once a week, and this should be a consideration before you buy.

What to look for in a healthy reptile or amphibian

Check that the nostrils are free from discharge. There should be no bad odour coming from the mouth; this could indicate an infection.

The eyes should be bright and not swollen (although they will normally become cloudy in snakes before skin shedding takes place – see pages 138–9).

Make sure that the animal can move freely, and that there are no injuries to the limbs or to any of the toes.

OBTAINING REPTILES AND AMPHIBIANS

There are now specialist outlets offering reptiles and amphibians for sale, as well as all the equipment and foodstuffs you will need to keep them healthy and happy (again, look in specialist magazines for names and addresses). Some general pet stores also stock these animals, although the range on offer may be more limited.

First of all, look generally at the displays, as this will give you an idea of how the animals are being looked after. Well-lit, clean enclosures with good labelling about the occupants suggest well-run premises. Ask about any species which interests you – particularly about its origins, how long the

animals have been in stock, and whether they are feeding. This is particularly important in the case of some snakes, notably the royal or ball python (*Python regius*) and monitor lizards (*Varanus* species), which often undergo periods of fasting (see also page 149).

If you are seriously interested in buying a reptile, ask to examine it at closer quarters. This will give you the chance to inspect its condition very carefully, and also to check for external parasites (see page 138) and for any signs of bodily injury that might not otherwise be visible: for instance, snakes sometimes suffer from burns after coming into contact with a badly positioned heater in the vivarium, and can be prone to ulcers caused by bacterial infections.

SEXING

If you are hoping to breed your reptiles or amphibians, you will need to establish the sex of the animals. Amphibians should not be handled directly if possible because of their sensitive skins, so transfer them to a clear-bottomed plastic container so that you can look underneath without touching them. This is also a useful technique for sexing some lizards, such as geckos. Sexing tortoises and terrapins is reasonably straightforward, but with snakes and some lizards an internal probe will be needed (see page 136), and this is where a specialist outlet or a breeder will probably be more helpful than a general pet store.

YOUNG OR OLD?

If you have a choice it may be better to start with young stock rather than with adults, whose age will probably be unknown. Younger animals will be likely to settle in more quickly than adults, and you may be able to tame them more easily.

External parasites such as mites and ticks may be visible on the skin of a reptile, and will need to be treated.

Look for any signs of skin damage, especially in amphibians, as this can lead to a fatal infection.

The body should be plump, not thin.

Housing and equipment

(Above) This typical vivarium is housing a leopard gecko. Note the heat source (an infrared dull-emitter bulb), and the retreat provided for the gecko to escape from public view.

(Right) Here, an aquatic set-up is used to house a Japanese fire-bellied newt; plants and rocks provide it with adequate cover.

The type of accommodation that you need will largely depend on the type of reptile or amphibian that appeals to you, although the equipment used for heating and lighting is fairly standard for all these creatures. Equipment suitable for housing is available from most pet stores, especially from those specializing in herptiles.

A VIVARIUM

In many cases you will be able to convert an unused glass aquarium successfully, although – especially with larger reptiles – a vivarium made from melamine-fronted chipboard or a similar easy-to-clean material may be better. It is best to start with a large enclosure even for a hatchling, because this will be cheaper in the long term, as well as being less disturbing for the animal.

If you use an aquarium, you will need to fit it with a suitable vivarium lid containing a ventilation panel, space for lighting and a sliding Perspex panel for access. The lid should fit snugly around the sides of the aquarium (lids are manufactured to correspond with the standard aquarium sizes). A purpose-built vivarium is likely to have ventilation panels already incorporated into the structure, with access given via a sliding front or through a door in the side. The box-like structure of such a unit can give nervous species a greater sense of security.

In either case, you must keep the access points of your vivarium securely closed to prevent any escapes. Snakes in particular are very adept at wriggling through even narrow openings.

Heating

You can provide heating within the vivarium in several ways. One option is to fit a special infrared dull-emitter bulb – which will give off heat rather than light – to the roof of the vivarium. For desert-dwelling reptiles, you can also create an additional basking area using a spot lamp. However, you should only keep this on during the day so that the temperature can drop back at night, to reflect what would happen in the reptiles' native environment.

A bulb or lamp in the vivarium can present a risk to snakes and climbing creatures such as geckos because they could be burned, so with these animals it is essential to place suitable screening around the heat source. Many people use wire-mesh boxes, or you could buy a heating pad. This acts rather like a radiator when attached to the back of a vivarium, and will warm the interior while remaining safely out of the occupants' reach. Heating pads are produced in various sizes, and can also be fitted under a tank if required. You should link your pad to a thermostat to regulate the temperature within the required range, while a digital thermometer at the front of the unit will provide a visual indication of the internal temperature.

Heating pads are equally useful for aquatic or semi-aquatic herptiles such as terrapins, and will warm the air space in the vivarium as well as the water. Another way of heating the water is with a heaterstat unit (sold for use with aquaria), consisting of a combined heater and thermostat. Always ensure that this is kept submerged when it is in operation.

Partitioning

If you plan to keep semi-aquatic herptiles you will need to install a suitable partition in the vivarium to provide an area of 'dry land'. A piece of either Perspex or glass – held securely in position at the appropriate height with aquarium sealant –

is ideal, but be sure to smooth off the top so that the animals can move back and forth with no risk of injury. Fill the dry area with coarse aquarium gravel, and include some rocks to provide easy access from the water out on to the land. A power filter will keep the water clean.

Lighting

You will need to provide lighting in the lid of the vivarium. Ordinary incandescent bulbs emit heat as well as light, but their spectrum of light – especially the output of ultra-violet light – is not the same as sunlight. Basking reptiles in particular, including many lizards and terrapins, need exposure to this type of light if they are to stay healthy and maintain a sufficient level of vitamin D_3, so you must fit special lighting in their quarters in the form of fluorescent tubes. Be sure to replace these as specified by the manufacturer, as their ultra-violet output will decline to a level of no significance before the tube actually ceases to work.

Decor

Decor in the vivarium is important, not only to make it look attractive but also to give the occupants a sense of security. At the same time, you must balance this with the need to be able to clean the interior easily.

For tortoises, it is best to provide a floor covering such as paper, which will be convenient to change; you should also include a retreat so that they can escape from public view. Other herbivorous reptiles such as green iguanas will also have to be kept in fairly bare surroundings, as they are likely to consume any plants. However, as they are arboreal creatures you should supply them with branches for climbing. Cut these to size and then fix them firmly in place in the vivarium, using a silicone sealant if necessary (bearing in mind that this can make cleaning rather awkward).

If you include any other types of decoration – particularly stones – set them firmly in place to avoid any risk of injury. Placing cork bark on the floor provides a useful retreat for smaller lizards and amphibians; the latter will also burrow readily

into damp moss, which you should always make available for them. Other types of substrate for amphibians are sold by specialist outlets.

You can also use a variety of additional materials for lining the floor of your vivarium. Whatever you choose, placing a layer of paper on the base will make cleaning easier. Bark chips are suitable for many species. Avoid using sand for desert reptiles, as this can stick to their food and may cause internal problems – notably compaction within the gut. In addition, never use sharp cacti, as these could injure your hands, quite apart from the reptiles themselves. If you do not wish to grow plants within your vivarium, you will be able to buy realistic substitutes which are hygienic and easy to clean.

Positioning a vivarium

Windows: If placed in direct sunlight, the temperature inside the vivarium could rise to a fatal level.

Cats: These may try to catch lizards, so keep them well away.

Lamps: Do not position these close to the vivarium, as they are likely to increase its temperature.

Household sprays: These could well be dangerous to reptiles and amphibians, so never use them in the same room.

Weight: A vivarium can be heavy and must sit on a strong base. Polystyrene placed under it will absorb unevenness and prevent leaks of water.

Central heating: Do not site the vivarium close to a radiator, as this is very likely to affect its internal temperature and also to lower the relative humidity.

Long, trailing flexes: These are dangerous, so position the vivarium close to a power point.

131

(Below) Provide adequate climbing opportunities in the vivarium for arboreal reptiles such as day geckos (see page 147), checking that all items are firmly positioned so that they cannot be dislodged and cause any injury to the occupants.

Feeding

Feeding reptiles and amphibians has become considerably easier in recent years, thanks to the increased availability of prepared foods. These creatures can be broadly divided into three categories on the basis of their dietary requirements: herbivores (plant eaters); carnivores (meat eaters) and insectivores (insect eaters).

HERBIVORES

The herbivorous reptiles include almost all of the tortoises and some lizards. It is important to provide adequate variety in the diet of these creatures, or nutritional deficiencies will quickly arise. A reptile that is suffering from health problems will be reluctant to eat, and this will exacerbate any deficiencies.

Some green foods, such as dandelion leaves and cress, are of greater value than others: for instance, ordinary lettuce consists mainly of water and has little fibre. If you gather green food outside the confines of your garden, be sure that it has not been subjected to chemical sprays. It is much better to cultivate your own supplies if possible. You can also easily grow other items such as beansprouts at home, but check that there are no moulds present on these foods, as this could threaten the health of your pets.

Wash all leaves thoroughly and chop them up before offering them to the reptiles in a ceramic container which cannot be tipped over easily (providing smaller pieces of food will lessen the likelihood of pieces being dragged out over the floor of the vivarium). You must supply adequate, fresh drinking water at all times, also in a suitable container which cannot be tipped over.

Breeders and pet stores often recommend using a special vitamin-and mineral-supplement for reptiles, and you can easily administer this by sprinkling it over food. There are also complete foods available in pelleted or canned form for some herbivorous reptiles, notably iguanas. These should be used according to the instructions on their packaging, and do not normally require extra supplementation – in fact, this can be harmful to the reptiles' health.

CARNIVORES

Snakes and some lizards, as well as terrapins, are carnivorous in their feeding habits. However, you should never offer a snake live rodents

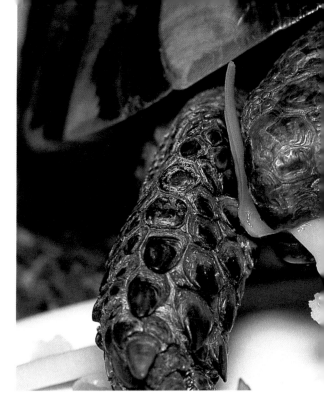

Tortoises will eat a wide range of vegetable matter, although they often ignore grass.

as prey: not only may this be illegal but it can also be dangerous, as the reptile may be attacked by its supposed quarry. Instead, you should buy frozen animal foods of suitable size from specialist suppliers, and then thaw them out as and when you need them. Mice of various sizes – from young so-called 'pinkies' upwards – are a popular choice, although dead gerbils may be favoured by royal or ball pythons (*Python regius*), which can be temperamental feeders. Snakes which would naturally hunt in the tree-tops will often prefer to eat dead day-old chicks.

Offering whole animals to these reptiles can be off-putting, but doing so will provide them with a relatively balanced diet in most cases. However, a recent breakthrough has been the development of special sausage-like foods formulated to meet a snake's nutritional requirements, which will prevent the need for you to handle and store dead creatures in your freezer.

Special diets of this type have also proved very useful for fish-eating snakes, such as the popular garter and ribbon snakes (*Thamnophis* species). These are particularly susceptible to dietary problems if fed entirely on raw fish, because of the presence of an enzyme known as thiaminase which destroys vitamin B_1; convulsions and ultimately death are likely to be the result. If you do feed fish you must cook it gently to inactivate the thiaminase enzyme, and allow it to cool before offering it to your snake. It may also be advisable to give a B-vitamin supplement.

132

The growth of interest in keeping herptiles has led to specialist diets being produced for them. This canned food is intended for carnivorous lizards, and contains all the ingredients required to keep them healthy; feeding a prepared diet will also eliminate the risk of your pet contracting *Salmonella* bacteria from its food.

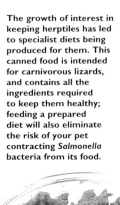

INSECTIVORES

Many lizards, as well as amphibians, feed on invertebrates. Creatures such as crickets are available from specialist breeders and suppliers, or you could breed your own if you wish, housing these in the type of accommodation that is recommended for invertebrates (see pages 178–9).

Crickets are particularly useful for feeding because they can be obtained in various sizes to suit different purposes: for example, hatchlings are ideal for young amphibians, while larger lizards will eat adult crickets. Special powders known as 'balancers' will correct any nutritional

shortcomings in the crickets; these are also suitable for the few insectivorous snakes which need to be fed on crickets. Use the powders as instructed on the packaging. The usual method is to sprinkle them over the insects, although it is also possible to feed the crickets themselves on a supplemented diet as an alternative. Chilling the crickets will make them easier to handle, and should stop them from hopping out at the wrong moment and escaping into your home. Avoid offering too many of the insects at once, as they will not all be eaten and could then escape.

Larger amphibians can also eat mealworms (*Tenebrio molitor*), but it is better to offer the mini-mealworms which will be more digestible. However, these are low in certain key ingredients such as vitamin A, and so do not constitute a balanced diet; they may also be difficult to digest because of their harder outer casing of chitin.

Soft-bodied invertebrates – such as waxmoth larvae – are available from specialist suppliers, as are whiteworm (*Enchytraeus*) in culture packs. Whiteworm will multiply readily in a container filled with damp compost, if regularly supplied with bread soaked in milk. Kept in a warm place, it will take about a month for the worms to multiply to a harvestable quantity. Remove them with a teaspoon and then float them in a saucer of water to separate them from the substrate.

Crickets are very useful for feeding, and you can easily breed your own if you wish. They range in size from hatchlings (top), which would be suitable for offering to young amphibians, to adult crickets (above), which you could feed to larger lizards.

133

FEEDING TERRAPINS

Terrapins will eat meat, but this is not advisable for three reasons. Meat will rapidly pollute the water, making the tank smell; there is a risk of introducing harmful bacteria (including *Salmonella*, present in raw meat); and finally, if meat is fed as the sole diet, vitamin and mineral deficiencies will soon arise. Instead, offer terrapins a complete prepared diet – in the form of food sticks (shown here) or pellets – which will contain all the ingredients to keep them healthy.

General care

When taking your herptiles home, the temperature is likely to be lower than that at which they have been kept. Although a slight fall-off will not be harmful, you must put them back in a suitably warm environment as soon as possible, as chilling will increase the risk of them falling ill. If the weather is cold, keep the heater on in your car, and when you reach home transfer the herptiles to their quarters without delay, switching on the heating at this point so that they are able to warm up again gradually.

Handling herptiles is relatively straightforward, but never grasp a lizard – such as this leopard gecko – by its tail, as it could snap off.

CARRIERS

A snake is best transported in a light canvas bag, which admits air through the fibres, tightly tied to prevent escape and placed in a cardboard box. Using this method, when you reach home you will simply need to undo the tie and place the bag in the vivarium, leaving the snake to emerge in its own time.

You can transport a large tortoise in a cardboard box with airholes in the lid. Line the base of the box well with paper to absorb any excreted liquid: handling and the unfamiliar sensations of travelling often elicit this response, and if the cardboard were to become wet the base could give way.

Small terrapins are usually sold in ventilated plastic containers with secure lids, although larger individuals can be transported like tortoises. Amphibians and small lizards are often carried like this; bigger lizards may have to be moved like snakes.

Carry herptiles in a covered container to prevent escapes.

HANDLING

As with any pets, handling reptiles and amphibians with great care is vital to avoid injury, either to the animal or to yourself.

Chelonians

It is a relatively simple matter to lift a chelonian out of its travelling container and into a vivarium. However, take care because, although the reptiles are unlikely to bite and will probably withdraw into their shells, they may well struggle quite fiercely with their hindlegs. Placing one hand on the top of the shell mid-way down the body, and supporting it from beneath with your other hand, is usually safer than holding the shell at the rear as is sometimes advocated. The shell itself is rather like a fingernail, and is likely to bleed if injured.

Snakes

Snakes can also be badly injured by careless handling. The aim here is to restrain the reptile's head and allow its body to curl around your other hand, providing support. Never grip a snake's body tightly as this is likely to result in internal bruising which, if severe, could even be fatal within a week or so.

Lizards

A number of lizards have evolved a unique means of protecting themselves from predators, using a detachable and often brightly coloured tail. The predator aims to seize this part of the body, but this will cause the tail to break away with minimum blood loss and twitch on the ground, diverting the predator's attention and allowing the lizard to escape. Stub-tailed lizards are sometimes available to buy, usually much more cheaply than their fully tailed relatives. In time the tail may re-grow, although it is likely to be a little shorter and a slightly different colour.

Wear a pair of disposable gloves when handling amphibians, as they often have toxic secretions in their skin. If at any time you have to handle them and do not have gloves available, wet your hands first, as dry hands may damage their sensitive skin and leave them at greater risk of infection.

Dropping part of the tail can be the only way of escaping from a predator. Stub-tailed lizards are occasionally available quite cheaply from pet stores or breeders.

of illness developing in reptiles or amphibians will depend to some extent on how many infective organisms are present in their environment, so good management depends on regular cleaning – even if the environment does not appear to be grossly contaminated. Only buy disinfectants produced specifically for use with herptiles (others could be toxic), and follow the instructions on the packaging very carefully.

(Below) When catching an aquatic amphibian, such as the Hong Kong newt (*Paramesotriton hongkongensis*) shown here, remove the decor from the tank first so that you can manoeuvre the net easily. Then carefully scoop up the amphibian, placing your hand over the net to prevent escape, and transfer your pet to a ventilated plastic carrier lined with sheets of damp paper towelling.

Always handle a lizard very carefully to avoid injuring the tail. Aim to restrain the front of its body by placing your fingers on either side of the head. This will prevent the lizard from biting, but watch its claws, as those of large lizards are often sharp. Use your other hand to restrain the remainder of the body.

Amphibians

It is best not to handle amphibians directly if possible, but if you have to do so you must wear disposable gloves as a precaution, since a number of species produce toxic skin secretions. Make sure, too, that your hands are wet: this will be less likely to injure an amphibian's sensitive skin covering, which would allow bacteria and fungi to attack its body. A net sold for fish-keeping is useful for catching amphibians easily, either in the water or on land; again, you must wet the material beforehand.

CLEANING

Tortoises and terrapins are likely to need their quarters cleaned more regularly than other herptiles (at least two or three times a week under normal circumstances). With other reptiles the need for cleaning will vary depending on their size, on how many animals are kept in the vivarium, and on whether they are breeding.

When emptying a vivarium, never suck water through a siphon tube because of the risk of swallowing dirty water; instead, use an aquarium siphon designed for the purpose. You should also change the water for less aquatic amphibians regularly, so that bacteria and other potentially harmful microbes cannot build up. The chances

135

Breeding

Breeding reptiles and amphibians will entail some additional expenditure on equipment, but it will give you a whole new dimension to your hobby and offer a unique insight into the natural world. There is considerable diversity in the reproductive habits of this particular group of creatures.

SEXING

The first potential difficulty with breeding lies in recognizing true pairs. There are visual clues in some species – such as tortoises and terrapins – where the tails of males are generally longer than those of females. Certain male lizards also have obvious femoral pores running down from the top of their legs for a variable distance, while crests and head embellishments may also serve to distinguish them from females. However, where such differences are not apparent, other methods need to be used for sexing purposes, as follows.

Probing

This sexing method must be carried out carefully to prevent any internal injury to the reptile. In this procedure a probe (these are available in different sizes) is lubricated and gently inserted into the vent, towards the tail. In a male snake or lizard the probe will penetrate further than in the female, passing into the copulatory organ known as the hemipenes.

If probing is not possible for any reason, you may be able to distinguish between the sexes by the fact that the tail of the female is slightly shorter and less broad when compared with that of the male.

Seasonal changes

These can be observed in the appearance of some amphibians. For example, male newts often develop crests, while male toads show swellings – called nuptial pads – on their feet which help them to clasp females during mating. The cloacal region at the base of the tail swells in male newts and salamanders, providing another means of distinguishing between the sexes at the onset of the breeding season.

MANAGEMENT FOR BREEDING

A number of different stimuli can be significant in triggering reproductive activity. One of the most significant of these in herptiles from subtropical and temperate areas especially is exposure to a relatively low temperature, to mimic the effects of hibernation in the wild. However, the animals must be healthy or this will affect their condition. In the case of adult snakes from temperate parts of the USA, for example, you should allow the temperature in their quarters to fall to 13°C (55°F). You must withhold food beforehand, or this could putrefy in the snake's gut, but leave out water to prevent dehydration. Use the same type of management with amphibians from this part of the world; mating and egg-laying will then occur once they emerge from hibernation in the spring.

With garter or ribbon snakes, it may help to house a female in the company of several males, as this also appears to increase the likelihood of successful breeding.

MATING AND EGG-LAYING

Mating may sometimes appear to be an aggressive encounter, especially with chelonians. The male will hit the female's shell repeatedly from the rear and, if she is not co-operative, will snap at her legs as well to stop her moving away from him. A male terrapin will often fan its front legs to create a slight current in the water and may bite the female's neck, maintaining his grip during mating (this rarely results in any injury).

With chelonians, mating prior to egg-laying is not always necessary. Females may lay fertile eggs often some years after their last mating, ensuring that solitary species can continue to reproduce even in the absence of a mate.

The majority of herptiles reproduce by means of eggs, although a few species – such as the boiid snakes and lizards such as the slow worm (*Anguis fragilis*) – give birth to live young. The method of egg-laying depends very much on the species concerned, as does the number of eggs that will be produced. Whereas geckos tend to lay just two eggs, often glued to the side of their quarters, other lizards such as skinks will bury them in the ground (you should provide a suitable container for this).

A female tortoise (below) typically has a shorter tail than the male (bottom). The underside of the male's shell may also be slightly concave.

136

The male tortoise has femoral pores: these are the scales with pores extending down the top part of each hindleg, roughly corresponding to the line of the femur.

This axolotl egg is on the point of hatching.

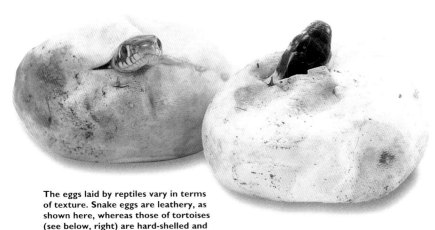

The eggs laid by reptiles vary in terms of texture. Snake eggs are leathery, as shown here, whereas those of tortoises (see below, right) are hard-shelled and have a similar feel to chicken eggs.

Prior to laying the female will usually swell with her eggs, so it is not difficult to recognize when laying has occurred (i.e., when this bulge disappears). Detecting egg-laying can be more problematical with chelonians, but increased restlessness on the part of the female is a likely sign of impending egg-laying activity, before she excavates her nest.

HATCHING AND REARING REPTILES

It is usually best to remove the eggs to separate quarters so that they can be hatched safely, although, among the snakes, female pythons will incubate their own brood by curling around their eggs. You can set up a simple incubator in a spare vivarium.

The most important aspect of hatching reptilian eggs is to avoid turning them (in marked contrast to the situation with birds). The eggs will need to be kept warm, at a temperature of between 28–30°C (82–86°F), and at a relative humidity (measured with a hygrometer) of approximately 75–80 per cent.

There is no set incubation period, so do not be in too much of a hurry to discard unhatched eggs. The outer shell may become discoloured, but this is not necessarily a sign that the egg will fail to hatch; however, in the case of eggs with parchment (leathery) shells, if the shell starts to shrivel it will be a warning of low humidity in the environment.

Rearing young reptiles is relatively simple. However, they are less able than adults to withstand temperature extremes, so it is not necessarily a good idea to hibernate young snakes or tortoises. The food that you offer should be of a suitable size. Some young snakes may be reluctant to feed on pinkies (young mice) at first, so you may need to force-feed them (this involves macerating the pinkies and feeding them with a special pump – ask a breeder or supplier for advice on how to do this). All snakes will only start to eat once they have moulted for the first time, soon after they have hatched (see also pages 138–9).

You will need to pay particular attention to the lighting in vivaria housing young lizards, tortoises and terrapins, as these animals will be most at risk of suffering from a deficiency of vitamin D_3 (see page 131). It may also be advantageous to provide a vitamin-and-mineral supplement at this stage. If you are in any doubt, seek advice from a vet.

REARING AMPHIBIANS

Amphibians' spawn will hatch more rapidly in relatively warm water, lessening the risk of fungal attack. The tadpoles will feed on their yolk-sac reserves at first, before they become free swimming, and will then start to eat flake fish food, which you should powder between your fingers. It is critical to avoid overfeeding so as not to pollute the water, so do not provide more food than the animals will eat at once.

Changing the water regularly and dividing the young tadpoles into smaller groups as they grow will be vital. Their hind limbs usually start to develop first, and their tails will shrink as they prepare to emerge on to dry land. Provide suitable rockwork in the water so that the young amphibians can start to clamber out here and use their lungs.

The young tortoise cuts its way out of its tough shell using a special projection called an egg tooth, located on its nose; this sloughs off after hatching. A trace of the tortoise's yolk sac, which nourished it through incubation, is likely to remain on its underside, but will soon disappear.

The milky coloration of the eye shows that this snake is about to shed its skin.

Health care

Selecting healthy stock initially is important, and one good indicator of health is that a reptile or amphibian which is eating is unlikely to be ill. While the cause of loss of appetite may be dehydration – in a tortoise, for example – it could equally be something more sinister. Mouth rot is relatively common in tortoises and snakes which have not been eating regularly, and can also prove to be a reason for continued refusal of food. An unpleasant odour may be detected close to the mouth and, when the jaws are parted, a whitish growth will be apparent within the oral cavity. Do not pick off pieces, but seek veterinary advice. Mouth rot is usually the result of a bacterial infection and can be treated successfully, provided that the reptile is not in a seriously weakened state. Careful force-feeding – based on your vet's advice – may then be necessary for a period.

EXTERNAL INJURIES

Injuries around the mouth – typically on or just below the snout – may result from a reptile rubbing itself on the clear front of its vivarium. Larger lizards such as monitors seem particularly susceptible to this problem. Sticking masking tape on the front to indicate the presence of a barrier should resolve the situation and allow the injury to heal uneventfully.

PARASITES

They may not be especially obvious to you, but parasites can seriously harm the health of reptiles, depressing their appetite and leaving them vulnerable to infection.

Snake mites (Ophionyssus natricis)

These parasites are a particular hazard, as they are almost invisible to the eye and multiply rapidly in the confines of a vivarium. You are most likely to spot these mites as dark specks around a snake's head, so check this area carefully. They can spread easily, so keep newly acquired snakes separate from established stock. A drug called ivermectin (available from your vet) can be used for treating an affected snake, and you will also need to kill off mites present in the vivarium by using dichlorvos (fly) strips suspended in a fabric bag.

Ticks and mites

Ticks are much more prevalent than mites, although they are only likely to be seen in stock caught in the wild. Ticks can spread blood-borne diseases, and should be removed using the same method as for ticks on dogs (see page 60).

Worms

Various intestinal worms have been identified in reptiles, with those animals caught in the wild most likely to be affected. Typical signs are usually fairly non-specific, and include loss of appetite and general malaise. While roundworms can be a problem in any kind of reptile, tapeworms tend to be found more often in carnivorous and insectivorous species, which acquire these parasites from their prey.

Your vet will be able to screen your pets and provide treatment for such parasites if necessary. Do not use proprietary remedies sold for dogs or cats on reptiles, as these could be harmful.

SKIN SHEDDING

Snakes shed their entire skins periodically, first breaking the skin at the snout by rubbing against hard objects and then crawling out slowly, leaving the skin turned inside out. Changes can be noted up to a week or so beforehand. Firstly, the skin – including the eye covering – will turn milky or opaque, giving the snake a blind appearance. After two days the eyes and skin clear again, and finally the skin is shed.

Snakes can suffer from a range of skin parasites, such as ticks (below) and snake mites (bottom). Once eliminated, ticks are unlikely to be a problem again, but mites can invade the vivarium, so you must treat this – by thoroughly cleaning and disinfecting it – as well as the snake itself.

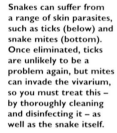

A snake sometimes has difficulty in shedding (or 'sloughing') its skin, particularly if it is in poor health or if the relative humidity is too low. Recently imported snakes are also more likely to have trouble shedding their skins than established captive-bred individuals. Pieces of old skin may stick to the snake, drying and hardening, and often the eye caps may not come off.

Skin shedding is important to the snake's health, and it is important that the old skin – especially around the head and the eye caps – is removed. If this is not done the snake may stop feeding, while the old skin over the eyes could cause an infection with a fatal outcome.

Removing old skin and eye caps

The best way of removing the old skin or eye caps is first to soak the snake by putting it in a box or bag with wet moss or saturated tissue paper for a few hours; this makes the skin soft and fairly easy to pull off. Hold the snake gently and firmly, and peel the skin carefully with a pair of tweezers or your fingers (if the skin is very soft, you may be able to rub it off). It is easiest to start at the head end and to work downwards because of the direction of the overlapping scales.

Removing eye caps must be done extremely carefully, because it is easy to take hold of the underlying tissue of the eye itself by mistake, which will cause injury. Using a pair of tweezers, very gently probe around the edge of the eye for the loose skin attached to the edge of the

transparent cover. Pulling gently at this will usually lift the edge of the cap so that you can remove it with the tweezers or your fingernails.

If you are unsure about how to remove the old skin, or you are not confident about doing so yourself, seek veterinary advice or obtain the assistance of an expert through a herpetological society or zoo.

BACTERIAL AILMENTS

These can be spread by the feeding activity of parasites such as mites, or acquired in the environment. Symptoms can vary from localized infections – such as abscesses – to sudden death if the infection is generalized. Respiratory infections are especially common in chelonians. Any symptoms of a runny nose in a tortoise, for example, need rapid attention as they may progress to a fatal pneumonia.

Salmonellosis

This is a serious infection which can arise in reptiles. There may be no obvious signs of illness, although the bacterium will be present in a reptile's droppings and can normally be identified here by clinical tests.

Salmonellosis could represent more of a potential threat to human health under these circumstances, but sensible hygienic precautions will eliminate any significant risk. Wear disposable gloves when cleaning out reptiles' quarters, and wash your hands well after handling them. Avoid tipping potentially contaminated water down the sink – use an outside drain instead.

FUNGAL AILMENTS

Aquatic species are most susceptible to these ailments, especially if they are in poor condition. Whitish strands on the skin are often indicative of this type of infection. Change the water in the vivarium frequently to lower the build-up of fungal microbes, and obtain suitable treatment from your vet. It can help to keep an affected terrapin out of the water for a period afterwards, if using a cream; for amphibians, proprietary fungus remedies sold for tropical fish are likely to be more effective.

VIRAL AILMENTS

These are becoming increasingly recognized in herptiles, although treatment is limited. However, viral papillomas – wart-like swellings, seen on green lizards (*Lacerta* species) in particular – can be treated by conventional surgery or by cryosurgery, which freezes the diseased tissue so that it sloughs off and is replaced by healthy skin.

(Top) Although this may look like a tumour, it is actually an abscess; this was later removed successfully by surgery.

(Centre) Sticky eyes are common in tortoises which are emerging from hibernation. Bathe the eyes gently with warm water and cotton wool, to ensure that your pet can see to find its food.

(Bottom) Ticks are sometimes a problem in tortoises, and will cluster on the soft parts of the animal's body.

Frogs and toads

This group of amphibians can make fascinating vivarium occupants, and are generally easy to maintain. They are often long-lived as well – many of the toads, for instance, have a life expectancy of over a decade.

African clawed frog (*Xenopus laevis*)

● 12.5 cm (5 in) ☺ the female is larger than the male, and has tiny swellings near the vent ⊕ up to 2000 eggs

The African clawed frog was originally kept in laboratories where, in the 1930s, it was used for diagnosing pregnancy in humans. This process involved injecting female *Xenopus* with urine taken from women who were thought to be pregnant. If this was the case the frogs would themselves produce eggs within a day, thus confirming the diagnosis.

African clawed frog

Although they are obviously no longer used for this purpose, *Xenopus* have since become popular as household pets – especially with children – while the hormonal spawning technique has been utilized for breeding other types of frogs and toads.

The African clawed frog is a fairly powerfully built, aquatic species which needs to be kept in a relatively large aquarium. Real plants are unlikely to thrive in the water of the aquarium because they will be continually disturbed by the frogs' swimming actions, but some of the very realistic plastic plants now available can make good alternatives if desired.

Dwarf clawed frog

Dwarf clawed frog
(*Hymenochirus boettgeri*)

● 3.5 cm (1½ in) ☺ the male has a swollen area located just behind the front legs ⊕ up to 1000 eggs

This is a similar but much smaller African species, which eats small invertebrates of suitable size. In the vivarium, dwarf clawed frogs should have a dry area where they can clamber on to a stone.

Males will call when they are in spawning condition, and the females lay their eggs at the water's surface.

Ornate horned frog
(*Ceratophrys ornatus*)

● 12.5 cm (5 in) ☺ the female has a lighter throat than the male ⊕ up to 1000 eggs

This frog is so called because of the horn-like swellings above the eyes. It has a very appealing appearance, but the large mouth indicates its predatory nature – this is not a species to be housed with others, even of its own kind. A thick floor covering is also important on the floor of the vivarium, as this is a burrowing species and will spend much of its time hidden away here. For food, you will need to provide invertebrates and pinkies for larger individuals.

Oriental fire-bellied toad
(*Bombina orientalis*)

● 5 cm (2 in) ☺ the male has nuptial pads (see page 136) ⊕ up to 300 eggs

The Oriental fire-bellied toad has distinctive reddish-orange underparts broken by black markings; its upper parts are a combination of bright green and black areas. This amphibian originates from northern parts of Asia and is very easy to maintain; it requires a semi-aquatic set-up.

Oriental fire-bellied toad

White's tree frog

Eggs will be laid among vegetation here, with the male calling loudly beforehand. In winter, allow the vivarium temperature to fall to 10°C (50°F); this will encourage breeding activity in spring when the water temperature is raised.

Less colourful but similar in their care requirements are the European fire-bellied toad (*B. bombina*) and the yellow-bellied toad (*B. variegata*).

TREE FROGS

These species spend much of their time off the ground and have specially adapted flattened tips to their toes – rather like those of the geckos (see page 147) – to enable them to climb and hold on to vertical surfaces.

White's tree frog (*Litoria caerulea*)

◑ 11.5 cm (4½ in) ♂ the female is larger and has a paler throat # up to 150 eggs

One of the most widely kept members of the group, this frog originates from parts of New Guinea and Australia. Its coloration tends to be greenish, although some individuals can have a decidedly bluish hue. Other variants – including pied frogs – are now available as the result of captive breeding.

Environmental manipulation is vital to encourage spawning – the temperature and humidity must be reduced and then raised to mimic the onset of the rainy season. You will need a tall vivarium containing branches and stout house plants for these frogs, with a container of water placed on the floor. They are generally long-lived amphibians and can be tamed quite readily.

Poison-arrow frogs
(Dendrobatidae family)

◑ 5 cm (2 in) ♂ the male has thicker front digits than the female # 5–10 eggs

These creatures are the jewels of the frog world. They occur in vivid colours ranging from red through green to blue, with great variation also apparent in the markings between individuals of the same species. They are frogs of the forest floor in the main, where they hunt small invertebrates. Warm, humid surroundings are essential for them.

The breeding habits of poison-arrow frogs are unusual because they do not spawn in water. Instead, the male carries the eggs until the tadpoles are ready to hatch and then deposits them in water: for instance, in the cup of leaves at the centre of a bromeliad plant. The female lays infertile eggs here as food, which the young then eat. In an emergency, grated egg yolk can be used for rearing.

Poison-arrow frogs have venom in their skin, so avoid handling them unless essential, and then only with gloves on.

Ranid frogs

The members of this group, which includes the common European frog (*Rana temporaria*) and the very similar leopard frog (*R. pipens*) which is native to the USA, can prove rather nervous vivarium occupants and are therefore more suitable for a garden pond. Here the females will lay huge numbers of eggs, in clumps, in the early spring, before leaving the water and spending the rest of the year on land. The tadpoles will grow fairly rapidly in pond surroundings, although they can also be reared very successfully in the home. The powdered flake food that is sold for fish makes a good diet for them.

Toads (*Bufo* species)

The toads tend to prefer a drier environment than frogs although, again, you should provide a good layer of moss for burrowing, as well as a bowl of water on the floor of the vivarium. They can be cannibalistic so you should avoid mixing large and small individuals,

Red-spotted toad

although several toads of the same size will live together without problems. This also usually provides the best way of achieving breeding success, with spawning typically occurring in water during the spring.

Bufo species vary considerably in size, from little more than 2.5 cm (1 in) in the oak toad (*B. quercicus*) to about 25 cm (10 in) in the giant or cane toad (*B. marinus*). All toads can become quite tame with patience, and feed on worms and grubs of various types.

Salamanders and newts

These amphibians can easily be identified by their rather cylindrical body shape. As a general rule salamanders tend to be less aquatic than newts, although they prefer to live in damp, moist conditions. Both can be kept quite satisfactorily at room temperature and may benefit from a slightly colder period over the winter months: perhaps as low as 7°C (45°F) in some cases.

Line the floor of the vivarium with moss, including sphagnum moss (available from florists or from pet stores specializing in herptiles). Another very useful item for a vivarium housing salamanders or newts is cork bark (also sold by pet stores), which you can simply place on top of the moss to provide a snug retreat for these rather secretive amphibians.

FEEDING SALAMANDERS AND NEWTS

Small invertebrates of a suitable size will make a good diet for newts and salamanders – worms are often particularly favoured. You should obtain the worms from a specialist supplier if possible, rather than from the garden where they could be contaminated. It is usually safer to place the worms in a damp container of grass, allowing them to void their gut contents for about three days before offering them to your amphibians.

Other food options that are commercially produced for salamanders and newts include crickets and waxworms.

Fire salamander

Fire salamander
(*Salamandra salamandra*)

◐ 25 cm (10 in) ◑ a cloacal swelling (see page 136) indicates a male # up to 75 eggs

This is one of the most popular of the salamander species. Individuals can show considerable variation in appearance: some are predominantly black with a few yellow spots, while others have vivid yellow stripes running down their bodies. This in part reflects the huge area over which they occur in the wild, from central and southern parts of Europe eastwards to Asia and south to North Africa. Some fire salamanders may even display orangish rather than yellow markings. The bright coloration of these creatures is indicative of toxic skin secretions, so always handle them with care, wearing a pair of protective gloves.

Tiger salamander

The fire salamander's breeding habits can be as diverse as its appearance. Some populations lay eggs, whereas in other groups the females give birth to live young in water. These young are larvae rather than miniature adults, and undergo metamorphosis in the water in the conventional way; it takes 12–15 weeks until they lose their gills and can emerge on to land.

Axolotl (*Ambystoma mexicanum*)

◐ 30 cm (12 in) ◑ the male has an enlarged cloacal area # up to 300 eggs

The axolotl is one of the most bizarre and fascinating of all amphibians. Like the fire salamander, it is very easy to care for and does not require heated surroundings when kept indoors.

This creature is a rare example of a phenomenon known as neoteny. This means that it can actually reproduce in its larval stage, with females laying eggs which hatch into miniature axolotls,

however, it is also important – especially in the spring – that the newts have sufficient swimming space available to them for the purposes of spawning.

The male produces a packet of sperm, called a spermatophore, which the female steers into her body via her cloacal opening. She will then lay eggs individually over a period of time, carefully hiding them under the leaves of cold-water aquatic plants such as Canadian pondweed (*Elodea canadensis*) and folding over the leaves to disguise the eggs' presence.

You will need to feed the newts well through the summer so that they can hibernate during the winter, which they will do in a frost-free locality. Mating and egg-laying will then take place in the spring. Hatching depends to some extent on the water temperature, but averages about 15 days. You should remove the adult newts at this stage so that their offspring are left unmolested.

Metamorphosis will be complete in a further 18 weeks. The tadpoles will be predatory through this period, so you should provide small daphnia and other livefood, such as whiteworm. When they leave the water, the young marbled newts will be about 5 cm (2 in) long. Lower the water level gradually, and provide easy access to dry land to facilitate their change in environment. Here, worms are often a favoured prey. It will take about three years for these newts to attain maturity.

Similar management is also suitable for most other species of newt.

Axolotl

barely 1.5 cm (½ in) long. However, if the tank's water level is lowered, the axolotl will start to metamorphose into an adult salamander. Adding iodine to the water in the tank will also trigger this process, as it does in other amphibians.

The axolotl has various other bizarre biological features, including the way it can regenerate its limbs if necessary.

There are a range of colour forms now in existence. The dark-blackish variant is the natural colour, although albinos are also well established. The

axolotl occurs in just two lakes in Mexico, where it is considered to be endangered, although it has bred in captivity on a large scale for many years and stock is readily obtainable.

These amphibians will eat worms and other live food. They are remarkably long-lived, with a life expectancy that may exceed 30 years.

Marbled newt
(*Triturus marmoratus*)

This is a colourful and easily sexed species – characteristics that have made it a popular choice with enthusiasts. As with most other newts, you should provide marbled newts with a fairly extensive area of moist land in the vivarium, rather than housing them in an aquatic set-up. Having said this,

Marbled newt

Tortoises and terrapins

Tortoises and terrapins (or freshwater turtles, as the latter are better known in the USA) are a popular group of reptiles, and have been kept as domestic pets for centuries. An early scientific study of the habits of tortoises was carried out by an English parson called the Rev. Gilbert White, whose own tortoise Timothy featured prominently in his writings.

It was thought for many years that Mediterranean tortoises could simply be allowed to wander around gardens in the summer, and to hibernate over the winter in more northerly latitudes. What happened in fact was that they frequently lost condition and died during their dormant winter period. Fortunately, the situation has changed for the better during recent years as we have gained a greater understanding of the needs of these very endearing reptiles, and, when well cared for, they can live for many years.

144

Leopard tortoise

Mediterranean spur-thighed tortoise (*Testudo graeca*) **and Hermann's tortoise** (*T. hermanni*)

⬭ 30 cm (12 in) ☯ the male has a longer tail than the female # 4–13 eggs

As our understanding of the tortoise has improved, so captive breeding has become quite commonplace, particularly with these two species. Young hatchlings are now more readily available than adult stock and will thrive in a heated vivarium, even if you do not have access to a garden during the summer months. The spur-thighed tortoise is so called because of the tubercles (small bony projections) on either side of its tail.

Both of these tortoises are primarily herbivorous, so you should offer a range of plant matter for them to eat, such as dandelion flowers and leaves, chickweed and similar items. Tomatoes may also be eaten, and it is easy to provide a vitamin-and-mineral mix by simply sprinkling the powder over the cut surfaces of the fruit.

Take care with the lighting in your vivarium to ensure an adequate production of vitamin D$_3$. This is especially important with young tortoises, so that they are able to absorb sufficient calcium and do not suffer from shell or skeletal abnormalities. You must also supply fresh drinking water, but make sure that the pot is of a suitable size so that the tortoise cannot become trapped in it.

Outdoors, you will need to house a tortoise either in a secure run (bearing in mind that tortoises do climb on occasions), or in a walled garden. You must also provide a snug wooden house

Red-eared turtle: the long claws indicate that this is a male.

as a retreat, to which the tortoise can rest when the sun is at its hottest or when the weather turns unexpectedly wet. Dampness can often lead to respiratory ailments, so do not leave a tortoise outdoors under these conditions. Hatchlings are especially vulnerable to bad weather.

Leopard tortoise
(*Geochelone pardalis*)

⬭ 70 cm (28 in) ☯ the male has a longer tail than the female # 4–15 eggs

Tropical tortoises are occasionally available from suppliers. In temperate regions these need to be housed in vivarium surroundings rather than being allowed to wander outdoors, unless the weather is very warm.

The leopard tortoise often has attractive yellowish and brownish-black shell markings, although some individuals are more heavily marked on the upper portion of the shell (known as the carapace) than others. This species is primarily herbivorous in its feeding habits and can grow to a large size. A female is likely to be mature when she reaches about 38 cm (15 in). The hatching period is very variable, and may extend from three to nine months.

Bell's hingeback tortoise
(*Kinixys belliana*)

◐ 20 cm (8 in) ⚥ the male has a longer tail than the female # 3–4 eggs

Hingeback tortoises are found in Africa; they occur more in areas of forest than on the plains, and so tend to be more frugivorous (fruit-eating) in their feeding requirements. The species is so called because of the movable hinge which can be used to close the shell around its hind limbs at any time if the tortoise feels threatened. Hingebacks need fairly humid surroundings in order to thrive, as well as a water bowl in which they can immerse themselves.

Bell's hingeback is the most commonly seen example of the species. These tortoises can vary greatly in coloration, and some individuals have plain shells while others are variegated.

Common box tortoise
(*Terrapene carolina*)

◐ 13 cm (5 in) ⚥ the male usually has redder eyes than the female # 3–7 eggs

This tortoise (or turtle) is a native of the USA. Hinges positioned at the front and rear of the shell allow it to seal itself in from any perceived danger.

Markings on the shell can be highly variable from one individual to another.

Common box tortoises are relatively easy to maintain, although they are far more insectivorous in their feeding habits than true tortoises. A diet based on a complete food sold for terrapins, combined with greenstuff, tomatoes and some fruit – such as blackberries when they are in season – will be required. Access to a bowl of water for bathing purposes is also important; again, you must ensure that this is of a suitable size, so that the tortoise cannot become trapped in it.

These chelonians prefer to live in relatively shaded conditions, and will hibernate in winter. Mating takes place soon after the tortoises emerge from hibernation in spring, with the incubation period lasting for up to three months.

Red-eared turtle
(*Chrysemys scripta elegans*)

◐ 30 cm (12 in) ⚥ the male has long front claws # 8–12 eggs

This turtle is bred on farms in the south-east USA and elsewhere in the world in large numbers, and is the most widely kept of all the freshwater chelonians. The distinctive red flash behind the eyes serves as an identifying feature; the carapace (the upper portion of the shell) is predominantly green, with some lighter markings which fade as the turtle grows older.

It is not a good idea to rely on raw meat, offal or fish as food for a red-eared turtle as, inevitably, it will develop signs of nutritional deficiencies on this diet unless careful supplementation is given. Typical indicators are swollen eyes (associated with vitamin A deficiency) and a soft shell (indicating a mineral imbalance or a shortage of vitamin D_3). To prevent this, give either special food sticks or pellets containing all the necessary ingredients to keep these reptiles in good health.

The red-eared turtle's alternative name of red-eared slider comes from its habit of regularly emerging from water to sun itself on land, so you must incorporate suitable facilities to allow for this into your vivarium. As the

(Top) Bell's hingeback tortoise
(Above) Map turtle

turtles grow, they will require suitably spacious accommodation. The female will bury her eggs on land; these should start to hatch after about 13 weeks.

Map turtle (*Graptemys geographica*)

◐ up to 23 cm (9 in) ⚥ the male only grows to about half the size of the female # 8–13 eggs

The map turtle is similar to the red-eared turtle in its general care and feeding requirements. The markings on the carapaces (upper shells) of the hatchlings are especially striking, resembling contours in appearance, although these will become less apparent as the turtles grow older.

Soft-shelled turtles (*Trionyx* species)

◐ 50 cm (20 in) ⚥ the male has a longer tail than the female # 10–22 eggs

Most turtles are quite social by nature, but members of the soft-shelled group are exceptions to this rule and should therefore be housed on their own.

These chelonians, with their leathery carapaces, will burrow into sand, using their long necks rather like snorkels to reach the water surface from here. They need a relatively low water level in their aquarium. In addition, regular water changes are important, because the turtles are highly aquatic and will be at risk from any fungus in the water.

Lizards

Lizards make up one of the most diverse groups of all the reptiles, with species ranging in size from just a few inches up to several feet in length. The likely adult size of a lizard must therefore be a very important consideration when you are selecting a species to keep in your home. Certain types of lizard are also likely to become much more friendly than others, which may well influence your choice. Feeding preferences can be significant, too: many lizards are insectivorous, some are primarily vegetarian, and others are carnivorous.

IGUANIDS

This group includes a number of popular species often kept as pets in the home, of which the green iguana is probably the best known.

Green iguana (*Iguana iguana*)

🔵 1.5 m (60 in) 🌓 the male can be distinguished by its larger crest
\# 20–40 eggs

Despite its name, this lizard can vary fairly widely in colour, with some individuals being distinctly bluish-green. Overall, older animals tend to be duller than juveniles in terms of coloration.

The green iguana is definitely a lizard with personality, and it needs large surroundings because it will grow quickly. Good lighting is also vital to its well-being. If you do not provide this, skeletal problems such as hindleg paralysis will become apparent and, by this stage, will be very hard to correct. In the summer months, allowing the iguana to bask in the sun will have a tonic effect, but you must always be careful that it cannot escape. An aviary-type structure equipped with a number of suitable branches for climbing is ideal for this purpose.

Special formulated foods are available for iguanas, but you can supplement these with some greenstuff and raw vegetables. However, if this type of food forms the basis of your iguana's diet, you should also give a powdered vitamin-and-mineral supplement.

You may need to trim or file your iguana's claws occasionally, as these can become sharp and inflict a painful scratch – particularly on a bare arm. Ask your vet for advice and, if necessary, for a demonstration of what to do.

Head-bobbing is associated with the display of males and, although successful breeding is unlikely to occur within the confines of the home, this has been accomplished on occasions. Hatching can take up to two months.

Green anole (*Anolis carolinensis*)

🔵 23 cm (9 in) 🌓 the male has a bigger dewlap under the chins
\# 2 eggs

This lizard is a much smaller member of the iguanid family than the green iguana, and will be quite at home in a standard vivarium with some branches for climbing. It needs a relatively humid environment, so you must spray its quarters regularly; ultra-violet lighting is also essential for good health.

The green anole is also sometimes called the American chameleon because of its ability to change colour to reflect its mood or surroundings. If challenged, these creatures will turn much darker – bordering on black in some cases.

Keep male anoles apart or they will fight, especially when in breeding condition. Egg-laying usually occurs about two weeks after mating, and the young should hatch in a further two to three months. These measure just 5 cm (2 in) at this stage, and must be kept in especially secure surroundings to prevent escape.

Green iguana

GECKOS

These are the most agile of all lizards, and many species have enlarged toe pads which help them to grip and to climb up vertical surfaces. This makes the height of the vivarium significant, and you must supply branches for climbing. Hollow bamboo tubes of suitable diameter are especially useful, too, as several species of gecko will lay their eggs within these.

Leopard gecko

Day geckos (*Phelsuma* species)

⬧ up to 25 cm (10 in) ⬧ the male has prominent femoral pores (see page 136) ⬧ 2 eggs

The area of distribution of these geckos is centred on the island of Madagascar. They are especially colourful creatures, with shades of brilliant green, red, blue and gold often showing in their appearance. They can be bred quite readily in vivarium surroundings, with females laying repeatedly under favourable conditions. Always house your male day geckos separately from one another, or they may fight viciously.

For food, you will need to supply small invertebrates dusted with a special vitamin-and-mineral powder, as well as a little honey dissolved in water and some grated cuttlefish bone to provide additional calcium for the developing eggshells (female day geckos often develop swellings around their heads, which are deposits of calcium). The incubation of the eggs is likely to take up to 12 weeks.

Bearded dragons

Tokay gecko (*Gekko gecko*)

⬧ 35 cm (14 in) ⬧ the male has prominent femoral pores ⬧ 2 eggs

The tokay gecko originates from south-east Asia, and is a widely kept and bred species. Its coloration is a combination of grey and red. This lizard needs similar care to the day geckos, but it is more aggressive by nature – adult tokays may feed on pinkies (baby mice) as well as large invertebrates.

The incubation period for the tokay gecko can range from four to seven months, or possibly even longer.

Leopard gecko
(*Eublepharis macularius*)

⬧ 25 cm (10 in) ⬧ the male has femoral pores ⬧ 2 eggs

This gecko differs from most others of its kind in that it lacks expanded footpads and spends much of its time on the ground. It will make an ideal introduction to keeping lizards, as it is easy to feed and care for, and pairs are likely to breed quite readily in the vivarium environment.

The homeland of the leopard gecko is western Asia, where the temperature becomes very hot during the day and then cools significantly at night. You will need to provide similar conditions and adequate retreats in vivarium surroundings, with the temperature

at night falling to about 20°C (68°F). You can use a heat pad attached to the vivarium (see page 130) to maintain the background temperature at night, and switch on a spotlight to raise it again in the morning.

Cooling over the winter period will encourage breeding. The eggs will be laid in a damp area (often close to the water pot). Incubation of the eggs typically lasts for two months. Young leopard geckos are banded at first, with alternating dark and light stripes encircling their bodies.

Bearded dragon (*Pogona barbatus*)

⬧ 50 cm (20 in) ⬧ the male has femoral pores ⬧ 15–30 eggs

Given this name because of the spines encircling its neck, the bearded dragon is actually a friendly species and can become very tame. Its readiness to breed in collections has led to an increasing availability of the hatchlings in recent years.

This lizard is essentially a desert dweller and, as a result, needs similar surroundings to those of the leopard gecko, with adequate opportunity to bask under ultra-violet light. It is insectivorous in its feeding habits.

The incubation period for the eggs is approximately three months. On hatching, the young measure about 7.5 cm (3 in) and usually grow rapidly.

Snakes

A wide range of snakes is now being bred in captivity, with some species being fairly widely available. However, before you buy, you must stop to consider what the full adult size of the hatchlings will be. Some snakes can grow up to 6 m (20 ft) or more, which means that not only housing but also handling may become problematical.

Boa constrictor

Garter snake

Garter snakes (*Thamnophis* species)

 78 cm–1.2 m (30–48 in)

🔢 8–30 young

These small, striped snakes originated in the USA. There are about 10 common species, as well as many subspecies and local colour variants; individuals are often beautifully coloured.

Garter snakes rank among the simplest and hardiest of all snakes to keep, and make an ideal introduction to this group of reptiles. They are alert and active, and usually feed well on a diet of fish and earthworms. Many of these snakes will also learn to take pieces of meat and chicken, although

such is their popularity that prepared diets are now available for them. Garter snakes seldom bite.

Commonly available species are the plains garter snake (*T. radix*), Butler's garter snake (*T. butleri*) and many races of the common garter snake (*T. sirtalis*).

Ribbon snakes are also fairly widely available, and have similar requirements.

Corn snake (*Elaphe guttata*)

90 cm–1.2 m (3–4 ft)

🔢 approximately 20 eggs

This is a very beautiful snake with a red, orange or grey background colour and red or orange markings. It will usually

thrive in a vivarium, and has proved to be a popular pet, bred in large numbers by enthusiasts and commercial breeders alike. Captive-bred specimens are normally healthy and hardy, but wild-caught specimens are sometimes prone to respiratory or intestinal infections.

The corn snake is gentle and rarely bites, making its handling relatively straightforward. The diet should consist mainly of mice.

Yellow, Everglades and Black rat snakes (*Elaphe obsoleta*)

1.2–1.8 m (4–5 ft)

🔢 approximately 15 eggs

These large mammal- and bird-eating snakes from the eastern USA are all races of the same species, and have the same habits. They are quite easy to look after, and breeding likelihood is good. These are handsome reptiles – especially the orange Everglades rat snake.

The rat snakes are largely arboreal in their habits, so you must provide branches for climbing. They are variable in temperament and many individuals bite freely, but they are tameable.

Corn snake

Sinaloan milk snake

Common king snake
(*Lampropeltis getulus*)

 1.8 m (6 ft) approximately 15 eggs

This is another attractive and easily kept snake. There are several races, with various patterns consisting of combinations of contrasting black and yellow, or white bands or stripes. They feed on mice or very small rats, and breed well in captivity. Most specimens that are commercially available are from captive-bred stock.

Sinaloan milk snake (*Lampropeltis triangulum sinaloae*) **and Honduran milk snake** (*L.t. hondurensis*)

 60 cm–1.2 m (2–4 ft) 6–24 eggs

These brilliantly coloured red-black-white or yellow-banded snakes, which originate from tropical and subtropical Central America, are commonly bred in captivity. Milk snakes are easy to care for and seldom bite, although they do not like being handled. They feed mainly on small mice.

Bull and Pine snakes
(*Pituophis melanoleucus*)

◗ 1.5–2.1 m (5–7 ft)
⊕ approximately 12 eggs

These are large, terrestrial snakes whose habitat is the Great Plains and eastern pine forests of the USA. They are handsomely marked reptiles, with yellowish, brown and white, or black and brown blotches. They seldom bite, but may hiss and bluff loudly. They feed on rodents and birds, and are bred in large numbers in captivity.

Indian python (*Python molurus*)

◗ 3–6 m (10–20 ft)
⊕ approximately 50 eggs

This is a very large snake from India and south-east Asia. Of the subspecies, the Burmese or 'dark-phase' python (*P.m. bivittatus*) is the most widely kept and bred. This handsome snake – marked with patterns of warm browns, yellows, tan and white – is robust, hardy and voracious. It has a calm temperament and is easily tamed if acquired young. It thrives exceptionally well in captivity and is simple to keep, making an excellent – if large – pet.

Often bred in captivity, the Indian python grows rapidly, reaching 1.8 m (6 ft) or more within two years and attaining its adult size the following year. Unless you are buying a long-term captive, it is advisable to buy only a young snake of between 60 cm (2 ft) and 1.2 m (4 ft) in length, which you will be able to tame easily.

You can feed a juvenile on mice; when it grows to over 90 cm (3 ft) long you should provide rats; and, when the snake is fully grown, small rabbits and/or chickens.

Royal or ball python (*Python regius*)

◗ 90–1.5 m (3–5 ft)
⊕ approximately 8 eggs

This is one of the most commonly available species of python. It lives in the tropical grasslands of West and Central Africa, and is a relatively shy, secretive snake. When first acquired it will often fast for months until it has settled into

Indian python

its new accommodation, and it is especially important that you do not disturb the snake before it is feeding regularly. At first it may only feed at night (pythons and boas are largely nocturnal reptiles); this species likes to hide during the day, and will do well if provided with a deep pile of hay.

Nearly all imported specimens of the royal or ball python will be carrying snake mites, which you will need to treat (see page 138).

This python is sensitive to cold, and will need extra heating during the winter months when it is kept in a temperate climate. Feed the python on gerbils at first to encourage its appetite, then wean it on to mice or on to very small rats by rubbing them together to transfer the gerbils' scent to that of the other rodents.

Boa constrictor
(*Constrictor constrictor*)

◗ 1.5–4 m (5–13 ft) ⊕ 20–60 live young

This is another of the popular bigger snakes, and several races are found throughout tropical and subtropical Central and South America. Although a large snake, this boa does not grow as big as some pythons will do. It is attractively coloured: light grey with black or brown saddle-like markings turning to wine-red, orange or tan towards the tail.

Like the pythons, the boa constrictor feeds mostly on rodents and birds in the wild; in captivity, mice, rats and small chickens are its normal diet. It will have a calm temperament if acquired when young and will seldom – if ever – attempt to bite, but it is not quite as hardy as the larger pythons.

Fish

Fish-keeping offers great scope and variety, from putting a few ornamental fish in a garden pond to filling a marine aquarium with stunning – and sometimes bizarre – reef fish, where they can be appreciated at close quarters. There are few activities more relaxing than watching fish swimming in a pond on a summer's evening, or looking at an aquarium from a favourite armchair. Nor is it mere coincidence that aquaria are often found in potentially stressful places such as dentists' waiting rooms, because studies have shown that fish-keeping can lower blood pressure and have positive health benefits.

A GARDEN POND

The origins of keeping fish for pleasure – rather than as a food source – date back over 3000 years to Ancient Egypt, when ponds were often built as purely decorative features. Subsequently, in the Far East, goldfish and koi, both of which are now universally popular as pond fish, were bred for centuries before being introduced to Europe and the USA.

Today, making a garden pond has been greatly simplified by the availability of butyl-rubber sheeting and pre-moulded pond structures, both of which are very easy to install.

Using a pond liner

If you take this option, calculate the size of liner you need by adding twice the maximum required depth of your pond to both the maximum width and length measurements. This will also provide sufficient overlap around the perimeter of the pond for support here. Then, once you have dug the hole, simply set the liner in place on a bed of sand or an underlay.

Avoid siting your pond near trees, as not only are leaves likely to fall and pollute the water, but – more seriously – the roots may in time penetrate through the liner, causing a leak. Under normal circumstances a butyl-rubber pond should remain watertight for at least 50 years, as it will be highly resistant to the ultra-violet component of sunlight which can rapidly destroy a plastic liner. If you plan to install a filter or a fountain you will need a power supply, so position the pond fairly close to your house. If you are in any doubt about laying an electrical supply to the pond, consult a qualified electrician.

Hold the liner in place with bricks or paving slabs around the edge while you fill it. The weight of the water will press down the liner, and you can make adjustments at the corners as it stretches. You can then plant the pond, and introduce your fish a week later.

One of the great appeals of a garden pond is its scope for design. You might decide on a formal style, for instance, or you could go for a much more casual approach with grass coming down to the edges of the water. Whatever

the design, you should include a marginal shelf of 30 cm (12 in) beneath the water's surface, around at least part of the edge – this will provide extra possibilities for planting, and may help to prevent cats from lurking at the edge and trying to scoop your fish from the water.

Installing a pre-moulded pond

This type of pond is obviously less flexible in shape than a liner, and may also be smaller. Avoid choosing a shell less than 91 cm (3 ft) deep, as this is likely to be a source of problems. In summer the water will warm up rapidly and algae will thrive, turning the water green and obscuring the fish; in winter the water may turn to ice and trap the fish. You can set a moulded pond in the ground in the same way as a liner, but check that the shell is absolutely level before you fill it or the higher edge will be visible above the water and spoil the look of the pond.

A sunken pond could be dangerous if you have young children, so another option is to stand the shell on a level surface – such as a patio – and enclose the sides with brick or stonework. Conceal any filter equipment in the base, with access via a door (this is rarely needed for goldfish).

Maintaining the pond

Once established, your pond will need minimal maintenance, although when leaves are falling you should cover it with a special net. You can also clean out any dead vegetation – such as water-lily leaves which have died back – at this stage. In winter, you could install a pond heater to stop the water from freezing solid. Fish are basically inactive in freezing water but they still need oxygen, and ice will form an impenetrable barrier and also trap poisonous gases. Never hammer the ice to break it: this could damage a pre-moulded pond, and the vibrations will upset your fish. Instead, hold a container of boiling water on the surface of the ice to create a hole.

In the summer, the level in the pond may fall. Keep this topped up by adding water, pre-treated with a conditioner (available from an aquatic store) to eliminate chlorine and similar chemicals. Low oxygen levels caused by the hotter weather and a lack of circulation will cause the fish to gasp at the surface, but moving water through a fountain can help.

KEEPING TROPICAL FISH

This is a relatively recent pastime compared with cold-water fish-keeping. Early this century, before electricity became widespread, tropical-fish pioneers faced almost insuperable problems in keeping their tanks heated to a constant temperature. Today, however, setting up an aquarium is quite straightforward – particularly for freshwater fish. Enthusiasts have also benefited in recent years from new equipment and an increasing range of foodstuffs, simplifying the process considerably and making it more enjoyable. You will find detailed information on setting up aquaria on pages 154–9.

Choosing and buying fish

The first step is to decide on the type of fish you would like. If you are aiming to create a community aquarium, check that your choice of fish will be compatible, while bearing in mind that some fish recommended for this purpose – such as angelfish (*Pterophyllum* species) – will actually grow quite large and may prey on their companions. It is definitely not a good idea to buy a species just because it appeals to you, especially where tropical fish are concerned. Find out as much as you can about the habits and needs of the species: for instance, if you are buying marine fish you should be aware that the attractive lionfish (Scorpaenidae family) is equipped with poisonous spines, and that it may go blind in brightly lit surroundings.

BUYING YOUR FISH

Choose an outlet fairly close to where you live if possible, as the water conditions are likely to be similar and the fish should re-adjust quickly once you get them home. You will be able to identify a good outlet by the condition of its tanks, which should be attractive and clearly labelled.

Some stores operate a 'spotting' policy, where a green dot means that a species is quite easy to keep and should live well in a community aquarium; an amber dot indicates that the fish may have some special requirements (such as needing salt to be added to the aquarium to create brackish conditions), or are likely to grow large; and a red dot denotes species that are definitely not compatible with others and may even be difficult to keep with their own kind.

When choosing your fish, try to think about the overall appearance of your aquarium. The most attractive display tanks have fish at varying heights in the water, from the top-swimming danios to the bottom-dwelling catfish and loaches, so plan your aquarium to have fish occupying all levels; this will also lessen the risk of conflict. As a guide, a 60 cm (24 in) aquarium will accommodate about 25 fish, measuring an average of about 3–4 cm (1¼–1½ in). Remember that this is the length of the adult fish and not the young stock, so check in advance on their likely adult size if you are in any doubt, and be careful not to overstock your aquarium.

TRANSFERRING FISH TO THE AQUARIUM

Once you have chosen your fish, they will probably be packed into a plastic bag with a small quantity of water and a larger volume of oxygen, where they will be able to survive with no ill-effects for several hours if necessary.

When you get the fish home, float the bag unopened in the aquarium for about 20 minutes to allow the water in the bag to warm up again to the temperature of the aquarium water. Once the water temperatures have equalized, rather than simply snipping off the top of the bag and letting the fish swim out it will be safer to catch and transfer them

What to look for in a healthy fish

A healthy fish should swim readily around its aquarium (the bottom-dwelling catfish, which tends to anchor itself here, is an exception). If a fish seems to be experiencing difficulty in swimming, it may be suffering from an incurable swim-bladder disorder.

Unless they are a feature of the species, the eyes should not bulge; this may be a sign of illness.

The underparts should not appear swollen, as this is likely to indicate that the fish is suffering from dropsy.

Look closely for any signs of damaged scales – causing an uneven appearance – on the sides of the fish, as these could become infected by fungus.

A fish in good condition should be reasonably rounded in shape; this also indicates that it has been feeding well.

Any damage to the fins could become infected by fungus, although the fins should soon re-grow properly provided that you avoid mixing notorious fin-nippers such as zebra danios (*Brachydanio rerio*) with fish which have trailing fins such as fighting fish (*Betta splendens*) or angelfish (*Pterophyllum* species).

individually, using a special aquarium net. This is because the water from the shop tank may contain potentially harmful microbes, which you will introduce in large numbers to your aquarium if you simply tip in the water from the bag (see also page 164).

Catching the fish in the bag will be fairly straightforward. In order to cause them as little disturbance as possible, dip the net into the water and scoop up a fish from underneath, rather than chasing after it with the net. Doing this will be easiest if you have a helper to hold the bag for you, but, if you are on your own, stand the bag in a bucket. Having caught a fish, transfer it without delay to the aquarium, keeping one hand close to the roof of the net to prevent it from jumping out.

If at any stage you have the misfortune to be confronted by a fish on the floor, you will need to retrieve it without delay. However, be sure to wet your hands first – this will minimize any damage to the covering of mucus on the fish's body, which helps to protect it from infection. Provided that a fish has not been out of the water for very long, it should recover without any problems.

Keep the aquarium light off until the fish have settled down, or they may become nervous, darting against the sides of the tank and possibly injuring themselves.

ADDING NEW FISH TO YOUR COLLECTION

There is an argument for adding all new fish to an existing aquarium at once, to lessen the likelihood of introducing disease (particularly if you inspected all the fish carefully before buying them). However, this may cause problems with the tank filtration (see pages 154–5), and in any case you may want to buy new fish at a later stage.

It is therefore a good idea to keep a second tank available so that you can quarantine new arrivals for two weeks to ensure that they are healthy and are feeding properly. If all is well, you can then transfer them to the main aquarium.

Housing and equipment

The aim of keeping tropical fish is to create an environment in which a community will live happily together over a long period. The first consideration – and in some ways the most important one – lies in the choice of aquarium, as many people make the mistake of buying one that is too small. The aquarium should be at least 60 cm (24 in) long by 38 cm (15 in) high and 30 cm (12 in) wide, with a volume of about 64 litres (14 gallons) of water. However, buying a larger aquarium – perhaps of 91 cm (36 in) or even 1.2 m (48 in) long – may actually be a better investment, as it will give you a great deal more scope without significantly affecting your setting-up and running costs.

A typical aquarium set-up for tropical freshwater fish, with the heaterstat located at the back of the tank.

TYPES OF AQUARIUM

Aquaria come in a very wide variety of styles, shapes and prices. The glass sides may simply be fixed together with a special silicone-rubber sealant, while more expensive models may have a decorative framework of plastic or aluminium strips. You can even buy an aquarium built into a cabinet as a decorative item of furniture.

You will also need to fit lights over the top of your aquarium (see below, right). This usually means buying a separate hood or cover, although some models have an integrated compartment for lights. You must also find somewhere to place your aquarium at a comfortable viewing height. Remember that a full aquarium is very heavy, so it is best to use a proper stand.

HEATING

Most tropical fish will require a temperature of 23–26°C (73–81°F), and the easiest way to maintain this is to use a thermostatically controlled heater intended for aquarium use. Designs do vary, but most heaters are enclosed in a heavy glass tube about 25 cm (10 in) long and 2 cm (¾ in) in diameter, and also incorporate a thermostat; these are often described as 'heaterstats'.

Your heater may already be pre-set to the required temperature, but will have a control at the top so that you can set it exactly as you wish. A heater's output is reflected by its wattage, and most aquarium heaters are rated between 75 and 150W. As a guide, you should allow about 100W per 100 litres (22 gallons) of water.

Handle the heater with great care to avoid breaking the glass, and use a clip with fixing suckers to keep it at least

WATER CHANGES

Whatever type of filtration you use, your fish will benefit greatly from a regular partial water change – especially during the first weeks – as this will dilute the toxic substances in solution. As a rough guide, you should replace about 20 per cent of the water every three weeks.

You will need to pre-treat the new water with a conditioner (available from aquatic stores) to remove chlorine or similar substances harmful to fish; you must also ensure that it is at the same temperature as the water in the aquarium before pouring it in.

2 cm (1 in) above the gravel so that water can circulate freely around it. Always unplug the heater and let it cool down for at least five minutes before removing it from the aquarium.

You will need a thermometer to check that the heater and the thermostat are functioning properly. Digital thermometers fix on to the outside of the aquarium and are easy to read, although 'dial'-type and old-style spirit scale thermometers (which stick on below the water level) are just as good.

LIGHTING

You will need lighting in your aquarium so that plants can grow and you can see the fish, and special fluorescent tubes are now available. For a tropical freshwater setting, a figure of roughly 10W of fluorescent light for each 0.09 sq m (1 sq ft) of surface area, switched on for 12 hours per day, will be adequate. You can vary the timing to suit yourself, but keep within the range of 10–14 hours per day for the best results.

Excessive light exposure will result in heavy algal growth (although in a marine tank, especially one containing anemones, more intense illumination is usually needed). Avoid placing your aquarium in front of a window because, although this will provide some light, the water could become excessively hot on a sunny day and be fatal for your fish.

and biological filtration, which uses the gravel in the aquarium to purify the water.

An air-operated filter is powered by an airlift, a plastic tube of approximately 1 cm (½ in) in diameter which is placed vertically in the aquarium. A steady stream of bubbles from the air pump is introduced into this tube near the bottom, and as the bubbles rush upwards they draw the water upwards too. This means that water is sucked into the bottom of the tube and expelled from the top.

Mechanical filters

The cheapest mechanical filter is a square or triangular transparent box which is fitted inside the aquarium – usually hidden in a back corner behind plants or a rock – with an airlift placed in the centre. To use this type of filter, remove the perforated lid and place a small handful of nylon floss inside (this looks similar to cotton wool but is far more efficient).

When you connect the filter to the air supply, the aquarium water is sucked through the nylon floss which will trap all the solid waste matter. When the floss is dirty (within a week or so), remove the filter from the aquarium, dismantle it and wash out the floss thoroughly in a bucket of conditioned water. You should renew the filter floss about every third time. Never be tempted to substitute any other material for the floss, even if it looks similar, as it could be harmful to your fish.

Another type of mechanical filter uses a plastic sponge to keep the water clean: with this, you simply squeeze out the sponge under a cold tap to remove the dirt, fit it back on to the airlift and replace it in the aquarium.

Biological filters

A biological filter uses a perforated plate which covers most or all of the base of the aquarium, placed beneath the gravel and attached to an airlift at one corner. Water is drawn down through the gravel, where the dirt and waste matter are trapped. This is broken down by beneficial bacteria here, with the toxic ammonia produced by the fish being converted to relatively harmless nitrate that will be used by the plants as a fertilizer. This forms the basis of the so-called 'nitrogen cycle'.

Special products are now available to seed the filter bed in a new tank, encouraging the bacteria to develop. The process is likely to take about six weeks, but during this time there is a risk that the level of toxic substances in solution could rise to harmful levels, causing so-called 'new-tank syndrome'. Watch for any signs of discomfort among your fish, such as gasping at the surface or swimming at abnormal angles. If you see these signs, check your equipment and carry out a partial water change if necessary (see box opposite).

AERATION

You will need to connect an air pump to the electricity supply; a length of small-bore plastic pipe then conveys the air to an air stone or a filter in the aquarium. If the pump is powerful enough you may want to operate two or more items at once (for example, a filter and a fountain), in which case a series of plastic airline valves will ensure that each receives the correct amount of air.

Keep your air pump working continuously, as your fish may become distressed when it is switched off and an undergravel filter (see below) will not function effectively. The pump will be very cheap to run, using about as much electricity in a day as a lightbulb uses in an hour. Make sure that the pump never gets near the water, as this could be very dangerous. It must also be fitted with a non-return valve. Choose a pump which operates quietly, as it will not be safe to cover it to mask unwanted noise.

An air stone will break up the air into a mass of tiny bubbles, helping to oxygenate the water and possibly also improving its circulation. Most air stones are round or oblong in shape and are quite small, but in a large aquarium you could use one of 10 cm (4 in) or more in length.

FILTRATION

A filter will remove the unsightly waste matter which would soon collect at the bottom of your aquarium, and will help to keep the water pure and clean for months at a time. There are two basic types of filtration: mechanical filtration, where the water is passed through a layer of nylon floss which traps the waste matter for you to wash out at regular intervals;

Setting up and planting an aquarium

There is a wide range of aquarium plants available today, but plan your planting scheme carefully before you buy. Some plants give much better cover at the water's surface than others, and these are useful when some shade is required.

Java moss

156

Pygmy chain-sword plant

Dwarf hygrophila

When setting up a new aquarium you will need to choose between living plants and plastic substitutes. The latter are often extremely realistic in appearance, but living plants do more than simply create an attractive natural aquascape – they also improve the aquarium environment. During daylight hours, aquatic plants convert carbon dioxide produced by the fish to oxygen; they also use the nitrate produced by the breakdown of the fishes' waste as a fertilizer. An aquarium that is devoid of living plants is therefore far more likely to be blighted by the growth of unsightly algae.

BUYING AND PREPARING PLANTS

The biggest range of aquarium plants is available by mail order from specialist nurseries (look in aquatic magazines for details). However, you should also find a good selection in a local aquatic store, and you will be able to buy these plants straight from the water and then return them to an aquarium environment with minimal delay (if allowed to dry out, their delicate foliage is easily damaged). You may like to buy a collection, rather than individual plants: these are intended for aquaria of specific sizes and will take much of the guesswork out of what you need, if you have no strong preferences about particular plants.

Always wash new plants in a solution of aquarium disinfectant, to avoid introducing any diseases or parasites which could harm your fish.

PLANTING THE AQUARIUM

Most aquatic plants are different from those which grow on land. Plants growing in water tend not to have highly developed root systems, but obtain their nutrients through their leaves. Even so, it may be better to set the plants in small pots disguised in aquarium gravel, to prevent their roots from clogging the pores of an undergravel filter (see page 155). Wash the gravel well before putting it into the tank, or it will create a scum on the water's surface. You will need to allow approximately 1 kg (2¼ lb) of gravel per 4.5 litres (1 gallon) of water, to give an adequate depth of covering above the undergravel filter. Coloured gravel is available, but this can detract from the natural colour of the fish.

The planting scheme that you use is up to you, but take some time to plan this carefully so that you do not need to disturb the plants as they grow. As a general guide, put taller plants at the back and around the sides of the aquarium, and use one as a centrepiece. Position smaller plants in the foreground and, if suitable, use some for growing over rocks and other tank decor. Cover over the plant pots with gravel to conceal them.

Although aquarium plants need little in the way of attention, proper lighting conditions will be essential if they are to thrive. Some aquatic plants need more light than others (the supplier will be able to advise you on this), and very effective fluorescent lights are now available to maintain the optimum conditions needed for them to grow (see page 154).

The following are some suggestions of suitable plants to include in your aquarium, all of which should grow well and will provide an attractive environment for your fish.

Java moss (*Vesicularia dubyana*)

Java moss is one of the most versatile aquatic plants, whose growth cannot be replicated by plastic substitutes. It originates in south-east Asia, ranging from parts of India eastwards and including the island of Java. True Java moss will grow well in an underwater setting, or you can allow it to spread above the water level as well (this also makes it useful in a vivarium housing amphibians). The moss is fairly slow-growing, but its dense growth underwater provides a safe spawning ground for egg-laying species, and also offers a retreat for young fry. Hold a mass of the moss in position on a piece of bogwood or rock using an elastic band until it has established itself.

Java moss prefers soft water, although it is very adaptable in its growing requirements. However, do not position it in a brightly lit part of the aquarium, as algae will soon develop and start to choke the dense fronds. The only thing that you can do under these circumstances is to discard the plant and start again.

Pygmy chain-sword plant
(*Echinodorus tenellus*)

This plant makes a good choice for the front part of the aquarium, and is easy to cultivate. In general, the plant grows no more than 5–7.5 cm (2–3 in) high, although if plants are crowded their pattern of growth will be more upright, making them appear taller. Space out the plants in the foreground at the outset, to create an attractive, low-growing and bright green array of vegetation in the aquarium. Pygmy chain-sword plants usually dislike hard water; this makes them ideally suited to an Amazonian-style tank (characterized by relatively soft, acidic water conditions), featuring fish such as cardinal tetras (see page 171).

Floating plants

These plants – such as the water lettuce (*Pistia stratiotes*) – can be very valuable in the aquarium, offering cover to the fish and also screening part of the water's surface, creating suitably darkened areas for catfish and others which tend to avoid bright light. Water lettuce will not thrive without good artificial lighting in the aquarium, but do not allow it to come into contact with the droplets of condensation on the cover glass. If water drips down persistently on to the plants, they will turn black and die. However, in favourable conditions water lettuce will grow very rapidly, with small plants developing as offshoots on stolons connected to the adult plant (rather like strawberry runners). These stems will rot away in due course, leaving the young plants on their own. As they grow, their white roots will turn black – this is quite normal, and not a sign of fungal attack, as you might expect.

Dwarf hygrophila
(*Hygrophila polysperma*)

Pests tend not to strike aquarium plants as readily as those in ponds, but snails can be a problem. Dwarf hygrophila is normally very easy to cultivate in an aquarium, provided that there is not a large population of snails (these would be very likely to strip the leaves of this plant, in preference to almost any others in the aquarium).

Weigh down the cuttings in groups, and they should soon root and grow to form a dense clump. You can also arrange the plants in a line to provide good cover at the back of the aquarium. Dwarf hygrophila is very undemanding in its growing requirements, but will tend to turn the aquarium water more acidic.

(Top) Carefully running in the water on top of a saucer, as shown here, will prevent the gravel on the aquarium floor from being churned up by the current.

(Above) After buying plants, keep them moist until you can replant them. Insert them into the gravel once the tank is about half full and the saucer has been removed; they should then not be disturbed as you top up the water. Do not bury the crowns of any plants, as this will cause rotting.

ARTIFICIAL PLANTS

Unfortunately, it is not always possible to grow plants successfully, even in ideal conditions, because certain fish – notably large cichlids – will dig them up, while others may eat them. In these cases, plastic plants are very useful. You can also add them to a marine aquarium (in which plants will not be a major feature), although they may look less realistic here.

Setting up a marine aquarium

The earliest successful attempts to keep marine fish were made in the seaside aquaria which developed in the resort towns of Victorian Britain, at a time when an elaborate system of pumps and saltwater storage reservoirs was needed to maintain the water conditions in the display tanks. The origins of marine aquaria in the home are much more recent and date back only to the 1960s, when

Specialist equipment

You will need some specialist equipment in the marine tank to maintain the quality of the water. This includes a protein skimmer to aerate the water, effectively whipping organic waste into a foam which is then trapped in the unit. An ozonizer is often run in association with the protein skimmer. This produces the gas ozone – a potent disinfectant – and converts both ammonia and nitrite into less toxic nitrates via a chemical reaction.

A diatom filter will remove harmful microbes directly, and is able to capture particles of just a micron (one-millionth of a metre) in diameter. Another method of maintaining the water quality is to use an ultra-violet sterilizer; this comprises a sealed chamber in which light is emitted as the water passes through it, destroying potential pathogens. The efficiency of the sterilizer will depend on the light output – this can fall quite rapidly, so you will need to replace it regularly.

Although marine aquaria do not feature plants in the same way as freshwater set-ups, the background can still be spectacular, with a careful mix of fish and invertebrates used to ensure compatibility (see also pages 188–9).

the availability of synthetic sea salts and specialist equipment, combined with efficient transportation by air, enabled spectacular reef fish to be obtained and kept with minimal difficulty for the first time.

ESTABLISHING AN AQUARIUM

Coral reefs are one of the most stable environments on earth, and the fish from such areas are far less able than many freshwater species to adapt to a change in conditions. Not surprisingly, therefore, setting up and maintaining a marine aquarium will be more costly. Saltwater is corrosive, so a metal-hooded or old-style metal-framed aquarium will be unsuitable for marine fish. Rubber is also likely to perish in this environment, so nylon is a better alternative. Make up the filter bed with cockleshell, rather than gravel, with a layer of coral sand on top.

Water

Only use water from the cold-water supply to dissolve the salt in a marine tank: this is likely to contain less copper, which can be toxic (especially to invertebrates). After filling the tank, aerate the water for a day or so to ensure that the salts are fully dissolved. The specific gravity (SG) figure of the salt solution is important. This is a measure of the concentration of dissolved salts present, and is measured with an instrument called a hygrometer, set for a particular water temperature. The majority of marine tropical fish require water with an SG

Caring for marine invertebrates has been simplified by the availability of special foods.

reading of 1.023, although those from Caribbean waters may require a slightly higher figure.

The salinity will be 35 parts per thousand. However, if the water evaporates this figure will rise and the oxygen content will fall. In this case, you will need to add tap water (rather than more of the salt solution) to restore the balance. If the SG becomes too low, the appetite of the fish will be depressed.

Aquarium decor

You must take care over the decor that you add to the aquarium. It must not lower the pH reading of the water, which needs to be maintained at between 8.0 and 8.4 in a marine tank; and you will need to clean it regularly, using a safe aquarium disinfectant if necessary.

Starting out

You will need to mature your aquarium in the same way as a freshwater set-up, in order to allow the bacterial population in the filter bed to build up

and function effectively (see page 155). Adding so-called 'living rock' will help with this process, and you can also put in a few relatively hardy fish during this initial phase. As a guide, you should keep the maximum stocking density in your aquarium to no more than 2.5 cm (1 in) of fish per 18 litres (4 gallons) in the first six months, after which you can double this figure.

You will need to take SG and pH readings twice a week at first, and make slight adjustments as necessary to retain these figures within the set limits. If there is a fall in pH, use a saltwater buffer solution initially; you should then carry out partial water changes in due course (see page 154), once the buffering capacity of the solution is no longer so effective.

Check the nitrite level in a new marine aquarium daily at first, as this is the stage at which you are most likely to encounter problems. If you have any specific worries, knowledgeable staff at an aquatic store will be able to advise you.

Lighting is very important for a marine aquarium. More powerful lighting may be needed here than in a tank for freshwater fish, especially when invertebrates are also included in the set-up.

(Left) Tufa rock provides a good growing medium for a number of marine invertebrates (see above).

Feeding

Gone are the days when fish food was little more than dried ants' eggs. Today's manufacturers have invested huge sums of money in technology to ensure that a wide range of aquarium fish can be provided with foods to keep them in the very best of health. And it is not only the fish that can be given specially formulated food, because diets are also now produced for filter-feeding invertebrates such as sponges and fanworms, which remove tiny food particles from the water.

Feeding fish presents no problems today, with the wide range of safe prepared foods available for them. Provide some variation in your fishes' diet; adding items such as bloodworm can also help to encourage spawning.

TYPES OF FOOD

In many cases, prepared diets reflect the feeding habits of the fish concerned, as well as their nutritional needs. For example, fish which feed near the surface are usually given flake food which floats readily, while bottom-dwelling catfish are typically fed on pellets which sink to the floor of the aquarium. The position of a fish's mouth will give a clue as to where it will feed. Those with upturned mouths – such as mollies – are likely to be surface feeders, taking their food with little effort; while those with mouths on the lower side of their bodies – such as many catfish – generally seek their food at the bottom of the aquarium.

Fish normally eat a wide variety of foods, but changes may occur in their diet during the year. In the Amazon region, for example, the waters may rise and fall significantly in the wet and dry seasons, affecting the abundance of foods. The availability of insect life is also an important conditioner for many species. In aquarium surroundings dry foods often make an ideal basic diet, but adding other items – such as livefood – can be useful, especially to trigger breeding activity. Unfortunately, however, aquatic livefoods such as tubifex worms can represent a hazard to fish, because they may introduce parasites, bacteria and other harmful microbes into the aquarium.

Freeze-dried and frozen foods

Rather than giving livefoods, it is better to rely on freeze-dried or irradiated frozen supplies. You can offer freeze-dried foods direct from the pack and they need no special storage, so they are a convenient option. Frozen items obviously need to be kept in a freezer and thawed before use. As only a little food is needed at a time, cut off the required amount rather than thawing out the pack, as you will not be able to re-freeze it safely.

Freeze-dried tubifex

Vegetarian food sticks

Freeze-dried bloodworm

The hatchetfish is a surface feeder. In all cases, the food that you offer should correspond to your fishes' natural feeding habits.

Culturing whiteworm

Another option is to culture your own foods – such as whiteworm – which should represent no threat to your fishes' health. Small starter cultures of whiteworm are advertised in aquatic magazines, and with one of these you should soon have enough of the tiny worms to supplement your fishes' diet on a regular basis.

Culturing the worms is very simple. Take a clean plastic container (such as an empty margarine tub), and punch some small ventilation holes in the lid. Fill the container with a peat substitute, make shallow holes on the surface with the end of a pencil, and place a little bread (previously soaked in milk) in each. Divide up the starter culture and place the worms on their food supply, covering over the surface but marking the site. Place the container in a warm spot, keep the surface moist and top up the food supply regularly.

Freeze-dried river shrimp

Cichlid pellets

Proprietary fry food

HOW MUCH TO FEED

Do not offer your fish excessive amounts of any type of food, as the surplus will pollute the water. Catfish are especially vulnerable to an excess of food, as it will accumulate on the gravel where they spend much of their time, and may cause skin ailments. It is always much better to feed a small quantity of food several times a day rather than one large meal; the food should then all be eaten within a few minutes.

In a new aquarium or pond the fish may skulk for a day or so before regaining their appetites. This phase should soon pass, but watch to ensure that all the fish are in fact eating – a poor appetite is often a sign of illness. In goldfish, for example, so-called 'mouth fungus' (which is actually caused by a bacterium) may result in a fish appearing to eat normally and then spitting out the food almost immediately. If left untreated the fish will soon lose its appetite entirely, but prompt treatment can rapidly resolve this illness. With patience on your part, some larger fish – such as Oscars – will become sufficiently tame to feed from your hand.

(Above, left) Vitamin-enriched tablet food
(Above, right) Dry flakes

161

Feeding pond fish

The appetites of pond fish will fall as the water temperature declines in winter. You should offer special, easily digestible foods prior to the onset of winter, and then again in the spring until the water warms up. Over the winter period itself, the fish are unlikely to feed regularly, and offering concentrated food at this stage can be harmful. A sudden cold spell may result in the food remaining in the fishes' gut for much longer than normal, where it could start to putrify with possibly fatal consequences.

The worms will start to multiply rapidly, and you should be able to harvest them for your fish within a month. Simply tip the tiny worms into a saucer to separate them from the substrate, or pick them out using a pair of fine tweezers. You can also culture microworms and grindalworms using this simple method.

Wingless fruitflies

No-one would want fruitflies buzzing around their home, but you can buy wingless fruitflies which will provide a valuable food for surface feeders such as hatchetfish. Special containers and food cultures for fruitflies are available, but many fish-keepers prefer to use the well-tested method of placing some fresh banana skins in a clean ice-cream container, adding the fruitflies and covering the top with muslin held by an elastic band. If you keep the container warm and add banana skins as necessary, the flies will breed rapidly. Tip a small number into the tank on a regular basis, and they will quickly be consumed.

HOLIDAY FEEDING

If you go away for a short period, you can supply your fish with slow-release food blocks, which will meet their nutritional requirements in your absence without polluting the water. Even so, you must still ask someone to check the aquarium for you. If, for example, the heaterstat stopped working or the filter system went wrong, your fish could die. Lack of food is actually the least significant factor as, if the fish are in good condition and housed in an established aquarium, most of them will find enough to eat here – browsing on algae, for example – to prevent any loss of condition for a week or so.

Fresh bloodworm

Breeding

Live-bearers such as guppies (*Poecilia reticulata*) are the easiest tropical fish to breed, as they give birth to their young every five weeks or so, with a female only having to mate once in order to produce up to six or seven broods in succession. Many of the species of egg-laying fish will also be quite straightforward to breed.

Fish vary greatly in the extent to which they will look after their offspring. Goldfish such as these red-capped orandas (top) are likely to eat their eggs or fry, while cichlids (centre) usually display a high degree of parental care. (Bottom) Here, young discus feed on the mucus present on the sides of the parent fish.

BREEDING LIVE-BEARERS

The biggest problem that you are likely to come across with these fish is that the small fry may be eaten by other fish – including their mother. The simplest and cheapest means of preventing this is to use a suitable breeding trap. This is usually a plastic box with small holes around the base, which allows water to circulate; a removable grid near the bottom allows the baby fish to drop through to the lower section where the mother cannot reach them. Place the female live-bearer in the trap a week or so before she is likely to give birth; afterwards, return her to the main tank as soon as possible and remove the grid.

Raise the young fish on a suitable fry food followed by finely powdered flake, taking care not to pollute the water by offering too much. Within about two weeks they will probably be large enough for you to tip them carefully into the main tank. Remember that confining them for long periods in a small container will seriously affect their growth; take care, too, that all the extra new fish do not overcrowd the aquarium.

Alternatively, you can simply invest in a separate aquarium for breeding purposes. Either fill this densely with plastic plants to provide cover for the young, or fit it with V-shaped panels of glass with a small gap along the centre for the babies to fall through. You must provide heating in the breeding aquarium, but lighting and aeration will not be necessary.

BREEDING EGG-LAYERS

Egg-laying fish can be broadly divided into four groups, based on their spawning habits: non-adhesive egg scatterers, adhesive egg scatterers, bubble nesters and egg guardians. Breeding these fish is not difficult, but you do need a mature, healthy and well-fed pair. You will be able to distinguish them by the fact that the female will appear quite plump with eggs, while the male will be more brightly coloured and is likely to chase after the female as the time for spawning approaches.

An aquarium of 45 cm (18 in) in length will make a sufficiently large spawning tank for most species. Unfortunately, however, it is not usually possible to leave the fish in the main aquarium with their eggs, as they are likely to eat these before they can hatch.

Fill the tank with about 20 cm (8 in) of fresh water, and use a small heaterstat (see page 154) to maintain the water temperature at about 25°C (83°F). Place the tank in a quiet spot where the fish will not be suddenly disturbed.

Once the young fish are free-swimming in their quarters, giving special liquid fry food is usually the simplest way of feeding them. As they grow larger, you will need to provide additional foods such as brine shrimp (*nauplii*).

Egg scatterers (non-adhesive eggs)

This group, which includes the zebra danio (*Brachydanio rerio*) and the white cloud mountain minnow (*Tanichthys albonubes*), will require a tank lined with a layer of marbles and a clump of bushy plants at one end. A pair of fish in spawning condition will usually produce eggs within 36 hours of being transferred here, with the male chasing the female up and down the aquarium beforehand. If you look carefully you should be able to see the minute, transparent eggs. Remove the parents to their own aquarium as soon as possible; the eggs should then hatch within 48–72 hours. The fry are likely to be free-swimming in a further four days, depending on the species.

Egg scatterers (adhesive eggs)

This category includes most of the barbs and characins. These fish require a similar set-up to the previous group, except that you should place dense clumps of fine-leaved plants at both ends of the aquarium. The parents will spawn in and around these plants, with most of the eggs sticking to the leaves. When spawning is complete and the female shows little interest in continuing, remove the parents or they will consume their eggs. Those which do survive will hatch, like the non-adhesive egg scatterers, within 48–72 hours.

Bubble nesters

Members of this group are the Siamese fighting fish (*Betta splendens*), which is quite easy to breed, and the gouramis. Their aquarium should have fine gravel over its base, no aeration or filtration, and a few small clumps of fine-leaved plants. Place the male into the aquarium first, then add the female two days later. If ready to breed, the male will construct a nest of bubbles at the water's surface; then, after mating with the female, he will collect the eggs in his mouth and place them in the nest. Even when these hatch out and become free-swimming, the male will usually continue to guard them for a short time. It may be better to remove the female after egg-laying has taken place.

Egg guardians

The cichlids are the main group included under this heading, and they often display a highly developed sense of responsibility towards their offspring. You will need a fairly large aquarium – about 90 × 38 × 38 cm (36 × 15 × 15 in) – for these fish, although you can house members of the dwarf cichlid group in a slightly smaller tank. With egg guardians it is better to use their regular aquarium for breeding purposes rather than moving the fish into a special tank, so you may have to move out other fish if you have a mixed collection.

The parents will select a suitable, flat, smooth surface – such as a stone or a piece of slate – and will clean it with their mouths. In due course the eggs will be laid here, will hatch out and become free-swimming, and will then start to develop into recognizable fish. The male will usually shepherd his brood together for safety. Discus (*Symphysodon aequifasciata*) and angelfish (*Pterophyllum* species) breed in this way.

The most remarkable example of parental care is found in some of the more specialist cichlids from the Rift Valley area of Africa, which are known as mouth-brooders. The female takes the eggs and hatches them in her mouth, and the fry will dart back here for a time if danger threatens.

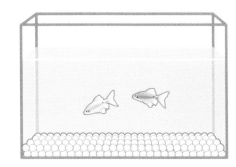

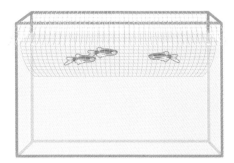

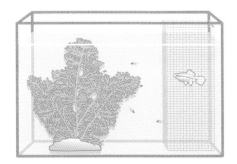

(Above) The breeding trap in this aquarium is being used to confine a female guppy; her young are contained in the body of the box.

(Left) It is possible to protect eggs or fry from adult fish in a number of ways. Marbles placed on the base of the aquarium will help to guard eggs which fall to the floor, while keeping other egg scatterers above a mesh screen – through which their eggs can fall – is another good method. Breeding traps can be used to house gravid females, to protect the young when they are born. It is then best to remove the young to a separate aquarium for rearing in safety.

163

Health care

When kept in suitable surroundings and well fed, fish rarely fall ill. However, their lifespan is often relatively short, particularly in the case of smaller species such as the guppy (*Poecilia reticulata*). If you obtain your fish as adults you will probably not know their age and they may only live for a few more months, but hopefully by then they will have bred and you will have had the enjoyment of watching the young fish grow up. Anywhere from one to three years is a good lifespan for most tropical fish. Species occurring in cold water, such as goldfish, tend to live for considerably longer: up to 40 years is possible, although 10 years or so is likely to be an average figure.

Keep a sick fish in isolation, as the medication needed to treat its condition may affect the tank's filtration system. The tank decor should be simple but provide some cover.

HEALTH PROBLEMS

Occasionally something can go wrong, and you will be faced with ailing fish. Assuming that the environmental conditions of your aquarium or pond are sound, the problem is likely to have been caused by the introduction of a new fish which already has a disease, even though it may appear to be healthy. This is why quarantining new fish is so important (see page 153), as it is obviously much more difficult to deal with an outbreak of disease in an established aquarium or pond rather than in an isolation set-up.

This fish is suffering from whitespot, a common parasitic ailment of fish. The infection will spread very readily through the aquarium water if prompt treatment is not given.

A swollen abdomen is typical of the condition known as dropsy, which can have both infectious and non-infectious causes. Treatment of dropsy is very difficult.

Whitespot

Fish seem especially prone to parasitic ailments, of which the most common – and also one of the most serious – is whitespot. This is also known (especially in the USA) as 'Ich', and is caused by the parasite *Ichthyophthirius multifiliis*. It results in the appearance of very small white dots – smaller in size even than grains of salt – which are often seen initially on the fins and then over the whole body of an affected fish. If it is not treated promptly, this infection can spread very easily and rapidly through the water in the aquarium to other fish. When the white spots break open, they can each release as many as 1000 further free-swimming parasites, which are known as tomites. These will die within a day or so if they do not find a host, but will have little problem in finding other fish to attack within the confines of an aquarium. The disease soon reaches epidemic proportions, and deaths will begin to mount up.

Preventive action depends first of all on trying to exclude the infection as far as possible from the aquarium in the first place. Do not tip the water from the bag in which you brought the fish home into the aquarium (see page 153), in case it contains tomites. If the disease does strike, you must take prompt action and treat all the fish with a remedy for whitespot (this will be available from an aquatic store). Changing the water in the aquarium (see page 154) will also help, as this will dispose of many of the potentially infective tomites.

Velvet disease

This infection is similar to whitespot, and is caused by a protozoon called *Amyloodinium*. It affects the gills rather than the whole body, and can be a particular problem in labyrinth fish and members of the carp family.

TREATING A SICK FISH

Treatments for a range of fish ailments are sold in aquatic pet stores. However, you must take care with these – especially with marine fish, if you have invertebrates in the tank – as copper-based remedies in particular may be toxic for them. Always set up a separate aquarium for a sick fish if possible, as a treatment could be inactivated by passing through a filter containing carbon, or may harm beneficial bacteria in the filter. Keeping the sick fish on its own will also allow it to recover without being molested by other fish.

Some vets specialize in treating fish, and there are even anaesthetics which can be used safely and successfully, simplifying the treatment of a number of parasites and diseases. For larger fish, injections of antibiotics, or the use of food that has been impregnated with these drugs, can resolve cases of bacterial illness.

Bacterial infections

Some diseases are caused by opportunistic bacteria in the water. These gain access to a fish's body following an injury to the scales, and do not normally spread to other, healthy fish. However, they can develop into ulcers, and may open the way for a fungal infection. Remedies are available to add to the water to treat fungus. Follow the instructions for use very carefully, as overdosing could be fatal to an already weakened fish.

Viral infections

Although uncommon in fish, viral infections are much more serious. The most significant of these is spring viraemia of carp, which, as the name suggests, usually strikes in the spring. Haemorrhaging around the gills and head is a typical sign, coupled with abdominal swelling and rapid death. There is no treatment for this virus.

Poisoning

Not all sudden deaths are due to disease: a fish could be the victim of inadvertent poisoning. Be particularly careful when using any household sprays, as these could waft into the aquarium and prove poisonous. Many flea treatments for dogs and cats can also be deadly to fish, so avoid using a spray near a tank or a pond. Chlorine and

similar chemicals used for purifying water supplies are liable to be harmful, which is why the use of a suitable water conditioner (available from an aquatic store) is so important.

GENERAL SIGNS OF ILLNESS

You will often first realize that a fish is ill because of a change in its behaviour: instead of being lively it will hide away in a corner, with its fins closed up and its body making a typical 'wriggling' motion without moving through the water. Other signs may include a swollen abdomen, bulging eyes and sometimes a loss of body colour.

Damage to a fish's scales will often be followed by fungal attack, as in this case of body fungus on a firemouth cichlid. If the fungus is caught at an early stage, treatment can be successful. Always isolate a sick fish if you can, so that the fungus cannot affect other fish.

Goldfish

Colour variants of small wild carp living in the waterways of southern China were first recorded in about AD 400, during the Chin dynasty. Instead of being the normal dull-brownish colour, some of these fish showed variable red areas on their bodies, and they created considerable interest.

Through selective breeding the Chinese were gradually able to increase the extent of this reddish coloration, and so began the evolution of the goldfish.

FURTHER DEVELOPMENTS

It was not until the 16th century that the first changes affecting the body shape and fins of these fish were noted, leading to the emergence of distinctive varieties of goldfish, such as the fantail (see opposite), which are well known today. Goldfish were exported to Japan during this period, but it was to be a further 200 years before they reached the UK and then spread to other European countries; from there they were finally introduced to the USA in the late 19th century.

Today a huge industry has developed, supplying goldfish to enthusiasts around the globe. Their ease of maintenance has made them the most popular of all the pet fish and yet, although there are now goldfish farms in countries as far apart as the USA, Singapore and Israel, fish of Chinese origin are still in great demand. Goldfish-breeding in China has always been fairly localized, with certain areas specializing in developing particular varieties.

The liberalization of trade in recent years has made it easier to obtain specific types of goldfish that were previously very scarce in the West, and these have found a ready market with enthusiasts.

Lionhead

Common goldfish

TYPES OF GOLDFISH

The following goldfish should be widely available from pet suppliers.

Common goldfish

This remains the most widely available and least expensive of all goldfish. It is very easy to care for – either in the home or in a garden pond – and can soon grow to 15 cm (6 in) or more. The common goldfish is also very hardy, making it a good choice for ponds in areas where the temperature frequently dips below freezing in winter.

Shubunkin

The shubunkins are the only goldfish varieties to have been developed in the UK to date. They are easily recognizable by their characteristic mottled coloration: a combination of reddish and black speckling on a silvery-blue background. The so-called Bristol shubunkin has a larger and more rounded tail fin than its London relative. Like the common goldfish, shubunkins show to good effect in ponds, and are almost as hardy.

Comet

This variety was developed in the USA towards the end of the 19th century. It is identical in body shape and coloration to the common goldfish, the only difference being that its tail is much larger and the other fins are slightly extended. The orange-and-white so-called 'sarassa comet' has become popular in recent years.

Fancy goldfish

There are many exotic varieties of fancy goldfish, which are characterized by a more rotund shape than the previous varieties. They are also less hardy and typically grow to a smaller size, rarely exceeding about 15 cm (6 in) in length.

Fancy goldfish are best suited to a spacious aquarium in which their

Lionhead and Oranda: The lionhead is characterized by the raspberry-like swelling on its head, which is said to resemble a lion's mane. It may take four or five years for this hood to develop to its full extent.

Closely related to the lionhead, but with a dorsal fin on top of its body, is the oranda. This goldfish can be bred in a variety of colours: chocolate and blue examples are now available, as is the red-capped oranda, whose bright red cap is in stark contrast to its white body.

Pearl scale: A recent introduction to the West, this fish originated in the Chinese province of Kwangtung. It has raised scales on its body, which produce a distinctively dimpled appearance and reflect light in such a way that they create a pearly image.

Black moor: This is another popular fish, whose coloration can vary from a distinctive velvet-black shade to a dark bronze in older fish, often combined with protruding 'telescopic' eyes.

Celestial: Another unusual-looking fancy goldfish, the celestial has upward-pointing, telescopic eyes which are positioned horizontally rather than on the sides of the head.

Bubble-eye: This is one of the most bizarre forms of the goldfish. Large, jelly-filled sacs under the eyes, which wave around as the fish swims, are its distinguishing feature. If you keep these fish, you must avoid any aquarium decor which could puncture these sacs.

KEEPING GOLDFISH INDOORS

You can keep goldfish satisfactorily in an indoor aquarium without a heater, but it is a good idea to include a power filter as they are rather messy fish. A range of prepared foods is available, and some of these have colour-enhancing properties. In an aquarium, suitable artificial lighting can also emphasize the coloration of the fish and will assist the growth of aquatic plants. Only select hardy cold-water plants – such as Canadian pondweed (*Elodea densa*) – for a goldfish aquarium, as tropical species will not flourish here.

(Top) Bristol shubunkin
(Centre) Pearl scale
(Bottom) Black moor

BREEDING

Sexing goldfish becomes easy during the breeding period (spring onwards) when the fish are in good condition. Male fish develop white pimples over their gill plates, behind the eyes, which may extend along the adjoining fins. They will also pursue females determinedly, fertilizing eggs as these are laid. If your goldfish spawn in the aquarium, move them elsewhere or they will eat the eggs before they can hatch (hatching typically takes four or five days).

Young goldfish are fairly easy to rear using fry foods and then powdered flake food. They are invariably olive-brown, not reddish, and it can take two months to a year for them to achieve their coloration. A few may never undergo this change, remaining the same colour as their wild ancestors despite having been domesticated for 1500 years.

individual features can be appreciated. They may well not survive a winter outdoors, although they can be kept in a pond during the summer. With their more highly developed fins and short, dumpy bodies, these fish are not very fast swimmers, so the more limited confines of an aquarium will be no handicap to them.

Some of the best-known types of fancy goldfish are as follows.

Fantail: This is probably the most common member of the group. It has a relatively long caudal fin and has been bred in a variety of colours.

Veiltail: In contrast to the fantail, the veiltail has the longest finnage of all, which flows behind the fish's body as it wriggles its way through the water. Veiltails are often interestingly coloured, with a patterning resembling that of the shubunkin in some cases.

Koi

Kohaku

The ancestors of today's colourful koi were dull brown carp. These were first introduced into Japan from China as a source of food in about AD 200, and it was not until the early 19th century that the first koi with colour variations were recorded there, in the Niigata region. These created great interest, and were soon being bred selectively as ornamental fish. From the 1930s onwards, koi were exported in increasing numbers to enthusiasts worldwide. Today, Japan still has an unrivalled reputation for the quality of its koi, but they are also produced elsewhere. Both Israel and the USA are big exporters of good fish, usually at lower prices than those of Japanese origin. Koi can sell for huge sums: sometimes for more than a house!

SHOWING KOI

The judging of koi at shows is carried out with the fish swimming in vats of blue-coloured water. Competition is invariably fierce, and the process of preparing the fish for a major event will begin weeks – if not months – beforehand. The condition of the koi is vital. Their scales must be unblemished, with a healthy sheen enhancing the natural coloration. Any markings must be balanced and colours should be clearly defined – white areas, for example, must be snow white with no hint of yellow. Koi are always judged from above, so a symmetrical body shape and a straight backbone are considered to be vital attributes. The fish must also swim elegantly through the water, using fins in proportion to their body size.

The appearance of koi may change somewhat as they mature, and the desired qualities – such as the sheen – may be less apparent on the bodies of older fish. As a result, the few adult fish which retain their winning characteristics as they approach a length of 91 cm (3 ft) are highly valued.

SPECIALIST FOODS

Good feeding plays an important part in the koi's condition. In Japan, special muddy pools – in which particular forms of algae, rich in nutrients and natural colouring agents, grow readily – are favoured by enthusiasts. However, for owners who do not have a muddy pool at hand a range of specialist foods is now produced for koi, so that feeding presents no difficulties. Floating pellets are popular, as they attract the fish up to the surface where, with time, they will become tame enough to feed from the hand.

MAKING A POND

Apart from the cost of buying the fish themselves (which is not prohibitive, especially if you choose fairly small fish), keeping koi is an expensive commitment. You will need a large pond if your fish are to achieve their

Kohaku

Shiro muji (left) and Orenfii ohgon (right)

Tancho

full potential, and deep water is essential to enable them to develop properly by swimming up and down.

Most koi keepers have ponds with a minimum depth of 1.5 m (5 ft). This helps to even out fluctuations in water temperatures near the surface, and also makes the fish less conspicuous to potential predators such as herons. You will need a good filtration system to keep the water clean and to enable you to view the fish easily. Using a butyl-rubber liner (see page 151) will make creating a koi pond fairly easy, and will save you having to mix vast amounts of concrete. When it comes to landscaping around the pond, many enthusiasts opt for a Japanese-style setting, incorporating bridges and bonsai trees. Unfortunately, however, it is not usually possible to include plants in the pond alongside the fish, as they are likely to destroy them.

BUYING KOI

Check for any signs of ulceration on the skin, as this is likely to be a problem and will require treatment. Koi are generally healthy fish once they are established in their quarters, although they may sometimes suffer from parasites such as anchor worms, which will burrow into their skin.

Bear in mind that it will be much harder to deal with any problems of this kind once your koi are in the pond, and that any existing healthy fish will also be at risk of infection. Ideally, you should therefore use a large quarantine tank to house small fish for the first two weeks after bringing them home. You will then be able to check that these new fish are healthy and eating well – and to treat them if necessary (see pages 164–5) – before releasing them into your pond.

BREEDING

Koi can be sexed once they are about 23 cm (9 in) long, when the ovaries of the female will give a more rounded outline to the body compared with the streamlined shape of the male. In the spring, spawning is likely to follow once the temperature reaches 18°C (65°F). Breeders often put nylon ropes in the water for spawning – the eggs will stick to the strands and can be removed before the adult fish eat them.

Young koi may take up to a week to hatch, depending on the water temperature. They will start swimming freely two to three days later, and you must then supply suitable fry food. By the time they are one month old, the fish should be about 1.25 cm (½ in) long. They have a good potential lifespan ahead of them – some koi are known to have lived for over 80 years.

169

KOI VARIETIES

The different varieties of koi are traditionally described in the West using an Anglicized version of their Japanese name. In recent years, a long-finned version of the fish has also been developed, although it is not universally popular. The name 'koi' is actually an abbreviated version of 'nishikigoi' ('colourful carp'). A selection of the common varieties and their names is shown on the right.

COLOUR	NAME
White	Shiro muji
Golden	Ohgon
Orange	Orenfii ohgon
Red	Aka muji
Red and white	Kohaku
White with red head	Tancho
Red with black spots	Aka bekko
Black with red areas	Hi utsuri

Tropical fish

Tropical fish can generally be divided up into two broad categories: the live-bearers, and those which reproduce by means of eggs. The relative ease with which live-bearers can be bred (see also page 162) has led to them becoming available in many different colour forms, far removed from their relatively dull wild ancestors and with significant alterations to the shape of their fins.

LIVE-BEARING FISH

Members of this group, which includes guppies, platies, swordtails and mollies, give birth to live young which will be swimming around the aquarium within a minute or two of birth. A female can produce between 20 and 100 young every five weeks or so, and, as long as there are plenty of plants to provide good cover, a number of them should survive the critical early stage when they are at risk of being eaten by the larger inhabitants of the aquarium.

Guppy (*Poecilia reticulata*)
This is probably the best known of the tropical live-bearers. The male has a brilliantly coloured, flag-like tail, while the female is rather larger and a drab colour.

Platies (*Xiphophorus* species)
These fish are also very varied in colour, ranging from yellow to black and displaying a multitude of markings and patterns over their bodies. They are always active, chasing each other about, and yet also become very tame. Some varieties of platy are known as 'wagtails': this merely signifies the presence of an all-black tail in combination with a red or yellow body colour.

Swordtail (*Xiphophorus helleri*)
This fish is rather larger than the platies, with the male featuring an extension of the lower edge of its tail into the sword shape that is responsible for its name. It is most commonly seen in all-red or 'red wagtail' varieties. Unfortunately, the swordtail is quite likely to become

Green variegated delta guppies

something of a bully in what would otherwise be a peaceful aquarium, and for this reason it is best kept with other fish of a similar size.

Mollies

Like the swordtail, mollies can grow rather larger than platies, although they are generally quite peaceful by nature. The black molly is one of the very few jet-black fish that are available for the aquarium, and is believed to be of hybrid origin. Adding some sea salt to the aquarium water of these fish is often recommended.

Other mollies include the sailfin (*Poecilia latipinna*), so called because of its enlarged dorsal fin.

EGG-LAYING FISH

This group comprises by far the most tropical species, and can be further split into a number of different families of fish. The members within each family will usually – but not always – share the same characteristics.

Barbs

These are some of the hardiest of all aquarium fish. They are small- to medium-sized, and tend to swim in the lower half of the tank. The tiger barb (*Barbus tetrazona*) is particularly beautiful, with several wide black bars running down a deep body and most of the fins coloured bright orange. It is very lively, and may occasionally bully

Neon tetras

other small fish. The black ruby barb (*B. nigrofasciatus*) is similar in appearance – although it lacks the coloured fins – and is more peaceful by nature.

The checker barb (*B. oligolepis*), cherry barb (*B. titteya*) and half-banded barb (*B. semifasciolatus*) are all fairly small, and make excellent aquarium occupants. The tinfoil barb (*B. schwanenfeldi*) should be avoided, as it will quickly devour all plants and will grow much larger in size.

Rasboras and danios
These fish are generally rather small and streamlined, are very fast swimming, and usually occupy the upper part of the aquarium. The zebra danio (*Brachydanio rerio*) and leopard danio (*B. frankei*) are identical except for their markings – the former has stripes running along the body, while the latter has spots. They are both very peaceful fish and make an excellent choice.

Another good option is the harlequin rasbora (*Rasbora heteromorpha*), which is rather deeper-bodied with a triangular-shaped black patch on either side. A little larger is the scissortail rasbora (*R. trilineata*), so called because of the opening and closing action of the tail as it swims along. Although not colourful, this is an active fish and a good mixer with other medium-sized individuals.

Other suitable members of this group include the white cloud mountain minnow (*Tanichthys albonubes*), which prefers cooler water than most tropical fish, and the pearl danio (*Brachydanio albolineatus*). For a larger aquarium, the giant danio (*Danio aequipinnatus*) develops into a beautiful fish with brilliant metallic-blue flanks.

Characins
This family includes the widest variety of species suitable for the aquarium and, many people would say, some of the prettiest. The neon tetra (*Paracheirodon innesi*), with a gleaming metallic-blue stripe running along its body, bordered by another of bright red on the lower part of its abdomen, is one of the best known of all fish; it is surpassed in brilliance only by the cardinal tetra (*Paracheirodon axelrodi*), which has a brilliant red stripe running all the way along the underside of its body. Neither of these fish will grow to more than about 3 cm (1¼ in) overall, so take care not to include them in an aquarium with other species that are boisterous or substantially larger.

The glowlight tetra (*Hemmigrammus erythrozonus*) has a plain silver body with a brilliant copper-coloured line running from nose to tail. As with many fish, this coloration will become even more pronounced as the fish grows older. Other attractive characins include the rummy-nose tetra (*Hemigrammus rhodoistomus*), the bleeding-heart tetra (*Hyphessobrycon erythrostigma*) and the rosy tetra (*H. rosaceus*). These fish are generally social, and are therefore best kept in shoals.

One group of characins – commonly known as pencil fish because of their slim, tapering body shape – makes an interesting study in its own right. Unless disturbed or frightened, these fish will often remain quite motionless in the water for half a minute or more at a time, with the rapid beating of their fins the only visible proof that they are still alive. Pencils tend to be very shy fish; they will require a well-planted aquarium and the company of equally peaceful co-habitees.

Gouramis
Members of this fish family have a special labyrinth organ which enables them to breath atmospheric air; as a result, they are commonly known as 'labyrinth fish'. Another characteristic feature of the gouramis is a pair of 'feelers' which they hold out ahead of them as they swim along. This family is extremely varied in its colours and markings. Probably the most beautiful of all is the male dwarf gourami (*Colisa lalia*), which has narrow, alternating bands of metallic blue and brilliant red covering the sides of its body (the female dwarf is much paler). These are

Tiger barb

(Above, top) **Siamese fighting fish**
(Above) **Corydoras catfish**
(Right) **Golden marbled angelfish**

shy fish and cannot compete with any boisterous individuals for food. Not quite so brilliant in coloration is the thick-lipped gourami (*C. labiosa*), although this grows a little larger and is a less timid fish than the dwarf gourami.

Another beautiful fish is the pearl gourami (*Trichogaster leeri*) which, although it grows to around 8 cm (3 in), remains peaceful towards smaller fish. Not suitable for inclusion with small fish is the three-spot gourami (*T. trichopterus*) or the gourami itself (*Osphronemus goramy*), while the male Siamese fighting fish (*Betta splendens*) must be kept apart from others of its kind or – as its name implies – battles will ensue.

Cichlids

This family includes many medium to large species, most of which cannot generally be kept with other fish. The angelfishes (*Pterophyllum* species) are some of the best-known cichlids, but they may eventually

Clown loach

grow up to about 12.5 cm (5 in) in size and so should not be kept with small fish. These fish have deep bodies and so they need a deep aquarium, which must also be well planted. Various colour varieties of the *Pterophyllum* species are now established.

The discus (*Symphysodon aequifasciata*) is another popular and very widely kept cichlid, but this is really a fish that needs to be kept on its own. So too is the colourful and friendly Oscar (*Astronotus ocellatus*).

OTHER EGG-LAYING SPECIES
There are many species belonging to other families of fish that will make excellent and often very unusual inhabitants for the aquarium. Look out for the snake-like coolie loach (*Acanthophthalmus kuhlii*); the long-nosed elephant fish (*Gnathonemus petersi*), which will benefit from having a sandy base in its aquarium; and the many forms of Corydoras catfish, which are ideal for the lower reaches of a community aquarium. All these fish should be fairly widely available.

Marine fish

The choice of occupants for a marine aquarium is potentially very large but, as with a freshwater set-up, you must ensure that any fish you choose are likely to be compatible before you buy them. Captive-breeding is limited at present, so many of the marine fish available to aquarium hobbyists originate from the wild. These are caught and sold to exporters rather than being eaten, providing a valuable sustainable-cash income for local communities and adding to the value of the reef itself.

As a guide, you should keep the maximum stocking density to no more than 2.5 cm (1 in) of fish per 18 litres (4 gallons) in the first six months, after which you can double it. The following are some suggestions for fish that will make good and attractive inhabitants for a marine aquarium.

Cowfish (*Lactoria cornuta*)

The amazing variety of body shapes in marine fish is exemplified by the cowfish, so called because of the two horn-like projections on its head. This is a gentle-natured fish, and grows to about 15 cm (6 in) in aquarium surroundings. The eggs of the cowfish float on the surface at first, and will hatch after about five days. Plankton is an important food in the early stages, before the fry are large enough to eat brine shrimp (*nauplii*).

Clown (anemone) fish

(*Pomacentridae* family)
This is one of the groups now being bred in captivity. The fish can be kept quite easily in an aquarium alongside

Clown (anemone) fish

sea anemones (see page 189), and will retreat into their poisonous tentacles if danger threatens. These fish get on quite well in groups of their own kind – which will increase your chances of having a pair for breeding purposes – although you can also keep them as part of a mixed group of fish. The eggs are usually laid on rockwork close to a sea anemone, and the fry will emerge about nine days later.

Seahorses

(*Syngnathidae* family)
These make fascinating occupants for a marine tank, but they generally have to be housed on their own or with non-aggressive companions. Seahorses are difficult to keep, mainly because of their feeding habits: they have small mouths and cannot be persuaded to take inert foods, so you must hatch brine shrimp (*nauplii*) for them on a regular basis.

Breeding seahorses successfully in aquarium surroundings is becoming increasingly common. The female lays about 200 eggs, which are then deposited in the male's pouch after mating. The eggs will take five weeks to hatch, by which time the young will be about 1.25 cm (½ in) long. By the age of eight weeks the young seahorses should have grown to nearly 6.25 cm (2½ in). They can live for up to three years.

173

Cowfish

Sea horse

Invertebrates may not be everyone's idea of ideal pets, but they have grown rapidly in popularity over the past few years. The exotic appearance of these creatures, coupled with their general ease of care, has been partly responsible for this change, and they often hold considerable fascination for children in particular. Invertebrates are essentially creatures to be looked at rather than handled. This is not only because they have relatively delicate bodies, but also because a number of these species have toxic secretions associated with them. This does not apply only to the large spiders commonly known as tarantulas, or indeed to scorpions; certain apparently harmless creatures – such as some stick insects and giant millipedes – also defend themselves in this way.

KEEPING INVERTEBRATES

Invertebrates are relatively inexpensive pets, and can be maintained with minimal financial outlay. They usually occupy little space and are suitable for a bedroom, provided that they are housed in escape-proof quarters. There is generally no unpleasant odour associated with them, and none of the species included in this section will be noisy. Some invertebrates can be surprisingly long-lived, at least in the home. For instance, a life expectancy of 30 years may not be unrealistic for some female tarantulas, although the males have a very much shorter lifespan.

Feeding is unlikely to be problematic, although some species are predatory by nature and hunt other invertebrates. However, while you should keep terrestrial invertebrates separately from other creatures, it is not uncommon to include both freshwater and marine invertebrates – ranging from apple snails to sea anemones – in aquaria alongside suitable non-aggressive fish.

LEARNING ABOUT INVERTEBRATES

There is a great deal still to be discovered about this group of creatures, and amateur naturalists can add considerably to our knowledge about them through home-based studies, writing up their experiences and observations for publication in specialist journals. This practice has been most marked in recent years with tarantulas, which – thanks to the efforts of enthusiasts – are now being bred on a regular basis.

There are also active study groups for these spiders, as well as for stick insects, about which there is still much to be learned. Only a tiny percentage of the world's species of stick insects have to date been kept in captivity: for instance, there are about 25 different types regularly available to collectors, of a total of approximately 2500 species. This does not mean that the others are difficult to keep or are rare, but simply

indicates that only a few have ever been obtained alive from the wild. The majority end up being collected and mounted as museum specimens.

Many of the invertebrates have a huge reproductive potential, often producing hundreds if not thousands of eggs, and so it will often only take a small number of specimens to become available for a species to be established successfully. Colonies of invertebrates suffer far less from the effects of in-breeding than vertebrates although, at the same time, colour variants are far less common.

CATEGORIZING INVERTEBRATES

There is often confusion about the different members of this group, as the descriptions of insect and invertebrate are not actually interchangeable. Insects are just one of a number of groups which lack a vertebral column, and so are considered to be invertebrates. The segmented body of the insect consists of three parts. There is the head section, followed by the thorax where the three pairs of legs are found; this segment of the body also provides the point of attachment for the wings (if present). The abdominal segment tends to be the largest of the three and contains the reproductive and other organs.

The simplest way of distinguishing insects from arachnids, a group which includes both spiders and scorpions, is on the basis of their respective number of legs, as arachnids have an additional pair. Other groups – such as millipedes – may have substantially more. Contrary to popular belief, however, they do not have a thousand legs but usually about 120 pairs, which create a ripple effect as the creature moves.

CAMOUFLAGE

Most invertebrates suffer from heavy predation, so they tend to hide away in their quarters. Some – such as stick insects – rely on camouflage to disguise their presence. They have even evolved behavioural patterns to provide better protection, so that, if they feel a breeze, they will rock gently back and forth to mimic the appearance of a twig more closely.

Very similar in this respect are the so-called leaf insects, which are occasionally kept as pets. These merge into the background by resembling leaves rather than twigs. This group of insects is known collectively as phasmids, meaning 'ghosts', because they are not what they appear to be, as well as being difficult to spot!

Other invertebrates will need suitable retreats in their quarters, because even those which have toxic substances to protect them – such as scorpions – prefer to hide away from possible dangers.

Choosing and buying invertebrates

There is a tremendous diversity within the invertebrate group. This is reflected in the care that these creatures require, which will affect your choice when buying them – especially if they are intended as pets for children. Many are relatively easy to house and look after as well as being inexpensive to buy, while others are more costly and also more demanding in terms of the environment and care they need in order to survive and thrive.

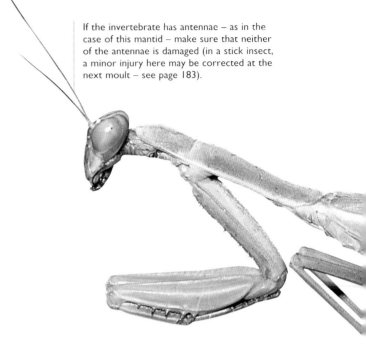

If the invertebrate has antennae – as in the case of this mantid – make sure that neither of the antennae is damaged (in a stick insect, a minor injury here may be corrected at the next moult – see page 183).

Marine invertebrates, such as this tropical fire shrimp (*Lysmata debelius*), can be highly colourful.

MARINE INVERTEBRATES

Marine invertebrates such as sea anemones (see page 189) tend to be the most costly invertebrates to accommodate, since they require the same environment as that of marine fish (see pages 158–9), which is expensive both to set up and to run. In some cases it may be possible to keep them in the company of fish, or you may wish to set up an aquarium consisting only of invertebrates. This need not be a static display, as there are various colourful shrimps and prawns which will thrive in these surroundings and will be very active occupants of the vivarium alongside more sedentary species such as starfish.

TERRESTRIAL INVERTEBRATES

These creatures are much easier to look after than their aquatic counterparts, and in many cases they will only need their vivaria cleaning out intermittently. Some terrestrial invertebrates are much more suitable than others as pets for children, with stick insects being a popular choice. In this case, though, it will be better to opt for one of the smooth-bodied species rather than any with sharp spines around their bodies, as the former will be easier to handle.

On this basis, neither the scorpions, with their ability to sting, nor tarantulas, which may not only inflict a painful bite but can also cause skin irritation with their body hairs, are recommended for children. In contrast, giant land snails can be handled easily by children, and can even be 'raced' on a suitable surface (two circles are drawn on a sheet of paper, and the snails are placed in the inner one; the first snail to cross the outer circle is deemed to be the winner).

SIGNS OF ILL-HEALTH

Recognizing symptoms of ill-health in invertebrates is not easy, especially since lack of activity is a normal feature of many species. However, you should check the legs for signs of injury. With sea anemones, look at the column which supports the creature on a rock. This should be broad, while the tentacles themselves should show no signs of shrivelling at their tips.

THE COST OF INVERTEBRATES

The feeding costs of invertebrates generally are negligible, and for the majority of phasmid species a supply of bramble leaves – replenished every few days – will suffice. Predatory invertebrates such as the arachnids will need to be offered live prey to feed on, and mealworms, crickets and waxworms are all available for this purpose (you can even breed your own crickets at home if you wish – see page 133).

The cost involved in buying invertebrates varies quite widely. Tarantulas are among the most expensive of these creatures to buy, and will not necessarily be within the pocket-money bracket, but it can often be a great deal cheaper and also more satisfying for many owners to start out with young spiders, which are known as spiderlings.

You should also be able to buy stick insects more economically from a pet store or a specialist supplier in the form of eggs or young nymphs, and will then have the added interest of watching them develop.

What to look for in a healthy invertebrate

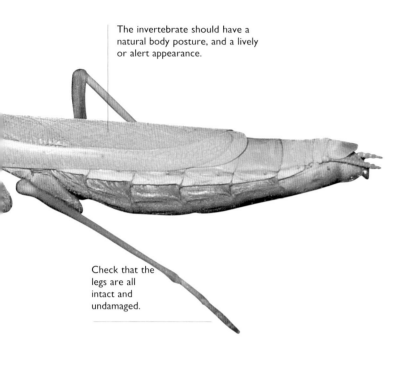

The invertebrate should have a natural body posture, and a lively or alert appearance.

Check that the legs are all intact and undamaged.

Buying eggs

In the case of stick insects, you may need to be patient with eggs bought for hatching out at home. Depending on the species concerned, hatching times can be very variable and, if the eggs have been laid recently, it may be nine months or more before the nymphs emerge.

With Indian stick insects, you can simply place the eggs in a container and leave them at room temperature, but other eggs – such as those of the giant spiny stick insect – will require more humid surroundings. The percentage of eggs which ultimately hatches will be variable, but patience can be rewarded as they will not all hatch at once. This is a survival mechanism which ensures that, in the wild, conditions should be favourable for at least some of the new stick insects.

Buying nymphs

This is another good option. Stick insects resemble adults on hatching, and then grow through a series of moults. It is much better to obtain nymphs – which should have a relatively long life ahead of them – rather than adults of uncertain age which may be approaching the end of their lives. Praying mantids, too, which are very short-lived as adults, should only be purchased as immatures.

This rule applies to most other invertebrates, including giant land snails, which will grow rapidly in good conditions.

WHERE TO FIND INVERTEBRATES

Most pet stores will only stock a very limited range of invertebrates. You are most likely to find them in stores also offering reptiles and amphibians, because the type of set-up required to display these can be similar. However, there are also specialist breeders and suppliers of invertebrates, as well as organizations catering for various species such as tarantulas. You may be able to find details at a public library, or by contacting a butterfly garden or the invertebrate section at a zoo.

It is often not essential to find a supplier close to where you live, although obviously this can be an advantage because you will then be able to see the stock on offer. However, many entomological dealers operate a mail-order service, and are permitted to send their stock through the mail in solid, escape-proof packaging. If you order your invertebrates by this method, it is obviously important that you arrange the delivery at a time when someone is likely to be at home. Open the package carefully and transfer the invertebrates to their quarters without delay. There is generally little need to keep them in quarantine, although this may be advisable in some cases; a number of species such as tarantulas will need to be housed on their own in any case.

Despite their appearance, tarantulas are very fragile and easily injured if they are dropped, so handle them with great care.

HANDLING A TARANTULA OR SCORPION

It will not usually be necessary to handle a tarantula directly, but you should wear a pair of thin gloves if doing so. Carefully slide your hand beneath the spider, and then cup your hands so that it cannot escape.

You should only pick up a scorpion by grasping the base of its tail with a pair of special forceps. This is rarely necessary, but, if you keep scorpions, you should have forceps available in case you need them.

Housing and equipment

You can keep terrestrial invertebrates in a variety of containers. For instance, large, clean sweet jars with ventilation holes punched in the lid are often recommended for young stick insects, although it is actually better to invest in a special plastic container with a ventilated hood (available from pet stores). Produced in a variety of sizes, these units are very versatile and inexpensive, which is useful if you have a large collection of invertebrates at different stages in their lifecycle.

After buying a tarantula and bringing it home in a safe container, transfer it very carefully to its new quarters (below). A suitable retreat will be required by terrestrial species (bottom), while arboreal tarantulas will need branches or even plants in their quarters for climbing purposes.

SECURE ACCOMMODATION

It is obviously important that you provide secure quarters for invertebrates, particularly for spiders and scorpions which are potentially harmful. The mesh on the roof of containers sold for invertebrates may be inadequate to restrain small stick-insect nymphs, which will have no difficulty in climbing around their quarters – including the roof. In these circumstances you will need to fix a piece of muslin over the roof, keeping it taut and secure with the aid of tape or elastic bands.

Although there will be an access flap in the centre of the container's roof, it is unlikely that you will be able to attend to the needs of your pets (especially stick insects) through this small area. When you lift off the lid, you must therefore always check carefully on the underside for any stick insects here before putting it down, as they can move surprisingly fast on occasions and may escape into the room.

Another alternative is to use a special fine-mesh cage, which you will be able to hang up (these cages are usually available from special entomological dealers, rather than from pet stores). One of the great advantages of this type of unit is that it will be secure even for small stick insects, and can also be folded flat when not in use.

Heating and humidity

The average room will be warm enough for many invertebrates, but there may be fluctuations during the day, with the temperature falling when the heating is off. A low-wattage heating pad will then

Be sure to provide a tarantula with a constant supply of fresh water. Dehydration can be a major killer of these spiders, especially in centrally-heated homes.

be useful. A slimline version of the type sold for reptile vivaria (see page 130) is the best option; these are manufactured in various sizes to correspond with the tanks themselves. You can place the heating pad under the unit or attach it to the back. Regulate the output of the heat pad with a thermostat if necessary, and keep a check on the temperature in the unit by fitting a digital thermometer at the front.

Do not try to economize on heating by placing the unit next to a radiator, because one of the major causes of mortality in invertebrates in the home is dehydration resulting from low humidity. This is a particular problem associated with central heating.

Lighting is not necessary for invertebrates, and it is better not to use an ordinary incandescent light bulb for heating as this could be dangerous for species which climb around their quarters; it will also dry out the atmosphere.

For giant land snails, a plant propagator which emits gentle bottom heat (widely available from garden centres) is another possibility for housing purposes. The ventilation grille of a propagator

Floor covering

The floor covering that you should provide in your invertebrates' quarters will depend very much on what species you have. For example, sand combined with retreats such as partially buried flowerpots will be suitable for scorpions originating from arid areas, whereas scorpions from a rainforest environment must be housed quite differently: in this case, the floor covering should consist partially of damp vermiculite (this is more likely to be sold in a garden centre than in a pet store, and is an inert substance which retains water and so helps to ensure a suitably humid environment; mix it with wood chippings or bark). Soak the vermiculite and squeeze it to remove excess water before placing it on the floor of the invertebrates' quarters. Vermiculite is also a good choice for a set-up accommodating a tarantula, although it does have the drawback that burrowing species will not be able to tunnel into it as effectively as they would do into sand. Choose the finest grade of vermiculite available, especially for young tarantulas.

Branches

A number of tarantulas are at least partially arboreal by nature, and this must be reflected in the design of their quarters. You should provide suitable branches for climbing, as well as fixing cork bark to the wall of the enclosure and placing it on the floor. This will make a secluded retreat for a spider, enabling it to spin its web.

It is not usually necessary to add plants to invertebrates' quarters, and you should never include cacti – even for desert-dwelling species – as their sharp spines could cause injury. However, you can set a simple succulent in a pot in the substrate if you wish, provided that it has not been treated with any pesticide.

Most stick insects will also require branches in their quarters for climbing purposes. It will help if you include growing brambles among these – despite their spines – as this will save you having to find new food sources so regularly. You can dig up some bramble runners and set them in pots of soil; these will sprout readily on a warm window-sill, even during the winter, guaranteeing a source of food at this potentially difficult time of year.

This is a typical tarantula burrow. Tarantulas are naturally shy creatures and prefer to hide away from view, so you must provide similar facilities – such as a length of plastic tubing of the appropriate size – in your vivarium.

has the advantage that it is confined to a fairly small part of the roof area, making it easy to build up a high degree of humidity.

Spraying the enclosure will be the easiest way of raising the RH (relative humidity) reading when necessary; it is also safer than providing a saucer of water on the floor of the enclosure in which young invertebrates could drown. In addition, to minimize this risk, you can cut a piece of sponge to fit the water pot and keep it moist, to allow the invertebrates to drink in relative safety. It is a good idea to invest in a special plant sprayer for your invertebrates; this will ensure that there are no toxic residues of insecticide left in the sprayer after you have treated house plants, for example. Always take great care when using any sprays in the home which could affect these creatures.

MONITORING HUMIDITY
You will be able to monitor the relative humidity in your pets' quarters quite easily using a hygrometer (available from garden centres). The simplest type has a dial-type face, which gives the relative humidity (RH) in percentage figures.

Breeding

The invertebrates' reproductive habits are remarkably diverse, but, as the enormous upsurge in the breeding of tarantulas in recent years has shown, it is generally not too difficult to achieve success in the home. In some cases you may not even have to worry about the sex of the invertebrates in order to be able to breed them.

STICK INSECTS

The fact that almost the entire population of the Indian stick insect (*Carausius morosus*) is female does not affect this creature's reproductive ability, with mature females often producing hundreds of eggs over several months. This process is known as parthenogenesis, and the young nymphs are actually clones of their mothers, as they derive their genetic material entirely from them.

Certain other species of stick insect – such as the pink-winged stick insect (*Sipyloidea sipylus*) – may reproduce both parthenogenetically and sexually. In these cases, the eggs produced by parthenogenesis often take longer to hatch, and may produce fewer offspring.

Rear the young stick insects in narrow-necked jars containing cut bramble in water, stuffed with tin foil around the top, as this will ensure that there is no risk of the stick insects drowning in the water. Misting the bramble very lightly will provide them with sufficient fluid in any case. You will probably need to change the stems once or twice a week when they wilt. Avoid any stems which have brown edges or appear to be tough, particularly for young nymphs, as they will not be able to eat these and are liable to starve.

Stick insects are fairly delicate at this stage of their lives, and, if you need to move them, it will be safest to do so by persuading them to walk on to a small paintbrush rather than trying to handle them directly.

SNAILS

Snails are also quite easy to breed without any worries about sexing. This is because they are hermaphrodite: in other words, they have both male and female sex organs in their bodies.

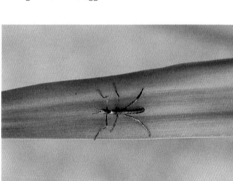

A stick-insect nymph will undergo a series of moults before reaching maturity. Stick insects do not pupate like some other insects; instead, their young bear a clear resemblance to the adults even when they have just emerged from the egg.

Young tarantula spiderlings. These will need to be separated and reared individually to prevent cannibalism.

Keeping two snails together will invariably result in the production of fertile eggs; in fact, you may well have to curtail their breeding activities. For instance, in the case of the giant land snail, assuming that it matures at nine months old and produces four batches of 150 eggs a year, and that all its descendants survive and go on to breed themselves, the potential number of offspring has been calculated at 16 trillion during its average five-year life! The simplest way to resolve this problem is to remove and destroy any unwanted batches of eggs.

A snail will usually bury its eggs in the substrate of its quarters. It will deposit the eggs in oval clumps approximately 5 mm (¼ in) long, in an area of moist soil if available (in this case you will need to keep a careful eye on them, as they could be attacked by fungus). If the eggs are kept at a temperature of roughly 25°C (77°F), hatching will take 10 days, and the young snails will emerge as miniature adults.

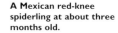

A Mexican red-knee spiderling at about three months old.

TARANTULAS

Pairing of these creatures needs to be carried out cautiously. You must carefully supervise the mating encounters of tarantulas, and ensure that the participants are well fed in advance to lessen the likelihood of aggression. Watch a male closely to find out when he is approaching breeding condition. He will weave a sperm web, where the sperm is deposited before being collected in the pedipalps (the first long, leg-like appendages attaching to the spider's head), with their swollen tips close to the mouth. The male can then be introduced to the female. He should start drumming with his feet almost immediately, and his mate should respond if she is receptive. Mating is a brief encounter of barely 30 seconds; the male will then retreat from the female, and you should transfer him back to his own quarters.

Eight weeks later the female will prepare an egg sac, in which she will deposit 100–400 eggs. She will remain with them until they hatch four months later, when you must move her out before she starts to feast on the offspring. They will need small livefood at first, such as hatchling crickets or fruitflies (see pages 133 and 161); as they grow, separate them to prevent cannibalism.

SCORPIONS

Female scorpions show a greater sense of familial loyalty than the arachnids, although there is little direct contact between the partners at mating. The male drops a packet of sperm during his courtship dance which the female retrieves, being dragged over to it as the scorpions embrace with their claws. She will then give birth to live young, which often break out of their egg cases as they are born. The female carries the young on her body for two weeks until they moult for the first time. If any of them fall off she will try to retrieve them; she will also guard her brood, which will feed on small invertebrates at first. As they grow, the young must be separated to prevent cannibalism.

(Above) The spur of the male tarantula (shown magnified) is present on each of the true front legs and provides a means of distinguishing the sexes. The spur is used to assist the mating process.

A female scorpion is likely to prove a highly dedicated parent.

Health care

Dehydration is a major killer of many invertebrates in the home, and all too often is not given enough thought by owners. In particular, you must be sure to provide drinking opportunities for newly acquired tarantulas: if you see a spider sitting on top of its water source, it will almost certainly be suffering from dehydration. However, as long as you recognize this in time and take action, the spider should soon recover.

PREVENTING DEHYDRATION

Once a tarantula has settled in its new quarters, you will need to maintain the relative humidity in the range of 70–80 per cent for most species, depending on their native environment. For instance, a rainforest tarantula such as the pink-toed (*Avicularia avicularia*) will benefit from a higher humidity than a species like the Mexican blond (*Aphonopelma chalcodes*), which occurs in arid areas. Nevertheless, the latter is a burrowing species and benefits from the dew which collects at the entrance to its underground tunnel.

Although tarantulas such as this Indian black-and-white tarantula (*Poecilotheria regalis*) come from hot parts of the world, the correct level of humidity is vital for their well-being, especially during the moulting period.

182

HANDLING

Careless handling of stick insects in particular may result in the loss of one or more limbs, which can be serious because the insects rely on their legs to climb and to feed. While the loss of one of their six legs may not be a great handicap, any more than this will almost certainly cause disability to the point that you will need to lay the bramble horizontally rather than vertically to allow the stick insect to continue feeding.

If a nymph loses a leg it may be replaced at the next moult, although this does not occur in every case. Do not handle nymphs directly; instead, use a paintbrush to move them (see page 180).

TREATING AN INJURED TARANTULA

Any damage to a tarantula's abdomen – which often occurs due to a fall – may be life-threatening, so you must carry out rapid treatment. One way of patching a wound is to apply a little dental cement, but there may be a greater chance of a problem at the next moult because of the injury. To stop seepage of haemolymph from a wound, use a pair of forceps to cover it over carefully with rice paper.

POISONING

Sudden and widespread death in a group of invertebrates is frequently indicative of poisoning, rather than disease. This may be related back to contaminated food which has been exposed to pesticides, and this is why it is preferable to grow your own supplies of bramble for stick insects, and only to rely on cultured invertebrates as a food supply for predatory species.

Chemicals kept around the house can also be dangerous, especially as they may be carried from one room to another on air currents. It is also worth remembering that cigarette smoke could possibly be dangerous, especially at close hand – nicotine can be a potent pesticide, so avoid smoking anywhere near your invertebrates.

MOULTING

Invertebrates need to moult their body casing in order to grow, and their behaviour beforehand changes. You will need to take certain steps to ensure that this stage passes without problems. With arboreal stick insects, for instance, it is important that their container is tall enough to allow them to suspend themselves from the roof and wriggle out of their old skins; otherwise they will have great difficulty in moulting.

Loss of appetite is a common indicator of the onset of a moult in tarantulas, and is likely to begin some weeks beforehand. If the spider is missing hairs on the abdomen, you will also notice the skin darkening here as the time of shedding approaches; this is the result of new hairs growing beneath the old layer of skin. Do not handle a moulting spider, as it will be particularly delicate at this stage. The tarantula will retreat to a web and you may notice it lying here on its back – this is quite normal behaviour.

Keep the relative humidity high (see page 179) to assist the moulting process, and do not feed the tarantula until its new skin has hardened and it is moving around its quarters again. As with stick insects, a spiderling which has lost a leg should grow another at the next moult. Adult females will continue to moult annually for the rest of their lives and can replace missing limbs at these times, but, in contrast, males will not moult again once they reach adulthood.

Moulting problems

In some cases, particularly if the relative humidity is low or if the spider is in poor condition, it may not shed its old skin cleanly. As a result, it could actually lose a leg or retain some of the old skin

A tarantula breaking away from its old skin. The relative humidity in a spider's quarters is extremely important for successful moulting: if the air is too dry, the spider will have difficulty in shedding its skin properly.

on the surface of its body. Do not attempt to pull this skin off as this could detach the underlying new skin as well. It may come away of its own accord in due course, or will be shed at the next moult when conditions are more favourable.

PARASITES
Among the invertebrates, tarantulas are especially at risk of suffering from parasites, although these are far less commonly seen in captive-bred stock.

Spider-hunting wasps
These wasps will bite and lay their eggs in a tarantula's abdomen and, when these hatch, the wasp larvae eat the spider's body from within, killing it. You should be suspicious of any swelling on the abdomen of a wild-caught tarantula (this could also be due to fly larvae, which bore into the spider's body).

Mites
Mites are parasites that are much more likely to affect a tarantula, multiplying rapidly and possibly resulting in its death. Young spiderlings are particularly at risk because of their smaller size,

The shed skin of a giant spiny stick insect. Note how the insect broke out at the front of the skin, and then wriggled its abdomen out of the resulting hole. A minor earlier injury – such as a damaged antenna – may be corrected following a moult; a nymph may also (but not always) be able to replace a lost leg.

and can be rapidly killed by mites. These parasites are able to live in the substrate and surrounds of a spider's quarters and are almost microscopic, although you should be able to confirm their presence with a magnifying glass.

If you are faced with an outbreak of mites, you will need to discard the contents of the spider's quarters, using hot water to kill any remaining mites. Then return the spider to the container, but keep a close watch in the following days, in case any mites have managed to survive.

Stick insects, mantids and giant land snails

Stick insects, or walking sticks, as they are better known in the USA, rank as the most popular invertebrate pet for children. Mantids are less widely kept, but can be a great source of interest; and children often enjoy keeping giant land snails because – unlike the majority of invertebrates – they are suitable for careful handling.

Indian stick insect

STICK INSECTS

These intriguing invertebrates are extremely easy to look after, and so make a very good choice as pets for children of any age.

Indian or laboratory stick insect

(*Carausius morosus*)

This stick insect, which is the most widely kept species, was originally kept for biological studies in the early years of this century. It has a smooth body, making it easy to handle: this should be done by gently grasping the sides of the stick insect's body, between the legs. Lift the creature off its branch with great care, because the hooks at the tips of its legs will enable it to maintain its grip on very thin leaves, as well as to climb vertical surfaces.

Indian stick insects are predominantly green in colour, with attractive red markings on the legs. Virtually all of them are female. The males are smaller in size, and have red markings running down the thorax; they are also short-lived and will not mate even when housed with females, which will start to lay eggs from about nine months of age onwards.

Hatching of the eggs will take about eight weeks, and the adults will live for approximately one year. Indian stick insects can be safely maintained at room temperature without the need for additional heat.

Giant prickly stick insect

(*Extatosoma tiaratum*)

Less hardy than the Indian stick insect, other species will benefit from being kept slightly warmer. One of the most spectacular of these is the giant prickly stick insect. Captive stock of these insects is descended from individuals that were collected in Queensland, Australia in the 1960s.

The females are significantly larger than their mates, growing to 20 cm (8 in) or so in length. Males are about 5 cm (2 in) shorter, with fully functional wings. Giant prickly stick insects can be sexed early in life, as females are darker in colour and have spikes on their bodies. Their eggs can take up to nine months to hatch.

(Above) Close-up view of a giant prickly stick insect, showing how it uses its mouthparts for eating.

(Below) Giant prickly stick insect

Pink-winged stick insect

(*Sipyloidea sipylus*)

This is another popular species. The delicate, paper-like wings are normally kept folded out of sight along the back and, although they rarely fly, the stick insects can move from one branch to another quite easily by this means.

Adult females may be recognized by their larger size, and they can breed parthenogenetically (without the need for fertilization). Pink-winged stick insects glue their eggs around their quarters – often on their food plant – so be careful not to discard eggs inadvertently when changing the supply. This species lays relatively few eggs – just 100 or so – which may hatch in just six weeks.

Giant spiny stick insect

(*Eurycantha calarata*)

Most stick insects conceal themselves on plants, but the giant spiny variety, which comes from New Guinea, is unusual in that it lives mainly on the ground, burying itself under leaf litter. It is well-equipped to defend itself, with painful spikes around its body. The males have a more pronounced spine at the top of their legs and are shorter in length than the females.

Females will bury their eggs in the substrate of their quarters, and these may not hatch for seven months or so. The young nymphs are often greenish in appearance, whereas adults are much browner in colour. This is a long-lived species, with a life expectancy of about 18 months. Provide a very shallow dish of water on the floor of the vivarium for the stick insects, as they will drink from a container like this.

Mediterranean mantid

MANTIDS

They may seem like stick insects in terms of their appearance and lack of movement, but the mantids are a much more sinister group. They are equipped with a powerful pair of forelegs, often reinforced with sharp spines. These legs are generally kept folded together and raised against the sides of the body so that the mantis looks as though it is praying, but if an insect of suitable size passes within reach it will be seized in a deadly embrace – with the strike completed in less than ten milliseconds.

Male mantids can be at risk of suffering this fate, so you must ensure that larger females are well fed, prior to pairing; afterwards you should remove the male immediately. Evidence of a successful mating may be indicated by the presence of the male's sperm sac on the floor of the enclosure – this will be just 2.5 mm (0.1 in) long and whitish in colour, then turning yellowish.

The female mantid will lay up to 400 eggs in a special protective egg case called an ootheca. If the eggs are kept at a temperature of about 29°C (84°F), the young should start to hatch after about 30 days. They resemble ants at this stage, and will need to be fed on fruitflies (*Drosophila*) and supplied with a dampened pad of cotton wool as a source of moisture. You should also provide a selection of thin branches in the vivarium for climbing.

The development of young mantids is rapid: they will undergo four moults, with their wings only appearing at the final moult. House females individually at this stage, although you can keep males together in relative safety. Mantids can breed when only two weeks old, and will lay up to six times at approximately 10-day intervals during their brief life of two to three months.

It can be difficult to identify different mantid species; there are more than 2000 in the world, ranging in size from 1.25–3.75 cm (½–1½ in).

African giant land snail

GIANT LAND SNAILS

(*Achatina fulica*)

These creatures are more suitable for handling than most invertebrates, although their shells can still be easily damaged, particularly if they are dropped. In time, these molluscs can become so tame that they will not retreat into their shells when picked up.

Originating in Africa – where they are farmed as food – giant land snails have long been kept in Europe, although they are not available in the USA because of fears that escapees could establish themselves in the wild. These huge molluscs can measure over 20 cm (8 in) as adults and weigh more than 227 g (8 oz), so they need spacious surroundings. A relatively humid and warm environment is also essential, so a heated, covered glass tank is ideal. They coast along on a trail of mucus, and are sufficiently large to dislodge a lightweight cover over their quarters.

These snails will eat a wide variety of vegetables and fruit: cabbage leaves, carrots, apple and dandelions are all likely to be consumed with relish. Calcium is also a vital component of the diet, or the snails' shells will become weak and easily damaged; you should provide a piece of cuttlefish bone to supply this. The snails will be able to rasp away at the soft underside of the cuttlefish with the aid of their powerful mouthparts, even though they have no teeth here.

Scorpions and tarantulas

The arachnids are a fascinating group of invertebrates, although they need to be handled very cautiously and only when strictly necessary. They have a long history on our planet. Scorpions are one of the oldest surviving life forms, having existed in a form not dissimilar to their present appearance for more than 400 million years. Their resilience is legendary – scorpions living in desert areas in which nuclear explosions have been carried out have been found alive and apparently unaffected by exposure to radiation up to 200 times greater than would be fatal for a human being.

Imperial or Emperor scorpion

SCORPIONS

There are now over 1500 species of scorpion known from around the world, and these range in size from barely 2.5 cm (1 in) in length right up to 25 cm (10 in) or even more.

All scorpions are similar in shape, possessing pincers and a potentially lethal sting at the tip of the tail. As a general rule, individuals with weak pincers have a more potent sting than those with powerful claws, and in some cases their venom can prove deadly to people.

While the keeping of such dangerous species requires a special licence (ask for information from a knowledgeable supplier on how to organize this), other scorpions are now being bred quite regularly by enthusiasts. Even so, do not attempt to handle these arachnids directly – instead, use a pair of special long-handled forceps.

Housing

It is important that accommodation for scorpions reflects their natural environment (see pages 178–9). All scorpions are shy and will require hiding places in their quarters; they will also use this cover to ambush their prey. You can use rocks, cork bark and even pieces of driftwood for this purpose and to create a scenic effect in the enclosure. Scorpions are reasonably social by nature, but you must not overcrowd them or they will fight.

Feeding

Feeding scorpions presents no problems, with mealworms, crickets and similar invertebrates being eaten readily. A healthy scorpion will rush out and seize its prey, before eating it rapidly.

Be very careful not to overfeed your scorpions, as this will be fatal for them. Obesity is indicated by a distinctive swelling of the abdomen, with the area between the plates on the back also starting to bulge when a scorpion is regularly overfed. As a guide, most adult scorpions which are healthy and in good condition will need to eat about once a fortnight.

Communication

Scorpions can communicate with each other by sound. Rubbing the mouthparts together – a process that is known as stridulation – creates a distinctive grating noise, and is often used as a warning.

Sexing

It is quite difficult to sex these arachnids by their appearance, although males are usually somewhat smaller and slimmer, and often have longer tails than females. In some (but not all) cases, the claws of the males may also appear less powerful.

Imperial or Emperor scorpion
(*Pandinus imperator*)
This is one of the most widely kept species. As with other scorpions, it will fluoresce under ultra-violet light because of an unusual chemical in its body casing. When viewed from beneath, the pectineal teeth of males are larger than those of females. These scorpions can grow up to 20 cm (8 in) long, and are mature by six years old. If a female gives birth in a colony, remove the other individuals or they may prey on her young.

Coming as they do from rainforest areas, these scorpions require an RH (relative humidity) of about 80 per cent and need to be kept warm.

Large-clawed yellow scorpion
(*Scorpio maurus*)
This species originates further north in Africa than the imperial scorpion, on the Mediterranean coast. Large-clawed scorpions can be kept at a slightly lower temperature – about 23°C (75°F) – and do not require such humid surroundings. Members of this species can be identified by their large claws and yellowish body coloration. They grow to about 7.5 cm (3 in) and will burrow, so provide a deep layer of substrate in their quarters.

TARANTULAS

This group of distinctively large spiders consists of about 700 different species, but at present fewer than 40 are well represented in breeding collections. Their distribution is also confined to the warmer parts of the world. While black and brown predominate in the coloration of many species, some of these spiders have very attractive markings.

Mexican red-knee tarantula

Mexican red-knee tarantula
(Brachypelma smithi)

This species is a typical example, as it has orangish-red areas – especially on its legs – and a contrasting blackish abdomen. It was the first species to become popular for keeping as a pet, but tarantulas have only been recently bred in any numbers. Although females may lay up to 400 eggs, these spiders are slow to mature and are unlikely to breed before they are six years old.

The Mexican red-knee is a burrowing species of tarantula, so provide a flower-pot set in the substrate of the enclosure. The surroundings must be humid, with an RH (relative humidity) reading of 70–80 per cent.

Mexican blond tarantula
(Aphonopelma chalcodes)

Also known as the Mexican palomino, this spider is named for its distinctive coloration. It is a popular – albeit fairly expensive – species, in spite of its rather nervous nature. It needs similar housing to the Mexican red-knee tarantula.

Costa Rican zebra tarantula
(A. seemanni)

This spider has distinctive striping on its legs, with brownish upper parts. Males can be identified by their coloration when adult, as they become entirely black on reaching maturity. This species needs warm, humid surroundings.

Pink-toed tarantula
(Avicularia avicularia)

This spider originates from northern South America, and is sometimes known as the bird-eater – essentially because of its arboreal nature rather than its diet. The patterning of a young spiderling is the reverse of the Costa Rican zebra, since, when it matures, it will develop pink toes in contrast to its black body. It requires tropical rainforest conditions in order to thrive, and favours crickets and/or flies as prey.

Chilean rose tarantula
(Grammostola spatulatus)

This species occurs much further south on the South American continent than the pink-toed tarantula; it is somewhat hardier and lives in burrows. This is a generally docile creature, so breeding can be more straightforward. The spiderling is pinkish with a contrasting dark abdomen.

Indian black-and-white tarantula
(Poecilotheria regalis)

This is one of a number of related species from this part of the world which have become popular in recent years. However, they are costly to buy and have a particularly nasty bite. In colour they are brown and grey, with yellow markings on the legs.

BABOON SPIDERS

These arachnids originate from Africa. They tend to be aggressive by nature, and will rear up on their legs if they feel threatened in any way.

Unusually, in a few cases, relatively high humidity in the quarters is likely to be harmful. This applies especially to varieties such as the popular East African horned baboon spider (*Ceratogyrus darlingi*), which is often found in arid grassland surroundings.

(Top) Costa Rican zebra tarantula
(Centre) Pink-toed tarantula
(Bottom) Chilean rose tarantula

Marine invertebrates

Most people naturally think of crabs as living in the sea, but there is a group of these creatures which have developed to spend most of their time on land, and which are known as hermit land crabs. Other marine invertebrates that may be kept as pets include sea anemones and living corals.

Hermit land crab

HERMIT LAND CRABS

(*Coenobita clypeatus*)
These crabs comb the beach for edible morsels of food, and even scavenge for their shells. They have five pairs of reddish legs, each of which has specific functions. The first pair is made up of one greatly enlarged limb, swollen into the form of a powerful pincer; this will deter gulls and other potential predators because it can inflict a painful nip. It can also be used to battle with other crabs, although these crustaceans tend to be quite social creatures. The smaller opposite leg is used mainly to hold food. The crab depends upon its next two pairs of legs for walking. The remaining legs act as anchors, holding the body in its shell and moving it along as required.

Housing and decor

Hermit crabs are often available from aquatic stores. They are not difficult creatures to look after, and make good first pets for children. They are best housed in an adapted aquarium. These crabs are surprisingly agile, so placing a cover on the tank will not only help to maintain the humidity (see opposite, above) but will also prevent them from escaping. You can use a variety of floor coverings, but well-washed sand is probably the best option as the crabs will be able to bury themselves in this without difficulty; sand will also allow you to create a natural environment.

Incorporate some suitable pieces of driftwood, both as a display feature and to give your crabs an opportunity to

HANDLING HERMIT CRABS

Handling these creatures is quite straightforward. You will usually be able to pick up a crab without fear of being bitten by holding the shell on each side between a finger and thumb. If you do have the misfortune to be grabbed by the large pincer, it may be difficult to persuade the crab to release its grip, but if you lower it into its water pot it should let go. Hermit crabs are fragile and a fall to the floor could be fatal, so always handle them carefully.

show off their climbing skills (they are also known as tree-climbing crabs). To give them sufficient room, it is best to use a tank with a depth of at least 45 cm (18 in). You can include pebbles and large stones in the decor, but be sure to position these in such a way that they cannot be accidentally dislodged. It is not worth trying to include live plants in your crabs' quarters, as they will destroy these, although you could use some of the realistic plastic plants produced for aquaria as an alternative if you wish.

Providing a regular supply of shells in the quarters is essential, because as the crabs grow they will look for new, larger shells. You can buy these from curio shops or specialist shell shops. Check the insides of the shells carefully before buying them to make sure that they are suitable: for example, although tiger cowrie shells are large and attractively patterned, the narrow slit-like opening makes them quite unsatisfactory for crabs. You will need shells with broad openings that you can leave lying around in the crabs' quarters, allowing them to select their own.

Hermit land crabs do not generally behave aggressively towards each other. However, it is unwise to mix individuals of widely differing sizes, because they are likely to fight over the occupancy of the shells as they grow.

Heating and humidity

Provide heat in the aquarium by fixing a lightbulb into a ventilated hood, and use a digital thermometer attached to the side of the tank, close to ground level, to monitor the temperature. A figure of between 21–26°C (70–78°F) suits these crabs well during the day; this can be allowed to fall slightly at night.

It is vital that you maintain a humid atmosphere in the aquarium if your crabs are to thrive. You should also set a shallow pot of water in the sand for bathing; salt water is preferable. You can make up a solution easily using specially formulated sea salt sold for marine aquaria: simply add the recommended amount of salt to the water and stir. In addition, spray the interior of the tank each day with tepid tap water.

High humidity is especially important during the moulting phase, when the crabs leave their shells and literally force themselves out of their existing body casings. At this stage they are completely defenceless and usually burrow into the sand, emerging after a period of rest to seek new shells.

Feeding

Although hermit land crabs are natural scavengers, they prefer food of animal rather than plant origin. Various prepared diets – in the form of flakes and pellets – are commercially available for them. In time, some crabs may become sufficiently trusting to feed on your hand. They will only eat small quantities, so avoid overfeeding them. The major benefit of using a prepared food is that you can easily remove any surplus from the tank, although various fish foods make suitable alternatives.

Signs of illness

A healthy crab will usually withdraw rapidly into its shell when picked up. A lethargic individual could be unwell, although hermit crabs are not normally prone to illness. It may simply be that the crab is dehydrated, in which case dunking it in a salt-water solution can aid recovery. Hermit crabs may live for up to 10 years in the home – a much longer time than would be likely in the wild – although they will not breed here.

SEA ANEMONES

In spite of their name, these are not plants but predatory animals. They are so called because of the appearance of the mouth, which – surrounded by its stinging tentacles – is said to resemble the anemone flower. There are over 9000 different species of sea anemone. The majority of these are found in tropical waters, reflecting the fact that they need sunny conditions.

(Above, top) Ritteri anemone
(Above) Blue-and-yellow sand anemone
(Below) Starfish

Housing

Living inside the sea anemone's body are algae which are vital to its well-being. Without this algal presence, the sea anemone will die off, although the precise role of these microscopic plants is unclear. In the marine aquarium, you must therefore install special high-intensity lighting – towards the blue end of the spectrum – in order to promote the growth of these algae.

Space the anemones around the aquarium so that their tentacles do not touch one another, as this may result in fatalities. Special foods are available for these creatures. They can be surprisingly long-lived, with a life expectancy that is measured in decades in some cases.

OTHER MARINE INVERTEBRATES
Many living corals also have algae within their bodies, and they will need a similar set-up to that of sea anemones. In common with many invertebrates, they are very sensitive to water quality.

Be very careful about mixing your invertebrates: for instance, starfish may well be attacked by harlequin prawns (*Hymenocera picta*). If you are in doubt about which species to choose, ask the advice of a specialist supplier.

INDEX

190

ACKNOWLEDGEMENTS

The author and Reed Books Ltd would like to thank the following for their assistance, and/or for supplying and loaning equipment and animals for photography:
Stuart Christophers, Ernest Charles & Co. Ltd (for seed samples); Ivor Grogan; Peter Gurney; Rita Hemsley; and Regent Park Pet Supplies.

Thanks also to Ray Fury and Paul Webb for their design assistance, and to Bertie Hedges for modelling for the photograph on page 65, top.

PICTURE CREDITS

David Alderton 13 bottom right,65 bottom,86,112 bottom,112 top,126,136 bottom left,136 top left,139,144 left,144 centre, 145 top,180,183 bottom; **Animals Unlimited** 59 top,71 centre left,71 right, 74/5,91 left,97 left,97 right; **Ardea** /Dennis Avon 121 left,121 right,125 right,/Hans & Judy Beste 4/5,/John Clegg 59 bottom, /John Daniels 4 centre left,17 bottom left,26, 38, 38/9,64,70 right,95 bottom,111 centre right, 111 bottom right,122 left,146,/Bob Gibbons 87 bottom,/Pascal Goetgheluck 180/1,183 top,/J.M. Labat 56/7,/Eric Lindgren 138 top left,/Pat Morris 179,/Donald & Molly Trouson 114 left,/A. Weaving 185 bottom; **Dennis Avon** 107 top right,111 top right, 114 right, 115, 116 left, 116 right, 117 centre,117 top right, 117 left, 117 bottom right, 118 top,119, 120 right, 121 centre, 122 right,123,125 centre.; **BBC Natural History Unit** 8; **Bruce Coleman Ltd** /Ingo Arnot 185 top,/Adriano Bacchella 94,/Jane Burton 22 centre left,27 centre,27 right, 28,28/9,34 top,39 centre,56 bottom, 88,176,188,/AJ Deane 187 bottom right,/ M P L Fogden 143 left,/Joe McDonald 148 top left,/Andy Purcell 184 centre,/Hans Reinhard 5 top left, 92/3,99,120 left,121 bottom right,144/5,152/3,/Alan Stillwell 180 top right,181 centre right,/Kim Taylor 136 right,/Norman Tomalin 135 left,/Jorg & Petra Wegner 125 left,/Rod Williams174, 186/7; **Sylvia Cordaiy** /Paul Kaye 66 bottom,67 top,/James Murdoch 68 top, /Nick Rains 189 bottom; **John Daniels** 3,66 top,67 bottom,68 centre,69 ; **Sue Derbyshire** /Dr Cecillia Gorrel,Veterinary Oral Health Consultancy 92; **John and Alex Hedges** 65 top right; **Marc Henrie** 9,39 top,53 centre right,53 top right,53 bottom right,58,75,83 centre right,95 right, 96; **Image Bank** /James Carmichael 128/9, 140/1,/Michael Schneps 98,125 bottom right; **Frank Lane Picture Agency**/ H B Brandl 52,/E & D Hosking 40 top,40 bottom,118 bottom, 124,140 left,/Chris Mattison 138 bottom left,/Francois Merlet 175,184 right,/Silvestris 147 right; **Cyril Laubscher** 19 bottom right,27 left,29,30, 31,32,33 centre,33 top,35 top right,35 left, 101,110 left,110/1,112/3; **Dermod Malley FRCVS** 24; **Chris Mattison** 2,4 top left,7, 126/7,132/3,138/9,141, 142,142/3,143 right, 147 left,148 bottom left,148 right,149,181 bottom right,182,184 left,186,187 centre right,187 top right; **Arend van den Nieuwenhuizen** 162 centre left,162 top left,172 top left,173 left; **Nishikigoi International** 168,169 ; **Oxford Scientific Films** /M.A.Chapell 5 bottom left,176/7, /Michael Leach 148/9; **Photomax** 5 centre left,7 bottom,140 top,145 bottom,151,159 top,162 bottom left,163,164 top left,165, 166 bottom,166/7,167,170,171 bottom,172 bottom right,172 bottom right,172 top right,173 bottom right,189 centre,189 top; **Reed International Books Ltd** /Colin Bowling 177,178 top left,178/9 top,178 bottom left,/Jane Burton; 73,76,77,78,79, 80, 81,82, 84 top,84 bottom,89,90/Paul Forrester 102 top left,103,106,106/7, 107 bottom right,108,154/5,156,157,160/1 bottom,160 centre left,160 bottom left,160 top left,161,164/5,/Nick Goodall 83 bottom l,/Rosie Hyde 4 bottom left, 43,44, 46 left, 51 bottom,54 bottom left,62 right,63,/Peter Loughran 42,70 left,84/5,87 top,/Ray Moller endpapers, 4 right, 44/5,68 bottom,71 left, 72,/John Moss 71 centre right,/Laura Wickenden 6,10 left,10/11,12/3,12 left,13 right,14,15,16,17 top left,17 centre right,17 bottom right,18,19 right,20,21,22 top,23 top, 25,36/7,37,46 bottom,46 top right,47, 48, 49,53 right,54 top,102 bottom,102 centre,104,105,130,131,132,132/3 bottom, 133,134,135 top right,135 centre right,135 bottom right,158,159 bottom; **M Sandford** 164 bottom left; **Tony Stone Images** /Robert Stahl 93; **Bruce Tanner** 55; **TFH Publications** 41 bottom; **Warren Photographic** /Jane Burton 22 bottom left,23 right,23 bottom left,33 bottom,34 bottom,35 bottom right,39 bottom,56 top, 62 left,74,91 right,137 bottom right,137 right, 137 right,137 top right,140 bottom,160/1, 171 top,/Kim Taylor 137 top left; **Elizabeth Whiting Associates** 109; **ZEFA Picture Library** /Lazclemoine 95 left,/Reinhard 5 right,/W. Townsend JR 150,173 top right; **London Zoo** 41 top.

FURTHER READING

Small mammals
Alderton, David *A Petkeeper's Guide to Rabbits and Guinea Pigs* (Salamander Books, 1986)
Alderton, David *Rodents of the World* (Blandford Press, 1996)
Gurney, Peter *Piggy Potions* (Kingdom Books, 1997)
Henwood, Chris *Rodents in Captivity* (Ian Henry Publications, 1985)
Mckay, J. *The New Hamster Handbook* (Blandford Press, 1991)
Sandford, J.C. *The Domestic Rabbit* (Blackwell Science, 1996)

Dogs
Alderton, David *Eyewitness Handbook: Dogs – the visual guide to over 300 dog breeds* (Dorling Kindersley, 1993)
Bailey, Gwen *The Perfect Puppy* (Hamlyn, 1995)
Carruthers, Barry and Bing, Keith *Love Me, Love My Dog – Complete Dog Ownership Manual* (TFH Publications, 1994)
Edney, Andrew and Mugford, Roger *The Practical Guide to Dog and Puppy Care* (Salamander Books, 1987)
Taylor, David *You and Your Dog* (Dorling Kindersley, 1986)

Cats
Alderton, David *Eyewitness Handbook: Cats – the visual guide to over 250 types of cat* (Dorling Kindersley, 1992)
Alderton, David *The Practical Guide to Cat and Kitten Care* (Salamander Books, 1997)
Evans, J.M. and White, Kay *The Catlopaedia: A Complete Guide to Cat Care* (Henston, 1988)
Neville, Peter and Bessant, Claire *The Perfect Kitten* (Hamlyn, 1997)
Wright, M. and Walters, S. (eds) *The Book of the Cat* (Pan, 1980)

Birds
Alderton, David *The Handbook of Cage and Aviary Birds* (Blandford Press, 1995)
Alderton, David *Looking after Cage Birds* (Blandford Press, 1995)
Alderton, David *You and Your Pet Bird* (Dorling Kindersley, 1992)
Harper, Don *Pet Birds for Home and Garden* (Salamander Books, 1986)
Trollope, J. *The Care and Breeding of Seed-eating Birds* (Blandford Press, 1983)

Reptiles and Amphibians
Alderton, David *The Reptile Survival Manual* (Ringpress Books, 1997)
Mattison, Chris *Keeping and Breeding Lizards* (Blandford Press, 1991)
Mattison, Chris *Keeping and Breeding Snakes* (Blandford Press, 1990)
Rundquist, Eric M. *Reptiles and Amphibians – Management in Captivity* (TFH Publications, 1994)
Staniszewski, Marc *Amphibians in Captivity* (TFH Publications, 1995)

Fish
Alderton, David *Looking after Freshwater Aquarium Fish* (Blandford Press, 1995)
Alderton, David *The Hamlyn Book of Tropical Freshwater Fish* (Hamlyn, 1997)
Andrews, Chris A. *A Fishkeeper's Guide to Fish Breeding* (Salamander Books, 1986)
Andrews, Chris; Excell, A. and Carrington, Neville *The Manual of Fish Health* (Salamander Books, 1988)
Mills, Dick *The Practical Encyclopedia of the Marine Aquarium* (Salamander Books, 1987)
Scott, Peter W. *A Fishkeeper's Guide to Livebearing Fishes* (Salamander Books, 1987)

Invertebrates
Alderton, David *A Step-by-Step Book about Stick Insects* (TFH Publications, 1992)
Baxter, Ronald N. *Keeping and Breeding Tarantulas* (Chudleigh Publishing, 1995)
Frye, Fredric L. *Captive Invertebrates: A Guide to Their Biology and Husbandry* (Krieger Publishing, 1992)
Hancock, Kathleen and John *Tarantulas: Keeping and Breeding Arachnids in Captivity* (R & A Publishing, 1992)
Haywood, Martyn and Wells, Sue *The Interpet Manual of Marine Invertebrates* (Salamander Books, 1989)
Pronek, Neal *Hermit Crabs* (TFH Publications, 1982)